POS Business Application   Product Brochure

Overview

The Point-Of-Sale (POS) Business Application accounting software is designed to operate on one or more IBM PC computers each running the Windows operating system.

This POS Business Application provides the following main features:

1. Distributed Encrypted Network Databases
2. System User Password Control
3. Single or Multiple Networked Computer Systems (Server & Client Stations)
4. Point-Of-Sale (POS) Terminal
5. Inventory Control Module
6. Accounts Receivable Module
7. Database Import and Export
8. Database Backup and Restore

What sets this product apart from other POS Systems

The principal features which set this POS Business Application Software apart from other POS accounting software systems are the following:

- Distributed databases which allow POS transactions even when the server or network fails.
- Quicker Data Access via Calendar Indexed Databases
- The Re-Posting of POS Sales transactions if database recovery is required
- Non-Destructive Database Backup and Restore Operations

POS Business Application — Product Brochure

Distributed Encrypted Network Databases

Other POS Accounting Systems

The main restriction with many Point-Of-Sale systems is their reliance on both the network and the Server computer system. These POS systems locate their central database on the server computer and the client computer systems must access this database via the network in order to perform any Point-Of-Sale operations.

A major cause for concern with users of such systems is with regard to what would happen if the network or the server were to fail. If either of these failures were to occur then the client computer systems would not be able to access the central database and would therefore not be able to perform Point-Of-Sale transactions. In this situation, the counter staff would then be required to make hand written sales receipts and refer to previously printed (and perhaps outdated) price lists. This method of operation is tedious, slow and can easily generate errors.

Later, when the Server and/or network are once more operational, the handwritten sale transactions have to be manually entered into the accounting system – another time consuming operation which is also fraught with possible errors.

The POS Business Application

This POS Business Application system, however, is designed to minimize these conditions. It uses a distributed encrypted database and is therefore not totally reliant on the network nor on the Server. Although our Server contains the central database, any changes to this database are passed on to database copies which reside on each Client computer system. If the Server or the network were to subsequently fail, each POS Business Application Client computer system would still contain copies of the latest relevant inventory and accounts receivable databases and may still be used to perform Point-Of-Sale transactions with the current inventory stock part numbers and prices.

Once the Server and network are once more operational, the transaction sales data collected by each POS terminal may then be posted to the Server thereby updating the central database. All Server and Client databases are encrypted to provide basic system security. For higher level security, the file system encryption features of Windows XP Professional may be utilized.

Calendar Indexed Databases

Other POS Accounting Systems

In general, accounting systems are very responsive when the system is first installed. As the days and months progress, more and more data history is created and the system can start to get sluggish. After several years of data history has been collected, the system can take a long time to scan an entire database in order to access and obtain specific information pertaining to a report.

In order to minimize this effect, some accounting systems impose database size limitations which restrict the amount of data history which may be retained.

POS Business Application   Product Brochure

The POS Business Application

Firstly, this POS Business Application has no size limitation regarding the number of years of data history which may be retained. Also, in order to have direct, fast, access to sales history information, the POS Business Application Sales History database has been indexed by calendar year and month sub-directories. This means that when searching for data pertaining to a specific year and month, the data file for that calendar period can be quickly accessed and the information speedily obtained.

POS Sales Transaction Re-Posting

Other POS Accounting Systems

Most POS accounting systems use the Server to contain the central accounting databases. This database may also include the Point-Of-Sale transactions for each POS terminal. At the end of a business period, these POS sales transactions are posted to the sales history database and certain inventory database parameters (eg. the "On Hand" quantity) are updated. Once this posting operation has completed, the original information is then deleted since it is no longer required.

Normally this approach is successful, except under conditions when the database has had to be recovered due to system related problems.

If the database is to be recovered, the current day's posted (and un-posted) sales transactions for each POS Terminal may be deleted during the server backup restoration process. The sales data for the period between the backup date and the current date will then have to be manually re-entered in order to bring the database up to date. This is another time consuming operation which is also fraught with possible errors.

The POS Business Application

This POS Business Application, however, keeps each POS terminal's sales information on local files within each respective computer system. At the end of the business period, the collected sales data is posted to the server and the sales history and Inventory database updated.

On our system, the sales data is never deleted. It is placed into a local database directory and given a unique name which includes the date and time when the posting operation occurred. If a Server related problem were to occur at this point and a prior database was to be restored, the intervening sales data still exists and can simply be re-posted thereby quickly bringing the Server central database up to date. No manual re-entry of POS Sales transaction data would normally be required.

During the re-posting operation, the POS Business Application software merges the new information with the currently existing information. Since Calendar Indexed Databases are used, only the sales history file for the re-posting day in question has to be scanned. The merging process ensures that no duplicate sales entries are stored in the database and that subsequent databases operations (ie. adjustment of the Inventory On-Hand quantity, etc.) only occur once. If multiple re-posting operations were to be performed in error using the same file, no harm would result to the database.

Other POS systems may not allow re-posting since the merging process would involve the scanning of the entire history database – a lengthy, time-consuming operation.

POS Business Application — Product Brochure

Database Backup and Database Restore

Other POS Accounting Systems

During Database Backup operations, some POS Accounting systems use the same backup storage file name and/or location, which may result in the previous backup file being overwritten.

During Database Restore operations the POS Accounting system's active directory database is overwritten. A healthy database can easily be destroyed if an incorrect restore operation was performed.

The POS Business Application

This POS Business Application Database Backup operation allows the various databases to be converted to a single backup file for transfer to removable media (eg. removable hard drive, DVD-ROM, etc.). The system generated backup file name includes the current date and time and is therefore easily identified as shown below:

For example: `POS_Database_Backup 2006-11-03 11-15-21.BAK`

Each database backup operation will create a new unique backup file and will never overwrite any previous backup file.

The POS Business Application Database Restore operation takes a specified backup file and expands it to create the required system directories and databases. Prior to performing the Database Restoration, the previously existing database directory is renamed and is therefore not overwritten during this process. The Database Restore operation also has the capability of restoring from a previous database directory.

The default Database Backup and Database Restore operations do not erase or modify any existing database files, therefore the user is never faced with the situation where the system database could be overwritten due to operator error. If the user wishes to overwrite the active database directory during a restore operation, an override option is provided.

Quantum Blue Technology LLC

POS Business Application   Product Brochure

Inventory Control

The Inventory Control module allows the user to edit and/or view the various inventory items. Inventory items are identified by a stock number and by one or more aliases. Each inventory item can have a four line description and can be associated as belonging to a specific category, brand and type. List and Markup pricing methods permit the item sale price to be defined as either a fixed price or as a percentage markup based on the last cost. Quantity price breaks may also be defined. Primary and alternate vendor information may be stored with the inventory item as an aid when ordering additional inventory.

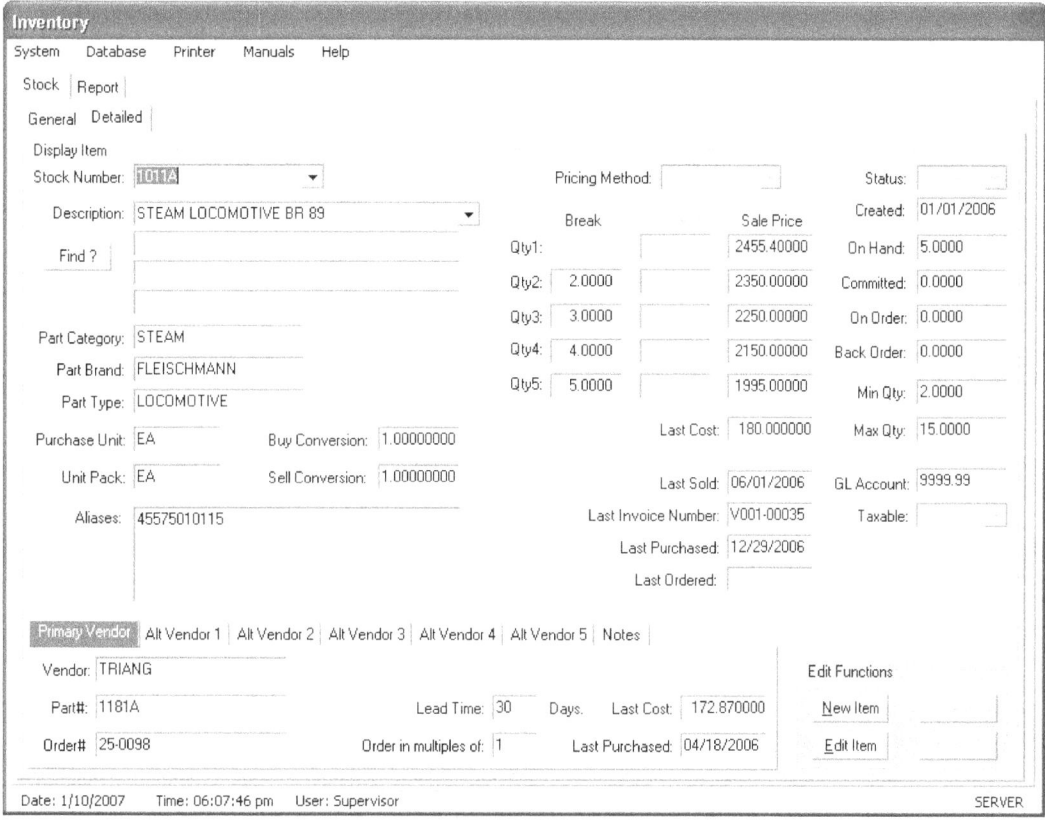

The Report section allows a specific report to be selected and generated. Report Parameters may be specified to extract specific groups of inventory items. Multiple nested sorts may be performed to allow the report to be ordered as required.

The following reports are provided which may be viewed and/or printed as required:

1. Quick Stock List Report
2. Price Book Report
3. Under Stock Report
4. Over Stock Report
5. Stock Value Report
6. Stocktake Worksheet Report
7. Stock Labels (with Bar Code 39 Generation)

POS Business Application   Product Brochure

Point-Of-Sale (POS) Terminal

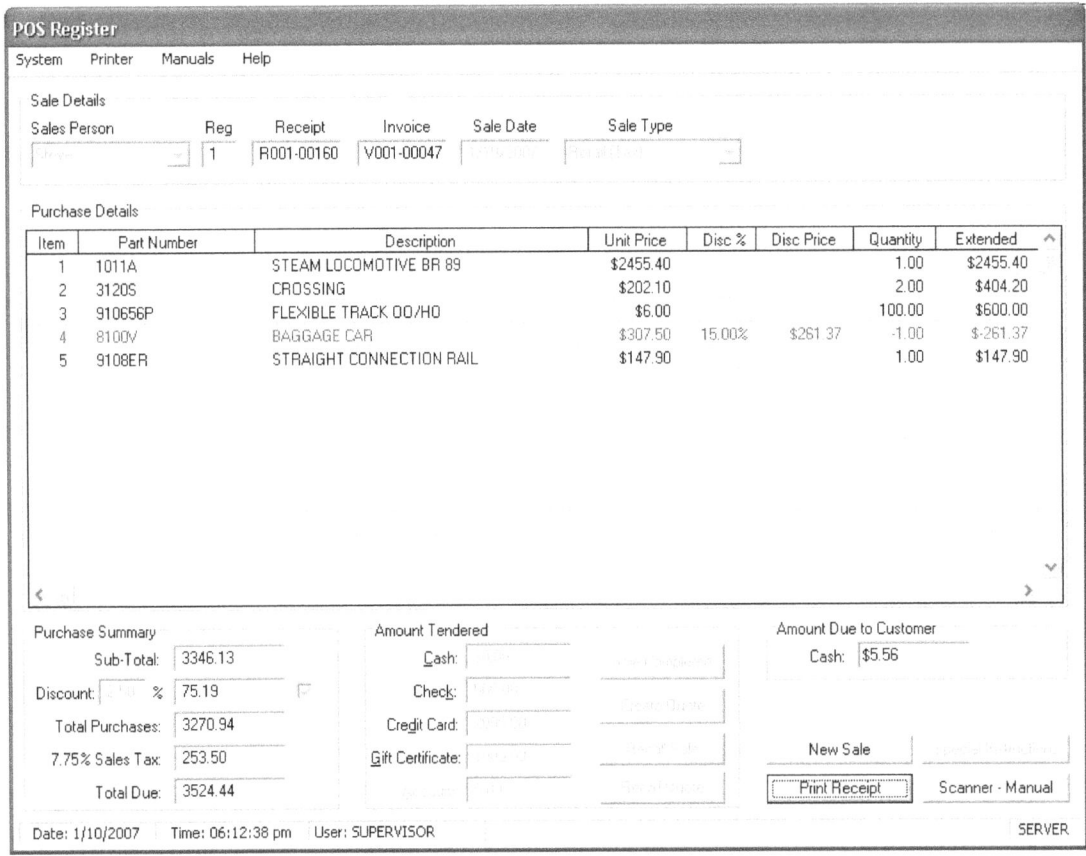

Note: Various options are included to control the manner in which purchase discounts may be applied.

    For example:
1. Account customers may be permitted or prevented from obtaining price breaks.
2. The total purchase discount may be permitted or prevented from being applied to price break items.
3. The total purchase discount may be permitted or prevented from being applied to discounted line items.

In the above example, the options "Total Discount Applies to Price Break Items" and "Total Discount Applies to Discounted Line Items" are both set to False. This prevents the price break item (ie. the Flexible Track OO/HO) and the returned "Baggage Car" from receiving the overall 2.5% discount which is why the discount amount is $75.19 instead of $83.65.

The POS Terminal permits the user to perform cash or account sale transactions as well as creating quote statements. Cash or account sale transactions are recorded and transferred to the Server at the end of the business day. The POS Terminal permits the use of a bar code scanner during sales line item entry. Only one listing of each purchased product is displayed on the screen and on the receipt. When an additional, previously entered product is input, the previously entered product quantity is adjusted accordingly. This helps to visually ensure that the correct number of items are charged to the customer.

POS Business Application　　　　　　　　　　　　　　　　　Product Brochure

If the network or Server were to suddenly fail, all Client POS Terminals would still continue to operate, thereby allowing the current sale to be completed and also allowing subsequent sales to be performed.

The user may identify which system printers are to be used for reports, account statements and till slips. An ESC/POS till slip printer interface is also provided.

The following POS Terminal features are available:

1. Price breaks for quantity purchases
2. Transaction line item price modification (specify price or discount percentage)
3. Overall discount for items not previously discounted
4. Indicate special handling instructions (ie. delivery information appended to receipt)

Sales data is stored in a hierarchical directory file structure which permits fast and efficient access to database records. Any number of sales transactions may be stored without adversely affecting the system performance. Previous Sales may be accessed and viewed. Quotes may be created and printed. Quotes may be converted into a sale without the need to re-enter purchase information.

The following POS Reports are provided:

1. Register Summary Report
2. Register Full Report (identify sales transactions)
3. Register Year Report (spreadsheet providing register totals for each day of the year)
4. Sales Tax Report

POS Business Application   Product Brochure

Accounts Receivable Module

The Accounts Receivable module permits the user to identify various customers who may purchase items on credit. The customer's name and address, credit limit, purchase terms and tax code may be specified. Customer Job Names and authorization information may also be defined – this information may be viewed during a POS sale and is used to identify which customer employee may purchase against which specific job. Various charge, account, credit and aging statistics are collected and may be viewed. A Transaction / Payment history can be viewed and Payments / Adjustments can be applied to the account.

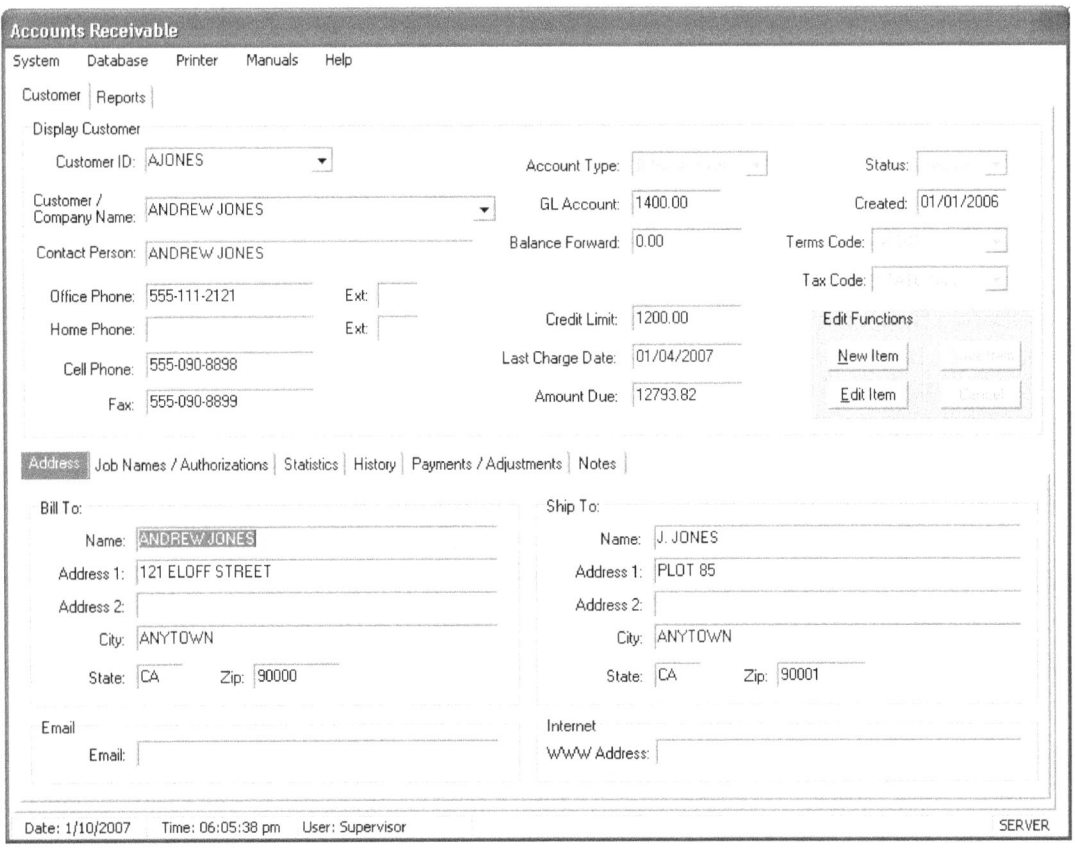

The following Accounts Receivable reports are available:

1. Customer Summary Report
2. Customer Full Report
3. Address Labels
4. Aged Analysis Report
5. Statements Report

POS Business Application   Product Brochure

System User Password Control

The POS Business Application software provides user login and password control to permit user access only to authorized system features. During POS Sales operations unauthorized users require a supervisor to enter an override password in order to change discount prices or select higher level features.

Single or Multiple Networked Computer Systems (Server / Clients)

The POS Business Application may operate either on a single IBM PC compatible computer system (Server) or on multiple networked IBM PC compatible computers (Server plus Clients).

Database Import / Export

The Database Import Section allows existing data from a different accounting system to be imported into the POS Business Application. Imported data must be in Comma Separated Variable (CSV) format. A conversion utility has also been provided to convert dBASE files to CSV format. The Database Import feature permits the user to specify the name/location of specific CSV variables to be imported as well as their destination position within the new database structure. Multiple databases can be combined during the import process into a single destination database.

The Database Export Section permits exportation of POS Business Application database data to CSV files.

System Requirements (Server / Client PC Computer Systems)

The Server / Client PC Computer Systems may use any one of the following operating systems:

1. Windows Vista
2. Windows XP (Professional or Home Editions, or later versions)
3. Windows 2000 (or later versions)
4. Windows 2000, 2003 Server (or later versions)

Note: The Server PC Computer System need not use a Windows Server Operating System unless high secure network access is required.

Hardware Requirements

The following minimum IBM PC compatible computer features are required:

- Pentium III 1GHz
- 512MB RAM
- LAN Network Interface
- Video Monitor (800 x 600 minimum)
- Mouse
- Keyboard

Quantum Blue Technology LLC

POS Business Application   Product Brochure

The POS Business Application program interface screens have been designed to fit on a monitor set to 800 x 600 pixel resolution. This permits the image to fill the entire screen thereby allowing the text to be easily read by both the customer and the counter staff.

Note: A DVD R/W device would be recommended for storing Server Database Backups.

Server / Client Operation

In a single computer environment, the computer will be configured as a POS Business Application Server.

In a multiple networked computer environment, one computer will be configured as a POS Business Application Server and the remaining computers will be configured as POS Business Application Clients.

The POS Business Application Server can execute the following modules:

1. Inventory Module
2. Point-Of-Sale Module
3. Accounts Receivable Module

POS Business Application Demo Version:

A demo version of the POS Business Application may be downloaded from the Quantum Blue Technology web site. This is a fully operational version with a trial period limitation. The demo version may be converted into a full version with the purchase of a POS Business Application software license.

POS Business Application Software License:

A POS Business Application software license may be purchased – please contact us or refer to the Quantum Blue Technology web site for details. This is a fixed price license and permits the user to utilize a system comprised of a POS Business Application "Server" with up to 99 associated "Client" computer systems.

Due to ongoing development, this brochure may be modified at any time.

For more information, please contact:

Quantum Blue Technology LLC 1424 Welsh Way, Ramona California 92065 U.S.A.	
Phone:	USA (858) 837-2160
Email:	info@QuantumBlueTechnology.com
Web:	www.QuantumBlueTechnology.com

Operator's Manual

Overview

(Read This Document First)

    Project: Point-Of-Sale
               Business Application
       Date: January 7th 2008
 Revision: 2.1.2
 Company: Quantum Blue Technology LLC.

Copyright Notice

Copyright ©2005, 2006, 2007, 2008 **Quantum Blue Technology LLC.** – All rights reserved worldwide. This document is proprietary to **Quantum Blue Technology LLC.** and may contain information that is to be maintained as Trade Secret. It is intended for use only by **Quantum Blue Technology LLC.** employees and its' contractors, customer employees, and authorized personnel. It may not be copied, translated, or transcribed in whole or in part without the express permission of the copyright holder **Quantum Blue Technology LLC.**

Quantum Blue Technology LLC
1424 Welsh Way, Ramona
California 92065
U.S.A.

Phone: USA (858) 837-2160
Email: info@QuantumBlueTechnology.com
Web: www.QuantumBlueTechnology.com

Please Note:

Due to ongoing design and development, **Quantum Blue Technology LLC.** may, at any time, and without notification, amend and update either this document and/or the associated "POS Business Application" software package.

Change History

Date	Version	Author	Reason for Change
11/13/06	1.0.0	Steve McClure	Initial Draft.
11/14/06	2.0.0	Steve McClure	General minor updates
11/20/06	2.1.0	Steve McClure	General minor updates.
1/9/07	2.1.1	Steve McClure	Minor updates.
1/7/08	2.1.2	Steve McClure	General updates

Table of Contents

1 **SCOPE** 1
   1.1   GENERAL 1
      1.1.1   *Operating System* *1*
      1.1.2   *Hardware Requirements* *1*
   1.2   SERVER / CLIENT STATIONS 2
      1.2.1   *Server Station* *2*
         1.2.1.1   License 3
      1.2.2   *Client Station* *3*
         1.2.2.1   License 3
   1.3   RECOMMENDATIONS 4
   1.4   END-USER LICENSE AGREEMENT (EULA) 4
   1.5   ABBREVIATIONS 5
   1.6   DOCUMENTS 5

2 **OVERVIEW** 6
   2.1   EASE OF USE 7
   2.2   DISTRIBUTED ENCRYPTED NETWORK DATABASES 7
   2.3   CALENDAR INDEXED DATABASES 8
   2.4   POS SALES TRANSACTION RE-POSTING 9
   2.5   DATABASE BACKUP AND DATABASE RESTORE 10

3 **MAIN FEATURES** 11
   3.1   SYSTEM USER PASSWORD CONTROL 11
   3.2   SINGLE OR MULTIPLE NETWORKED COMPUTER SYSTEMS 11
   3.3   POINT-OF-SALE (POS) TERMINAL 11
   3.4   INVENTORY CONTROL MODULE 12
   3.5   ACCOUNTS RECEIVABLE MODULE 13
   3.6   DATABASE IMPORT AND EXPORT 13
   3.7   DATABASE BACKUP AND RESTORE 14
   3.8   OPERATOR MANUAL 14

POS Business Application — Overview

1 Scope

This document provides the Overview of the Point-Of-Sale Business Application. This manual should be read first.

1.1 General

The Point-Of-Sale (POS) Business Application is designed for the small business and provides networking capabilities not normally available to general Point-Of-Sale systems.

1.1.1 Operating System

The POS Business Application software executes on a standard IBM Personal Computer System (or compatible) which executes one of the following operating systems:

1. Windows Vista
2. Windows XP (Professional or Home Editions, or later versions)
3. Windows 2000 (or later versions)
4. Windows 2000 Server (or later versions)

Note: The POS Business Application may operate correctly on previous versions of Windows, however, at this time it has not been verified.

1.1.2 Hardware Requirements

The following minimum IBM PC compatible computer features are required:

- Pentium III 1GHz
- 512MB RAM
- LAN Network Interface
- Video Monitor (800 x 600 minimum)
- Mouse
- Keyboard

The POS Business Application program interface screens have been designed to fit on a monitor set to 800 x 600 pixel resolution. This permits the image to fill the entire screen thereby allowing the text to be easily readable by both the customer and the counter staff.

Note: A DVD R/W device would be recommended for storing Server Database Backups.

POS Business Application   Overview

1.2 Server / Client Stations

The POS Business Application executes as either a:

1. Server Station
2. Client Station

Note: The term "Server" and "Client" refers to the type of POS Business Application installation and not to the type of operating system executing on the computer.

Note: The POS Business Application computer software may be installed on a computer system as either a Server Application or as a Client Application. The same software program is used for both these types of installations.

1.2.1 Server Station

In a single computer environment, the computer will be configured as a POS Business Application Server.

In a multiple networked computer environment, one computer will be configured as a POS Business Application Server and the remaining computers will be configured as POS Business Application Clients.

The computer system which is configured to be the POS Business Application Server contain the central databases. These databases are shared over the network with the POS Business Application Client computers. The Server Station is used to perform database import and export operations, as well as database backup and restore operations.

The POS Business Application Server can execute the following modules:

1. Inventory Module
2. Point-Of-Sale Module
3. Accounts Receivable Module

Note: Other modules are in the process of being developed.

POS Business Application   Overview

1.2.1.1 License

The POS Business Application (POSBA) may be installed on one or more networked computer systems. Of these computer systems, one is designated the POS Business Application "Server" since it holds the primary databases. Up to 99 POS Business Application "Client" networked computer systems may be associated with this Server system.

The POS Business Application license is a single fixed price license. This license permits the user to install the POS Business Application software on a POSBA Server computer system and also on up to 99 networked POSBA Client computer systems all for one fixed price.

The POS Business Application license is installed on the POSBA Server system.

1.2.2 Client Station

In a single computer environment, the computer will be configured as a POS Business Application Server.

In a multiple networked computer environment, one computer will be configured as a POS Business Application Server and the remaining computers will be configured as POS Business Application Clients.

The computer systems which are configured to be the POS Business Application Clients contain copies of various Server databases. The Client Stations constantly monitor the Server databases and download new copies of required databases whenever they have detected that the databases have been updated.

Note: The POS Business Application may utilize up to 99 client stations.

1.2.2.1 License

Each Client Station accesses the license stored on the POSBA Server system. No additional client license need be purchased.

1.3 Recommendations

It is important to note that computer systems are totally dependant upon a clean and reliable power source. If they are not provided with such a power source, hardware disk drive errors may occur – for example, the system power fails during a disk write to a database file. Such events can corrupt disk files making them unusable.

With this in mind, we strongly suggest the use of an uninterruptible power supply (UPS) which will provide a clean power source during normal operation and also supply power for a limited time in the event of a power failure. All computer systems and network Ethernet hub modules should be powered by the UPS. Either a single UPS which can handle the entire load, or several smaller UPS units each handling individual computer systems may be used.

When a power fail condition occurs, the UPS unit(s) will allow the counter staff to continue using the computer systems to complete their current sales. Once all sales have been completed, the computer systems should then be shut down as per the Windows Operating System procedure. The size of the UPS units should be such to provide at least ten (10) minutes of power for each computer system to safely complete this task.

Also, it is important to remember that hard disk drives are electro-mechanical in nature (ie. they have electronic and mechanical internal mechanisms) and do not have an infinite life span. They can either fail gradually or suddenly. When they fail gradually the computer system can appear to operate normally under most conditions but sluggishly when performing certain tasks (ie. performing retries when writing to a specific region of the disk drive). This can be an indication of a drive failure in progress. When a disk drive fails suddenly, it just stops. No amount of begging or pleading will help.

For this reason and since the POS Business Application relies on various database files it is important that database backups are performed frequently and stored off site. This will allow the system to be easily restored if database corruption or disk failure occurs.

1.4 End-User License Agreement (EULA)

Please refer to the Installation Manual for a complete description of the End-User License Agreement.

1.5 Abbreviations

CSV   Comma Separated Variable
LAN   Local Area Network
PC   Personal Computer
POS   Point-Of-Sale
UPS   Uninterruptible Power Supply

1.6 Documents

The following documents describe the entire POS Business Application system and should be read in the following order:

1. Overview
2. Installation
3. System
4. Inventory
5. Point Of Sale
6. Accounts Receivable
7. Import Database (General)

POS Business Application — Overview

2 Overview

The Point-Of-Sale (POS) Business Application accounting software is designed to operate on one or more IBM PC computers each running the Windows operating system.

This POS Business Application provides the following main features:

1. Distributed Encrypted Network Databases
2. System User Password Control
3. Single or Multiple Networked Computer Systems (Server & Client Stations)
4. Point-Of-Sale (POS) Terminal
5. Inventory Control Module
6. Accounts Receivable Module
7. Database Import and Export
8. Database Backup and Restore

<u>Note</u>: Other accounting modules are currently under development.

POS Business Application — Overview

What sets this product apart from other POS Systems

The principal features which set this POS Business Application Software apart from other POS accounting software systems are the following:

- Ease of Use
- Distributed Encrypted Databases
- Quicker Data Access via Calendar Indexed Databases
- Re-Posting of POS Sales transactions if database recovery is required
- Safe Non-Destructive Database Backup and Restore Operations

2.1 Ease of Use

Many POS Systems require their users to have in-depth accounting experience in order to understand how to use their software. The POS Business Application has been designed to be easy to understand and to use.

2.2 Distributed Encrypted Network Databases

The main restriction with many Point-Of-Sale accounting systems is their reliance on both the network and on the Server computer system. These accounting systems locate their central database on the server computer and the client computer systems must access this database via the network in order to perform any Point-Of-Sale operations.

A major cause for concern with users of such systems is with regard to what would happen if the network or the server were to fail. If either of these failures were to occur then the client computer systems would not be able to access the central database and would therefore not be able to perform Point-Of-Sale transactions. In this situation, the counter staff would then be required to make hand written sales receipts and refer to previously printed (and perhaps outdated) price lists. This method of operation is tedious, slow and can easily generate errors.

Later, when the Server and/or network are once more operational, the handwritten sale transactions have to be manually entered into the accounting system – another time consuming operation which is also fraught with possible errors.

The POS Business Application

This POS Business Application system, however, is designed to minimize these conditions. It uses a distributed encrypted database and is therefore not totally reliant on the network nor on the Server. Although our Server contains the central database, any changes to this database are passed on to database copies which reside on each Client computer system. If the Server and/or the network were to subsequently fail, each POS

POS Business Application Overview

Business Application Client computer system would still contain copies of the latest relevant inventory and accounts receivable databases and may still be used to perform Point-Of-Sale transactions with the current inventory stock part numbers and prices.

Once the Server and network are once more operational, the transaction sales data collected by each POS terminal may then be posted to the Server thereby updating the central database.

All Server and Client databases are encrypted to provide basic system security. For higher level security, the file system encryption features of Windows XP Professional may be utilized.

2.3 Calendar Indexed Databases

General POS accounting systems are very responsive when the system is first installed. As the days and months progress, more and more history data is created and the system can start to get sluggish. After several years of history data has been collected, the system can take a long time to scan an entire database in order to access and obtain specific information pertaining to a report.

In order to minimize this effect, some accounting systems impose database size limitations which restrict the amount of data history which may be retained.

The POS Business Application

Firstly, this POS Business Application has no size limitation regarding the number of years of data history which may be retained.

In order to have direct, fast, access to sales history information, the POS Business Application Sales History database has been indexed by calendar year and month sub-directories. This means that when searching for data pertaining to a specific year and month, the data file for that calendar period can be quickly accessed and the information speedily obtained.

POS Business Application — Overview

2.4 POS Sales Transaction Re-Posting

Most POS accounting systems use the Server to contain the central accounting databases. This database usually also includes the Point-Of-Sale transactions for each POS terminal. At the end of a business period, these POS sales transactions are posted to the sales history database and certain inventory database parameters (eg. the "On Hand" quantity) are updated. Once this posting operation has completed, the original information is then deleted since it is no longer required.

Normally this approach is successful, except under conditions when the database has had to be recovered due to system related problems.

If the database is to be recovered, the current day's posted (and un-posted) sales transactions for each POS Terminal may be deleted during the database backup restoration process. The sales data for the period between the backup date and the current date will then have to be manually re-entered in order to bring the database up to date. This is another time consuming operation which is also fraught with possible errors.

The POS Business Application

The POS Business Application, however, keeps each POS terminal's sales information on local files within each respective computer system. At the end of the business period, the collected sales data is posted to the server and the sales history and Inventory database updated.

With the POS Business Application, the sales data is never deleted after the posting operation. Instead, it is placed into a local database directory and given a unique name which includes the date and time when the posting operation occurred. If a Server related problem were to occur at this point and a prior database was to be restored, the intervening sales data still exists on all POS Terminal computers and can simply be re-posted thereby quickly bringing the Server central database up to date. No manual re-entry of POS Sales transaction data would normally be required.

During the re-posting operation, the POS Business Application software merges the new information with the currently existing information. Since Calendar Indexed Databases are used, the speed of the merging process is optimized since only the sales history file for the re-posting day in question has to be scanned. The merging process also ensures that no duplicate sales entries are stored in the database and that subsequent databases operations (ie. adjustment of the Inventory On-Hand quantity, etc.) only occur once. If multiple re-posting operations were to be performed with a previously posted file no harm would result to the database.

Other POS systems may not allow re-posting since the merging process would involve the scanning of the entire POS history database – a lengthy, time-consuming operation.

POS Business Application — Overview

2.5 Database Backup and Database Restore

During Database Backup operations, some POS Accounting systems use the same backup storage file name and/or location, which may result in the previous backup file being overwritten.

During Database Restore operations the same POS Accounting system's active directory database is overwritten.

With this procedure a healthy database can easily be destroyed if an incorrect restore operation was performed.

The POS Business Application

The POS Business Application Database Backup operation allows the various databases to be converted to a single backup file for transfer to another storage location or to removable media (eg. removable hard drive, DVD-ROM, etc.). The system generated backup file name is always unique and includes the current date and time and is therefore easily identified as shown in the example below:

    For example: `POS_Database_Backup 2007-01-09 11-15-21.BAK`

Each database backup operation will create a new unique backup file and will never overwrite any previous backup file.

The POS Business Application Database Restore operation takes a specified backup file and expands it to create the required system directories and databases. Prior to performing the Database Restoration, the previously existing database directory is renamed and is therefore not overwritten during this process. The Database Restore operation also has the capability of restoring this or any other previously created database directory.

The default Database Backup and Database Restore operations do not erase or modify any existing database files, therefore the user is never faced with the situation where the system database could be overwritten due to operator error. If the user wishes to overwrite the active database directory during a restore operation, an override option is provided.

POS Business Application — Overview

3 Main Features

3.1 System User Password Control

The POS Business Application provides user name / password protection access to the various sub-modules. For example, a user may be given access to the Point-Of-Sale module but may be restricted from overriding prices or discount information. If such a request is required a user with the correct authority may log in temporarily to perform the override operation.

The following features are provided:

1. Unlimited number of users
2. Specify access to various system operations

3.2 Single or Multiple Networked Computer Systems

The POS Business Application may operate on a single computer system or on a network of computer systems. A single computer installation may be performed initially and some time in the future be converted into a multiple computer system. When a multiple computer system is used, certain server databases are copied to the client system (ie. distributed databases) thereby allowing the client systems to function during network or server failure conditions.

The following features are provided:

1. Single or Multiple Computer System Operation.
2. Up to 99 client stations may be utilized.
3. Descriptive lockout details when another user has locked a database

3.3 Point-Of-Sale (POS) Terminal

The Point-Of-Sale screen allows the recording of sales transactions for cash or account customers. The purchase details of the sale are displayed along with discount price and percentage information. A cash sale may utilize cash, check, credit card and gift certificate tender in a single transaction.

The POS terminal may utilize a bar code scanner (keyboard interface). An option is available to place the scanner into manual operation (user enters item quantity manually) or automatic operation (a quantity of 1 is entered automatically).

POS Business Application   Overview

The following features are provided:

1. Quotes – Create, List, Convert to Sales
2. Sales – Create, List or Retrieve a current sale or a sale from the history database
3. Associate a special instruction message to a quote or to a sale
4. Store customer information if sale above a specific value
5. Specify start of business, paid in, paid out till amounts
6. Re-Printing of Receipts (original or copy)
7. Balance Register Screen and printout
8. Reposting of previous sales data to bring an old restored database up-to-date
9. The ESC/POS or Windows Driver Till Printer Interface

The following POS Register Reports are provided:

1. Register Summary/Full Reports (identify sale items)
2. Register Year Report (Yearly takings)
3. Sales Tax Report

3.4   Inventory Control Module

The POS Business Application Inventory Control Module is used to identify all the information associated with a specific inventory part.

The following Inventory features are provided:

1. Stock number, description, aliases and price break information
2. Category, Brand and Type details
3. Find utility for quick search
4. List, Markup, Level List, Level Markup Pricing (Margin Pricing added later)
5. Storage for Vendor Information and Notes
6. Stock Adjustment screen
7. History display of Inventory transactions

The following Inventory Reports are provided:

1. Quick Stock List
2. Price Book
3. Under Stock Report
4. Over Stock Report
5. Stock Value Report
6. Stocktake Worksheet
7. Stock Labels (prints Bar Code 39)
8. History Report

3.5 Accounts Receivable Module

The POS Business Application Accounts Receivable Module is used to identify all information pertaining to an account customer.

The following Account Receivable features are provided:

1. Customer ID, name, phone numbers, billing and shipping addresses.
2. Storage for email and WWW addresses
3. Term Codes and Tax Codes
4. Job Names and Authorization (information displayed on POS screen)
5. Account Statistics (charges, statement, payment, finance charge and aging info)
6. Posted account transaction history
7. Payment / Adjustments (including generation of finance charge transactions)
8. Notes

The following Accounts Receivable Reports are provided:

1. Customer Summary Report
2. Customer Full Report
3. Address Labels
4. Aged Analysis Report
5. Statements

3.6 Database Import and Export

The POS Business Application has a database import module which allows data from other POS accounting software systems to be imported. The database import screen allows the user to indicate which data items from specific data files are to be imported into the system.

Data may be imported into the following POS Business Application databases:

1. Accounts Receivable
2. Accounts Receivable History
3. Inventory
4. Inventory History
5. POS Sale History Register
6. POS Sale History Transaction

Data may be exported from the following POS Business Application databases:

1. Accounts Receivable
2. Inventory

Note: Future enhancements will include the exportation of other databases.

3.7 Database Backup and Restore

The database backup operation is used to keep system backups such that if the need ever arose, a previous copy of the system database may be restored.

The POS Business Application backup and restore operations when compared to other systems is unique in that no files or databases are ever deleted and can easily be recovered. A description of the processes involved is described earlier in this document.

3.8 Operator Manual

The various operator manuals may be easily accessed from the main menu. The user may specify which PDF reader is to be used to display the manuals.

The following manuals may be displayed:

1. Overview
2. Installation
3. Systems
4. Inventory
5. Point Of Sale
6. Accounts Receivable
7. Import Database

Operator's Manual

Installation

Project: Point-Of-Sale Business Application
Date: April 14th 2008
Revision: 2.1.8
Company: Quantum Blue Technology LLC.

Copyright Notice

Copyright ©2005, 2006, 2007, 2008 Quantum Blue Technology LLC. – All rights reserved worldwide. This document is proprietary to **Quantum Blue Technology LLC.** And may contain information that is to be maintained as Trade Secret. It is intended for use only by **Quantum Blue Technology LLC.** Employees and its' contractors, customer employees, and authorized personnel. It may not be copied, translated, or transcribed in whole or in part without the express permission of the copyright holder **Quantum Blue Technology LLC.**

Quantum Blue Technology LLC
1424 Welsh Way, Ramona
California 92065
U.S.A.

Phone: USA (858) 837-2160
Email: info@QuantumBlueTechnology.com
Web: www.QuantumBlueTechnology.com

Please Note:

Due to ongoing design and development, **Quantum Blue Technology LLC.** May at any time and without notification amend and update either this document and/or the associated "POS Business Application" software package.

Change History

Date	Version	Author	Reason for Change
8/11/06	1.0.0	Steve McClure	Initial Draft.
8/26/06	2.0.0	Steve McClure	Pre-Release 1
11/8/06	2.0.1	Steve McClure	Pre-Release 2
11/14/06	2.1.0	Steve McClure	Released – Added screen shots.
11/20/06	2.1.1	Steve McClure	Minor corrections.
12/04/06	2.1.2	Steve McClure	Added new installation screens.
1/8/07	2.1.3	Steve McClure	Minor additions.
7/5/07	2.1.4	Steve McClure	Modified installation description.
12/7/07	2.1.5	Steve McClure	Vista Operating System Execution
1/7/08	2.1.6	Steve McClure	General updates
1/11/08	2.1.7	Steve McClure	Added Vista OS installation details.
4/14/08	2.1.8	Steve McClure	Installation Procedure updated.

Table of Contents

1 SCOPE 1
   1.1 GENERAL 1
      1.1.1 *Operating System* *1*
      1.1.2 *Hardware Requirements* *1*
   1.2 SERVER / CLIENT STATIONS 2
      1.2.1 *Server Station*... *2*
         1.2.1.1 License 3
      1.2.2 *Client Station* *3*
         1.2.2.1 License 3
   1.3 OVERVIEW 4
   1.4 RECOMMENDATIONS 5
   1.5 END-USER LICENSE AGREEMENT (EULA) 6
   1.6 ABBREVIATIONS 10
   1.7 DIRECTORY OVERVIEW 11
      1.7.1 *Directory Sharing* *11*
      1.7.2 *Drive Mapping* *11*

2 SOFTWARE INSTALLATION PROCEDURE 12
   2.1 POS BUSINESS APPLICATION SOFTWARE INSTALLATION (CD-ROM) 13
   2.2 POS BUSINESS APPLICATION SOFTWARE INSTALLATION (INTERNET DOWNLOAD) 14
   2.3 CONFIGURING THE POS BUSINESS APPLICATION 16
      2.3.1 *Single Computer Installation* *18*
         2.3.1.1 The Application Type 19
         2.3.1.2 The POS Cash Register Number.. 19
         2.3.1.3 The Server Shared Directory Name 19
         2.3.1.4 The Project Directory Name 20
         2.3.1.5 Finalize Installation 20
         2.3.1.6 Demo Database Installation 20
         2.3.1.7 Edit POS Configuration File 21
         2.3.1.8 POSBA Server Configuration File Example 22
      2.3.2 *Multiple Computer Installation*... *23*
         2.3.2.1 Server Installation 25
            2.3.2.1.1 The Application Type 25
            2.3.2.1.2 The POS Cash Register Number.. 26
            2.3.2.1.3 The Server Shared Directory Name 26
            2.3.2.1.4 The Project Directory Name 26
            2.3.2.1.5 Share Server Directory 27
            2.3.2.1.6 Finalize Installation 28
            2.3.2.1.7 Demo Database Installation 29
            2.3.2.1.8 Edit POSBA Configuration File 30
            2.3.2.1.9 POSBA Server Configuration File Example 31

		2.3.2.2 Client Installation 32

- 2.3.2.2.1 The Application Type 33
- 2.3.2.2.2 The POS Cash Register Number... 34
- 2.3.2.2.3 The Server Drive 34
- 2.3.2.2.4 The Server Shared Directory Name 34
- 2.3.2.2.5 The Project Directory Name 34
- 2.3.2.2.6 Server Computer Network Name.. 34
- 2.3.2.2.7 Map Network Drive 34
- 2.3.2.2.8 Finalize Installation 36
- 2.3.2.2.9 Edit POSBA Configuration File 37
- 2.3.2.2.10 POSBA Client Configuration File Example 38

3 APPENDIX A 39

3.1 SYSTEM CONFIGURATION FILE 39
3.1.1 System Section... 39
- 3.1.1.1 Application 39
- 3.1.1.2 Sound 40

3.1.2 Drives Section 40
- 3.1.2.1 Server 40
  - 3.1.2.1.1 POS Business Application Server.. 40
  - 3.1.2.1.2 POS Business Application Client 41
- 3.1.2.2 Server Name... 41
- 3.1.2.3 Server Shared Directory... 41
- 3.1.2.4 Local Drive Low Limit 42
- 3.1.2.5 Server Drive Low Limit 42

3.1.3 Directories Section... 42

3.1.4 Options Section.. 43
- 3.1.4.1 Register 43

3.1.5 General Section.. 44
- 3.1.5.1 Currency Symbol 44
- 3.1.5.2 Minimize Screens 44
- 3.1.5.3 Fixed Forms 45
- 3.1.5.4 Display Network Messages.. 45
- 3.1.5.5 Auto POS 46
- 3.1.5.6 Auto Shutdown 46
- 3.1.5.7 Exit Block 47

3.1.6 Programs Section... 47
- 3.1.6.1 PDF Reader 47

3.2 MICROSOFT VISTA OPERATING SYSTEM INSTALLATION.............................. 48
3.2.1 Directory Sharing 48
- 3.2.1.1 Protected Shared Directory 48
- 3.2.1.2 Un-Protected Shared Directory... 49

3.2.2 Compatibility Mode 50
- 3.2.2.1 POS Business Application desktop icon................................... 50
- 3.2.2.2 Microsoft Vista Program Compatibility Wizard....................... 51

POS Business Application   Installation

1 Scope

This document is the Installation Manual for the Point-Of-Sale Business Application. The procedures in this document are used to install the POS Business Application software on both Server and Client computer systems.

1.1 General

The Point-Of-Sale (POS) Business Application is designed for the small business and provides networking capabilities not normally available to general Point-Of-Sale systems.

The principal features which set this POS Business Application Software apart from other POS accounting software systems are the following:

- Ease of Use
- Distributed Encrypted Databases
- Quicker Data Access via Calendar Indexed Databases
- Re-Posting of POS Sales transactions if database recovery is required
- Safe Non-Destructive Database Backup and Restore Operations

Please refer to the Overview document for a more detailed description of these features.

1.1.1 Operating System

The POS Business Application software executes on a standard IBM Personal Computer System (or compatible) which uses one of the following operating systems:

1. Microsoft Windows Vista (See Appendix for Vista Compatibility)
2. Microsoft Windows XP (Professional SP2 or Home Editions, or later versions)
3. Microsoft Windows 2000 (or later versions)
4. Microsoft Windows 2000 Server (or later versions)

Note: The POS Business Application may operate correctly on previous versions of Windows, however, at this time it has not been verified.

1.1.2 Hardware Requirements

The following minimum IBM PC compatible computer features are required:

- Pentium III 1GHz
- 512MB RAM
- LAN Network Interface
- Video Monitor (800 x 600 minimum)
- Mouse and Keyboard

Quantum Blue Technology LLC.

POS Business Application   Installation

The POS Business Application program interface screens have been designed to fit on a monitor set to 800 x 600 pixel resolution. This permits the image to fill the entire screen thereby allowing the text to be easily readable by both the customer and the counter staff.

Note: A DVD R/W device would be recommended for storing Server Database Backups.

1.2 Server / Client Stations

The POS Business Application executes as either a:

1. Server Station
2. Client Station

Note: The term "Server" and "Client" refers to the type of POS Business Application installation and not to the type of operating system executing on the computer.

Note: The POS Business Application computer software may be installed on a computer system as either a Server Application or as a Client Application. The same software program is used for both these types of installations.

1.2.1 Server Station

In a single computer environment, the computer will be configured as a POS Business Application Server.

In a multiple networked computer environment, one computer will be configured as a POS Business Application Server and the remaining computers will be configured as POS Business Application Clients.

The computer system which is configured to be the POS Business Application Server contain the central databases. These databases are shared over the network with the POS Business Application Client computers. The Server Station is used to perform database import and export operations, as well as database backup and restore operations.

The POS Business Application Server can execute the following modules:

1. Inventory Module
2. Point-Of-Sale Module
3. Accounts Receivable Module

Note: Other modules are in the process of being developed.

POS Business Application Installation

1.2.1.1 License

The POS Business Application (POSBA) may be installed on one or more networked computer systems. Of these computer systems, one is designated the POS Business Application "Server" since it holds the primary databases. Up to 99 POS Business Application "Client" networked computer systems may be associated with this Server system.

The POS Business Application license is a single fixed price license. This license permits the user to install the POS Business Application software on a POSBA Server computer system and also on up to 99 networked POSBA Client computer systems all for one fixed price.

The POS Business Application license is installed on the POSBA Server system.

1.2.2 Client Station

In a single computer environment, the computer will be configured as a POS Business Application Server.

In a multiple networked computer environment, one computer will be configured as a POS Business Application Server and the remaining computers will be configured as POS Business Application Clients.

The computer systems which are configured to be the POS Business Application Clients contain copies of various Server databases. The Client Stations constantly monitor the Server databases and download new copies of required databases whenever they have detected that the databases have been updated.

Note: The POS Business Application may utilize up to 99 client stations.

1.2.2.1 License

Each Client Station accesses the license stored on the POSBA Server system. No additional client license need be purchased.

POS Business Application   Installation

1.3   Overview

When the POS Business Application is started, the main screen will be displayed as shown below:

The main screen provides the following information:

1. The Company Name

   The top line indicates the authorized user of the POS Business Application software.

2. The Main Menus

   The main menu identifies the various POS Business Application modules available to the user. If a menu label is in bold letters then that specific module is available to the user currently logged onto the POS Business Application system.

3. System Status

   The System Status is located at the bottom of the display. It identifies the current system date and time, the user currently logged on (if any), an information message and finally Server availability.

   Server Availability is indicated as follows:

   a) Local   - Client is operating in local mode (ie. Server is not available)
   b) Server - Client can communicate with the Server
   c) SERVER - This computer system is the Server

1.4 Recommendations

It is important to note that computer systems are totally dependant upon a clean and reliable power source. If they are not provided with such a power source, hardware disk drive errors may occur – for example, the system power fails during a disk write to a database file. Such events can corrupt disk files making them unusable.

With this in mind, we strongly suggest the use of an uninterruptible power supply (UPS) which will provide a clean power source during normal operation and also supply power for a limited time in the event of a power failure. All computer systems and network Ethernet hub modules should be powered by the UPS. Either a single UPS which can handle the entire load, or several smaller UPS units each handling individual computer systems may be used.

When a power fail condition occurs, the UPS unit(s) will allow the counter staff to continue using the computer systems to complete their current sales. Once all sales have been completed, the computer systems should then be shut down as per the Windows Operating System procedure. The size of the UPS units should be such to provide at least ten (10) minutes of power for each computer system to safely complete this task.

Also, it is important to remember that hard disk drives are electro-mechanical in nature (ie. they have electronic and mechanical internal mechanisms) and do not have an infinite life span. They can either fail gradually or suddenly. When they fail gradually the computer system can appear to operate normally under most conditions but sluggishly when performing certain tasks (ie. performing retries when writing to a specific region of the disk drive). This can be an indication of a drive failure in progress. When a disk drive fails suddenly, it just stops. No amount of begging or pleading will help.

For this reason and since the POS Business Application relies on various database files it is important that database backups are performed frequently and stored off site. This will allow the system to be easily restored if database corruption or disk failure occurs.

1.5 End-User License Agreement (EULA)

The Quantum Blue Technology LLC End-User License Agreement (EULA) is a legal statement for the POS Business Application software product in which this EULA is contained, which includes computer software, and may include associated media, printed materials and "online" or electronic documentation (collectively the "POSBA Software Product"), and exists between you and Quantum Blue Technology LLC.

By installing, copying, or otherwise using the POSBA Software Product, you agree to be bound by the terms of this EULA. You must indicate your agreement to be bound by the terms of this EULA by pressing the "I ACCEPT" button on the Software Product's installation program, or else you will not be able to install the Software Product. If you do not agree to the terms of this EULA, you may not install or use the POSBA Software Product; you may, however, within 30 days of your initial purchase of a copy of the POSBA Software Product, return the entire copy of the POSBA Software Product (including all computer media, packaging and documentation) to Quantum Blue Technology for a refund after which event your rights under this EULA are immediately terminated.

If you are installing the Software Product on a computer that is not owned by you, you are bound to the terms of this EULA both in your individual capacity and as an agent of the owner of the computer, and your actions will bind the owner of the computer. You represent and warrant to Quantum Blue Technology LLC. that you have the capacity and authority to enter into this Agreement on your own behalf as well as on behalf of the owner of the computer the POSBA Software Product is being installed upon. For purposes of this EULA, the "owner" of a computer is the individual or entity that has legal title to the computer or that has the possessory interest in the computer if it is leased or loaned by the actual title owner.

COPYRIGHT
The POSBA Software Product is protected by copyright laws and international copyright treaties, as well as other intellectual property laws and treaties. All title and copyrights in and to the POSBA Software Product (including but not limited to any images, photographs, animations, video, audio, music, text, and "applets" incorporated into the Software Product) are owned by Quantum Blue Technology LLC. or its suppliers.

GRANT OF LICENSE
The POSBA Software Product is licensed, not sold. The licensee shall use the POS Business Application Software only for its own internal business purposes.

Provided you comply with all applicable license terms and conditions contained in this EULA, Quantum Blue Technology LLC. grants you the right to reproduce, install and use one copy of the POSBA Software Product on each of your networked computers that is running a validly licensed copy of the POSBA Software Product.

POS Business Application — Installation

The Licensee may make a single copy of the Software for archival or backup purposes, provided that such copy shall include the Licensor's copyright and other proprietary notices as originally contained with the Software.

No other use, copying or distribution of the POSBA Software Product is permitted. You may not rent the POSBA Software Product, nor may you offer use of it to others through a service bureau or application service provider. If you are installing this copy of the POSBA Software Product as an upgrade, update, patch or enhancement of a prior release of the same POSBA Software Product which was installed on the same computer, your rights under the prior license agreement for the POSBA Software Product are terminated, and all of your use of the POSBA Software Product (including its prior versions) are solely under the terms of this license agreement.

The Licensee is solely responsible for installation, configuration and use of the POSBA Software Product and do so at their own risk.

LIMITATIONS
The Licensee may not reverse-engineer, decompile or otherwise translate the POSBA Software Product. You may not modify, amend, or create derivative works of the POSBA Software Product, in whole or in part.

Limited Money Back Warranty.
The Licensee shall have thirty (30) days from the Effective Date of the initial term of this Agreement (the "Warranty Period") to test the POSBA Software Product to its satisfaction. If the Licensee is not fully satisfied with the POSBA Software Product, the Licensee may, within the Warranty Period, return the Software to the Licensor for a full refund of any license and maintenance fees actually received by the Licensor from the Licensee pursuant to this Agreement. All POSBA Software and associated directories and/or files must be removed from all Licensee computer systems. Upon such return, this Agreement shall immediately terminate.

POS Business Application Versions
The POSBA Software Product may be distributed as either:

1. A Trial Version
2. A Limited Full Version
3. An Unlimited Full Version

1. Trial Version
The trial version of this software is licensed solely for use during the trial period (normally 30 days). The trial software may limit the number of licenses and options, and also may limit the number of database records which may be stored.

POS Business Application Installation

If you do not have a valid licensed copy of this software, you are not authorized to install, copy or otherwise use this software and you have no rights under this eula.

At the end of the trial period, the Licensee must discontinue any and all use of the software. The Licensee must then remove the unlicensed POS Business Application software from all Licensee computer systems.

2. Limited Full Version

When the POSBA Software Package is purchased, the licensee may initially be provided with a Limited Full Version of the software package. If the licensee originally downloaded the POSBA Software Package from the Internet, Quantum Blue Technology LLC. may provide the licensee with a license key which, when installed, will convert the demo version of the software to one with limited full version status.

The Limited Full Version software will provide full functionality of the software for the warranty period. Quantum Blue Technology LLC. may then send a license key to the customer to convert the software to an unlimited full version for the purchased number of licenses and options.

If you do not have a valid licensed copy of this software, you are not authorized to install, copy or otherwise use this software and you have no rights under this eula.

If the purchaser decides to return the product for a refund during the warranty period, the Licensee must discontinue any and all use of the software. The Licensee must then remove the unlicensed POS Business Application software from all Licensee computer systems. If unlicensed use of the POSBA Software Package is continued, the limited full version license key will expire (normally 10 days later) and the POSBA Software Package applications will no longer function.

3. Unlimited Full Version

When the POSBA Software Package is purchased, the licensee may be provided with an Unlimited Full Version of the software package. If the licensee originally downloaded the POSBA Software Package from the Internet, Quantum Blue Technology may provide the licensee with a license key which, when installed, will convert the demo version of the software to one with unlimited full version status.

The Unlimited Full Version software will provide full functionality of the software for the purchased number of licenses and options. There is no expiry time duration associated with this software version.

POS Business Application　　　　　　　　　　　　　Installation

If you do not have a valid licensed copy of this software, you are not authorized to install, copy or otherwise use this software and you have no rights under this eula.

If the purchaser decides to return the product for a refund during the warranty period, the Licensee must discontinue any and all use of the software. The Licensee must then remove the unlicensed POS Business Application software from all Licensee computer systems.

The following section is applicable to all license types:

Disclaimer of warranties: To the maximum extent permitted by applicable law, Quantum Blue Technology LLC. and its suppliers provide to you the POS Business Application components, and support services (if any) AS IS and with all faults; and Quantum Blue Technology LLC. and its suppliers hereby disclaim all other warranties and conditions, whether express, implied or statutory, including, but not limited to, any (if any) implied warranties, duties or conditions of merchantability, of fitness for a particular purpose, of reliability or availability, of accuracy or completeness of responses, of results, of workmanlike effort, of lack of viruses, and of lack of negligence, all with regard to the POS Business Application components, and the provision of or failure to provide support or other services, information, software, and related content through the POS Business Application components or otherwise arising out of the use of the POS Business Application components. Also, there is no warranty or condition of title, quiet enjoyment, quiet possession, correspondence to description or non-infringement with regard to the POS Business Application components.

Exclusion of incidental, consequential and certain other damages: To the maximum extent permitted by applicable law, in no event shall Quantum Blue Technology LLC. or its suppliers be liable for any special, incidental, punitive, indirect, or consequential damages whatsoever (including, but not limited to, damages for loss of profits or confidential or other information, for business interruption, for personal injury, for loss of privacy, for failure to meet any duty including of good faith or of reasonable care, negligence, and any other pecuniary or other loss whatsoever) arising out of or in any way related to the use of or inability to use the POS Business Application components, the provision of or failure to provide support or other services, information, software, and related content through the POS Business Application components or otherwise arising out of the use of the POS Business Application components, or otherwise under or in connection with any provision of this EULA, even in the event of the fault, tort (including negligence), misrepresentation, strict or product liability, breach of contract or breach of warranty of Quantum Blue Technology LLC. or any supplier, and even if Quantum Blue Technology LLC. or any supplier has been advised of the possibility of such damages.

POS Business Application   Installation

Limitation of liability and remedies: Notwithstanding any damages that you might incur for any reason whatsoever (including, without limitation, all damages referenced above and all direct or general damages in contract or anything else), the entire liability of Quantum Blue Technology LLC. and any of its suppliers under any provision of this EULA and your exclusive remedy for all of the foregoing shall be limited to the amount actually paid by you for the POS Business Application components. The foregoing limitations, exclusions and disclaimers shall apply to the maximum extent permitted by applicable law, even if any remedy fails its essential purpose.

1.6   Abbreviations

CSV   Comma Separated Variable
POS   Point-Of-Sale
UPS   Uninterruptible Power Supply

POS Business Application   Installation

1.7 Directory Overview

The POS Business Application uses the Microsoft Window's mapped drive and shared directory features in order to allow the client computer systems access to the server computer databases. This concept may sound complicated, however, this installation procedure describes step by step instructions regarding how the drive mapping and directory sharing process is implemented. The Microsoft Windows Explorer program (part of the Windows Operating System already installed on the computer system) is used to perform the directory sharing and drive mapping process.

1.7.1 Directory Sharing

A Microsoft Windows disk drive can contain various directories and files. Each directory can contain sub-directories as well as files. Any directory (or sub-directory) can be shared over a computer network such that other computers may have access to that directory and the files it contains. The POS Business Application uses this feature in order to share its Server database directory with each of its Client computer systems.

When a directory is to be shared, the following information is required:

    a) the name of the directory (also called a "folder") that is to be shared, and
    b) if other network users are allowed to change the files in the directory.

The installation instructions in this manual will specify what settings to use.

1.7.2 Drive Mapping

Microsoft Windows assigns an alphabetic letter A-Z for each disk drive that can be accessed on the computer system. For example, Drive A: is usually the floppy drive, Drive C: the main hard disk drive, etc.

In the POS Business Application, the drive mapping feature allows a client computer system to map (ie. associate) a specific unused drive letter with the shared directory residing on the server computer.

When a drive is to be mapped, the following information is required:

    a) the Client's drive letter to be used to map to the Server's shared directory,
    b) the Server computer's name and directory (ie. the "folder" which is being shared),
    c) if the drive mapping is to be reconnected at logon (ie. each time the Client system is powered on).

The installation instructions in this manual will specify what settings to use.

POS Business Application   Installation

2   Software Installation Procedure

The POS Business Application software and associated documentation may be obtained on a CD-ROM disk or may be downloaded over the Internet. This section will discus the CD-ROM disk installation procedure as well as the Internet download installation procedure.

The POS Business Application CD-ROM may be used to install the POS Business Application on each computer system. The POS Business Application must be installed as a POS Business Application Server on one computer system (usually the fastest computer system on the network, which also contains the largest hard drive and a CD or preferably a DVD writer drive). The POS Business Application is also installed as POS Business Application Clients on the remaining networked computer systems.

If the POS Business Application is to be installed from the Quantum Blue Technology Download web page then use the computer's Internet Web Browser to select the Quantum Blue Technology home page at http://www.quantumbluetechnology.com and then select the "Download" page from the main menu. Select "POSBA Demo Installation" hyperlink to start the download / installation operation. This process is performed on each of the required computer systems. As described earlier, one computer system will be configured as the POS Business Application Server and the remaining computer systems will be configured as POS Business Application Clients.

Note: The Server / Client terminology used here refers to the POS Business Application software and not to the type of computer operating system. The POS Business Application Server may reside on a PC computer system running the Microsoft Server operating system but this is not a requisite. It is only required if enhanced database protection is required.

In a single computer system, the POS Business Application is configured as the POS Business Application Server.

In a multiple networked computer system, one computer is configured as the POS Business Application Server whereas the remaining computer systems are configured as POS Business Application Clients. When installing the POS Business Application software on multiple computer systems please install the Server application first.

Please Note:

Please refer to the Appendix for Vista compatibility mode and directory sharing.

POS Business Application Installation

2.1 POS Business Application Software Installation (CD-ROM)

The CD-ROM installation of the POS Business Application software for both Server and Client computer systems is performed as follows:

1. Power up the computer system and Window Operating System (logon as Supervisor if required).
2. Insert the POS Business Application CD-ROM into the CD or DVD drive.
3. The Installation Wizard should start executing. If this does not occur then use Windows Explorer to view the CD-ROM disk contents and execute the "POSInstall.exe" application.
4. Once the Installation Wizard has been started it will display the Welcome screen.
5. Press the [Next] button to continue.
6. The License Agreement screen will display the End User License Agreement (EULA). If you agree to the use of this program, select "I accept the terms of the license agreement".
7. Press the [Next] button to continue.
8. The Choose Destination Location screen is displayed. The Destination Location indicated is the directory location on the computer hard drive where the POS Business Application software will be stored. If a different location is required, press the [Browse] button and select or create the required directory.
9. Press the [Next] button to continue.
10. The "Set Program Shortcuts" screen is displayed. The Point-Of-Sale Business Application name and shortcuts can now be modified (if required).
11. Press the [Next] button to continue.
12. The "Confirm Setup Settings" screen is displayed. If any changes are required, press the [Back] key to select a previous page and make any required modifications.
13. If the settings are acceptable, press the [Next] button to continue.
14. The POS Business Application software will now be installed to the destination folder on the hard drive.
15. The "Setup Complete" screen is displayed.
16. Press the [Finish] button to complete the process.

Note: The POS Business Application program has now been installed on this specific computer system and is identified by an icon on the desktop, an icon in the Start menu and identified in the program list. The first time the POS Business Application is started the configuration screens will be displayed – see the section entitled "Configuring the POS Business Application" for more details.

Note: If the POS Business Application is to execute on a group of networked computers, the POS Business Application Software Installation process must then be repeated on each of the remaining computer systems in the network group.

POS Business Application   Installation

2.2 POS Business Application Software Installation (Internet Download)

The Internet Download installation of the POS Business Application software for both Server and Client computer systems is performed as follows:

1. Power up the computer system and Window Operating System (logon as Supervisor if required).
2. Start the computer's Internet Web Browser and access the Quantum Blue Technology Home Page at http://www.quantumbluetechnology.com.
3. Select the "Point-Of-Sale" main menu option from the Quantum Blue Technology Home Page - the "Point-Of-Sale Business Application (POSBA)" screen will be displayed. This page provides an overview of the POS Business Application, access to download the demo version of the application and the opportunity to purchase user licenses.
4. Step down the page until the "Free Software Evaluation Download" section is displayed. Select "Download POS Business Application" to start the download process. The demo version of the software will be downloaded to the user's computer. Please note that the Demo version of the software may have time and database size limitations. Purchasing and installing a license key converts the demo version into a fully functional version.
5. Once the demo version has been downloaded, the Installation Wizard will be started and the Welcome Screen will be displayed.
6. Press the [Next] button to continue.
7. The License Agreement screen will display the End User License Agreement (EULA). If you agree to the use of this program, select "I accept the terms of the license agreement".
8. Press the [Next] button to continue.
9. The Choose Destination Location screen is displayed. The Destination Location indicated is the directory location on the computer hard drive where the POS Business Application software will be stored. If a different location is required, press the [Browse] button and select (or create) the required directory.
10. Press the [Next] button to continue.
11. The "Set Program Shortcuts" screen is displayed. The Point-Of-Sale Business Application name and shortcuts can now be modified (if required).
12. Press the [Next] button to continue.
13. The "Confirm Setup Settings" screen is displayed. If any changes are required, press the [Back] key to select a previous page and make required modifications.
14. If the settings are acceptable, press the [Next] button to continue.
15. The POS Business Application software will now be installed to the destination folder on the hard drive.
16. The "Setup Complete" screen is displayed.
17. Press the [Finish] button to complete the process.

POS Business Application — Installation

Note: The POS Business Application program has now been installed on this specific computer system and is identified by an icon on the desktop, an icon in the Start menu and identified in the program list. The first time the POS Business Application is started the configuration screens will be displayed – see the section entitled "Configuring the POS Business Application" for more details.

Note: If the POS Business Application is to execute on a group of networked computers, the POS Business Application Software Installation process must then be repeated on each of the remaining computer systems in the network group.

POS Business Application — Installation

2.3 Configuring the POS Business Application

The following description is applicable to all POS Business Application installations (CD-ROM Installation and Internet Download Installation).

The POS Business Application program must now be configured to run either as a Server Application or as a Client Application. In a network of several computers only one computer system is configured as a POS Business Application Server and the remaining computer systems are configured as POS Business Application Clients.

To perform the configuration process, proceed as follows:

1. Start the POS Business Application program
2. The POS Business Application will start up and a Welcome Screen will be displayed. The following screen shows the demo version welcome screen.

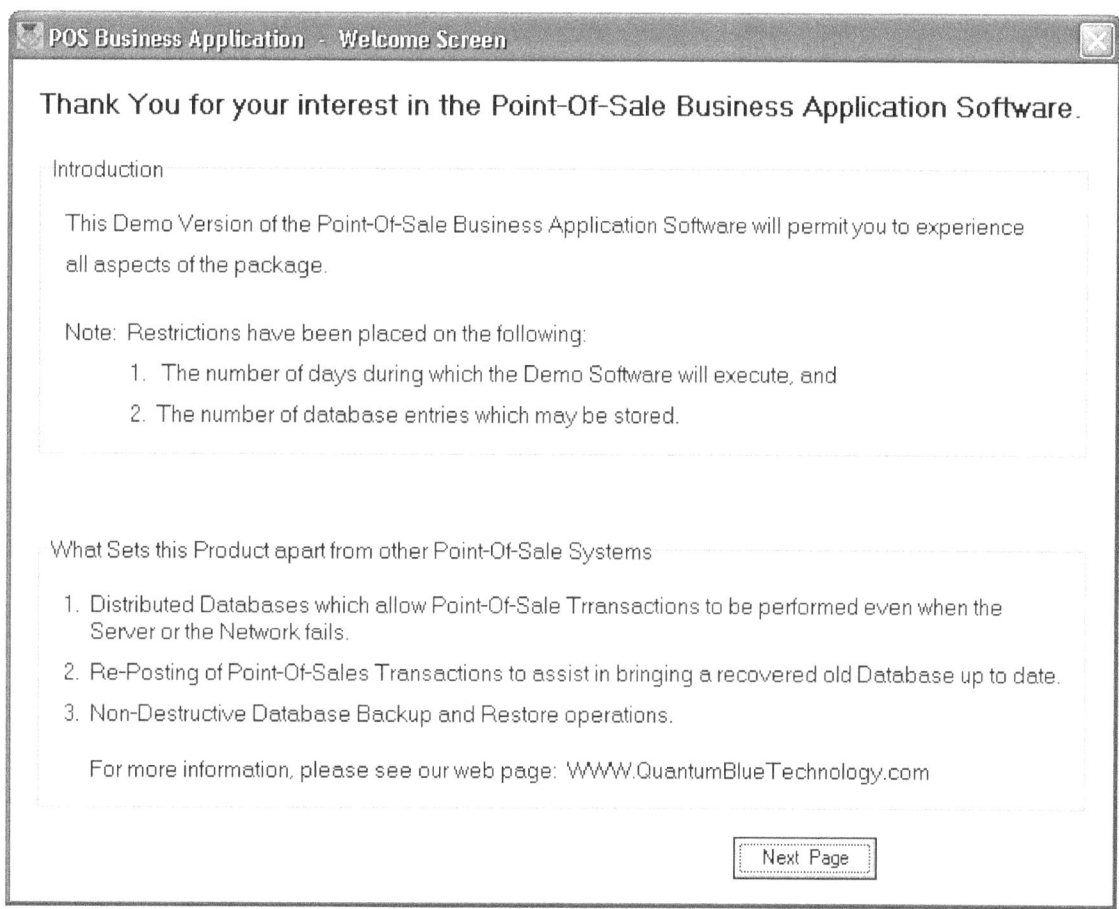

POS Business Application   Installation

3. After reviewing the Welcome Screen, press [Next Page] to step to the Server / Client Overview Screen.

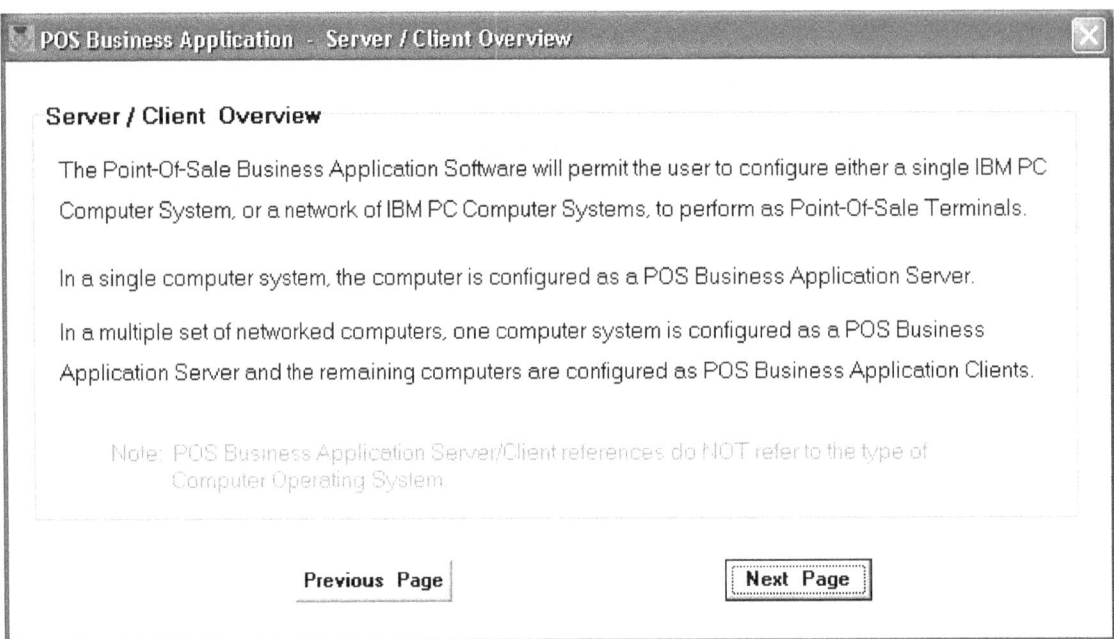

4. After reviewing this screen, press [Next Page] to step to the Single / Multiple Computer Installation Screen.

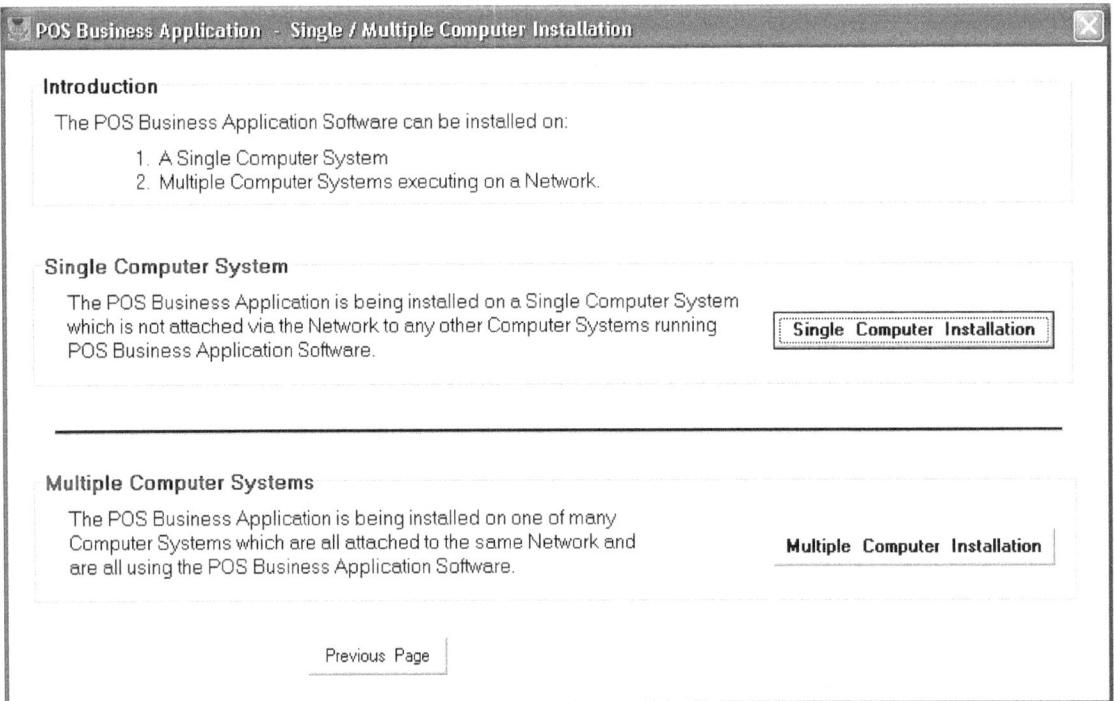

POS Business Application — Installation

After reviewing the Single / Multiple Computer Installation Screen, the user may press one of the following buttons:

1. The [Single Computer Installation] button, or
2. The [Multiple Computer Installation] button

The [Single Computer Installation] button is used when the software is being installed only on a single computer. Such a computer is configured as a Server.

The [Multiple Computer Installation] button is used when the software is being installed on multiple networked computers. One computer will be configured as the server and the remaining computers will be configured as clients.

2.3.1 Single Computer Installation

When the Single Computer Installation button is pressed, the following screen will be displayed:

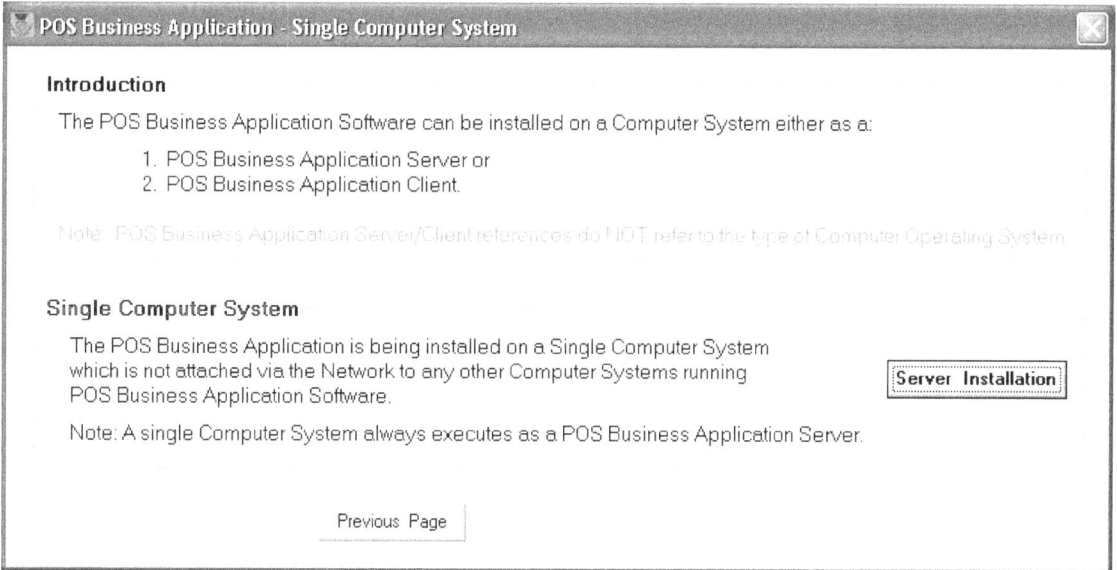

Note: If the Multiple Computer Installation option is required, please refer to the relevant chapters later in this document.

POS Business Application   Installation

Pressing the [Server Installation] button displays the following screen:

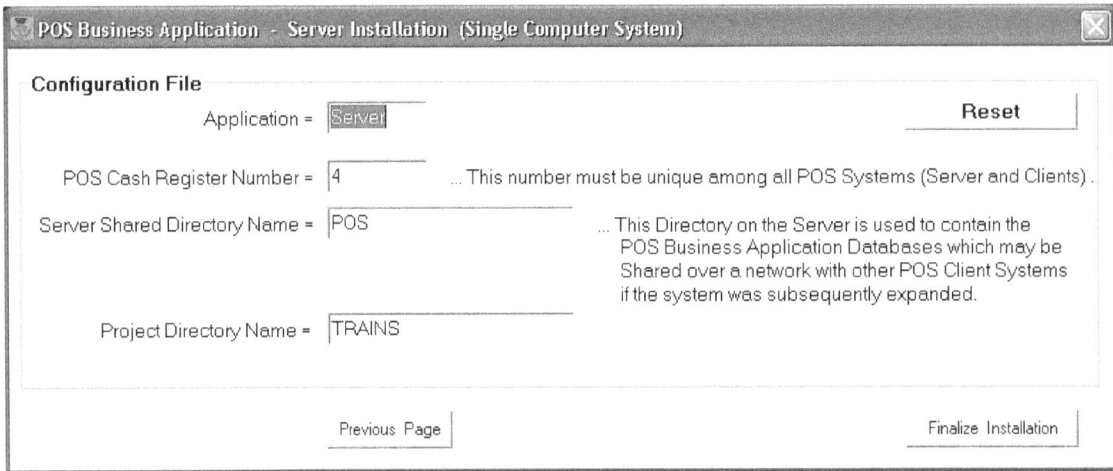

The Server Installation (Single Computer System) screen displays the following information:

1. The Application Type
2. The POS Cash Register Number
3. The Server Shared Directory Name
4. The Project Directory Name.

Note: If an incorrect Server/Client installation type was selected, the user may press the [Previous Page] button to return to the previous screen.

2.3.1.1 The Application Type

The Application Type is set to 'Server' indicating that this application is currently being configured as a POS Business Application Server. This value may not be changed.

2.3.1.2 The POS Cash Register Number

The current POS Cash Register Number is displayed. Any number in the range of [1..999] may be entered. Each computer system must use a unique register number.

2.3.1.3 The Server Shared Directory Name

In order to permit client computer systems to have access to the Server databases, it is necessary to create a shared directory on the Server. Although this directory need not be shared in single computer systems, the Server Shared Directory Name is identified for the future when additional computer systems may be added to the network.

POS Business Application   Installation

2.3.1.4 The Project Directory Name

The Project Directory Name identifies the directory which will hold all the accounting databases. When the system is initially configured, a demo project directory name called "TRAINS" is used. The project directory name can be changed later when a new empty database is to be created for the user's company database (See "Select Project Database" in the System Manual).

2.3.1.5 Finalize Installation

The [Finalize Installation] button may now be pressed to accept the data fields and to automatically update the POS Business Application Configuration File.

The POS Business Application program will be automatically restarted and the various database directories and databases will be automatically created.

2.3.1.6 Demo Database Installation

The user is given notification that the Demo Database will be installed. The Demo Database called "Trains" (providing train toy store inventory data) contains various database files which allows the user to immediately try various aspects of the POS Business Application.

Once the Demo Database has been successfully installed, the user is then informed regarding how to log into the system. The Supervisor password has been set to "super" and all the general user names have the same password "user" – do not include the quotation marks when entering these passwords; passwords are also case sensitive. These user names and passwords are associated with the Demo Database.

Some of the pre-defined user names and passwords that exist in the Demo Database are:

User Name	Password
Supervisor	super
Steve	user
Colin	user

When the System User Login Screen is displayed, the operator may login using any one of these user names and passwords.

Note: The Supervisor User Name permits full access to all system features whereas the other user names provide various limited access. Please refer to the "System" Operator's Manual in order to be aware of the implications of changing these features.

Note: Once the user is logged on, the system may now be used.

POS Business Application — Installation

2.3.1.7 Edit POS Configuration File

The POS Business Application uses the POS Configuration file to determine various operating criteria (eg. whether to run as a Server or as a Client). The previously described configuration process automatically changes the configuration file. If the user wishes to manually change these configuration parameters (or change additional parameters) the configuration file may be edited by a standard text editor. If the configuration file is changed, the POS Business Application must be restarted for the new values to take effect.

The POS Configuration file (called "POS_Configuration.ini") resides in the destination folder which was selected when the POS Business Application was installed.

This folder is usually the location: c:\Program Files\QuantumBlueTechnology\POSBA

The POS Configuration file may be edited by using the WordPad text editor which is supplied with the Microsoft Windows Operating System. Please refer to the Microsoft Windows documentation regarding the operating instructions for the WordPad editor.

2.3.1.8 POSBA Server Configuration File Example

A Typical Server POS Business Application Configuration file is as follows:

```
; File: POS_Configuration.ini
;
; This file identifies the various POS initialization variables.
;
; Note: Each POS Register must have a unique POS Register number.
;
; NOTE: THESE SETTINGS ARE ONLY READ AT SYSTEM STARTUP!!!
;

[System]
Application           = Server         ; Server, Client
Sound                 = Off            ; On, Off


[Drives]

Server = C:                            ; Drive letter + colon (eg. C:)
Server_Name           = Orion          ; The Network Name of the Server
Server_Shared_Directory = POS          ; The shared directory on the Server

Local_drive_low_limit  = 5.0           ; Gigabytes  (Will be implemented in a future release)
Server_drive_low_limit = 5.0           ; Gigabytes  (Will be implemented in a future release)


[Directory]
Project               = "Trains"


[Options]
Register  = 1                          ; Number (This number must be unique!!!)


[General]
Currency_Symbol       = $              ; Currency Symbol, $, L, R, etc.
Minimize_Screens      = Off            ; On, Off - Only for Main Screen at present
Fixed_Forms           = None           ; All, None, POS
Display_Network_Messages = On          ; On, Off

Auto_POS              = Off            ; On, Off
Auto_Shutdown         = Off            ; On, Off - Only used by Clients (future release)
Exit_Block            = Off            ; On, Off - Only used by Clients


[Programs]
PDF_Reader = "C:\Program Files\Adobe\Acrobat 5.0\Reader\AcroRd32.exe"
```

POS Business Application   Installation

2.3.2 Multiple Computer Installation

To configure the POS Business Application on Multiple Computer Systems, please press the Multiple Computer Installation button on the Single / Multiple Computer Installation screen as seen below:

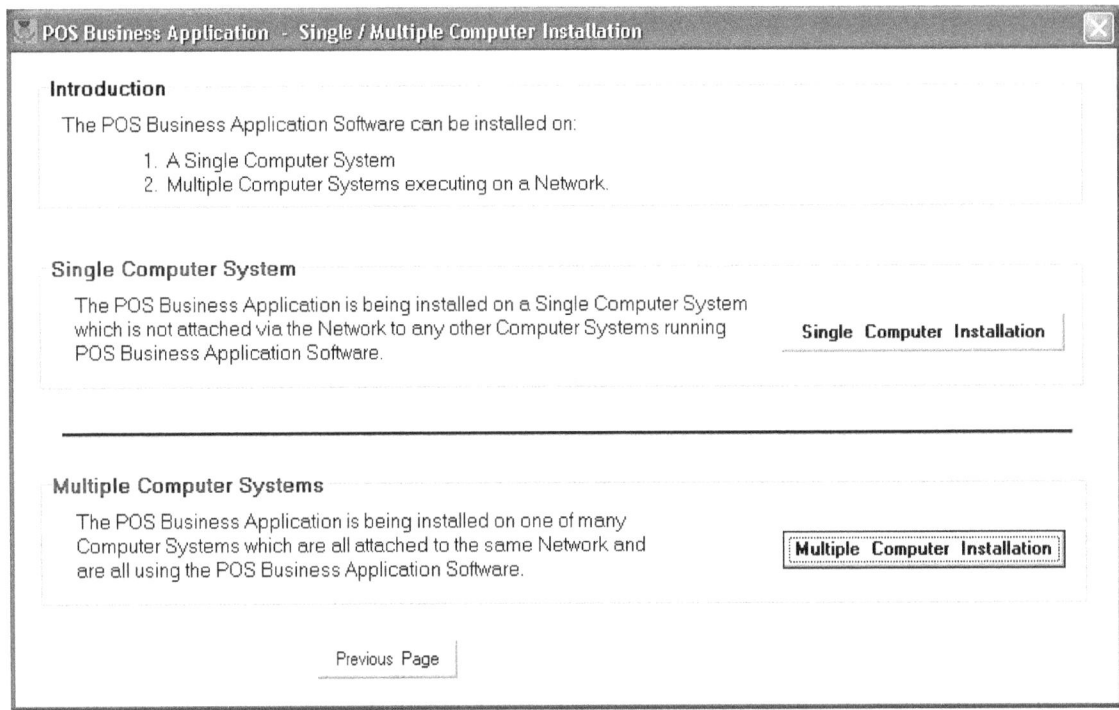

POS Business Application   Installation

When the Multiple Computer Installation button is pressed, the following screen will be displayed:

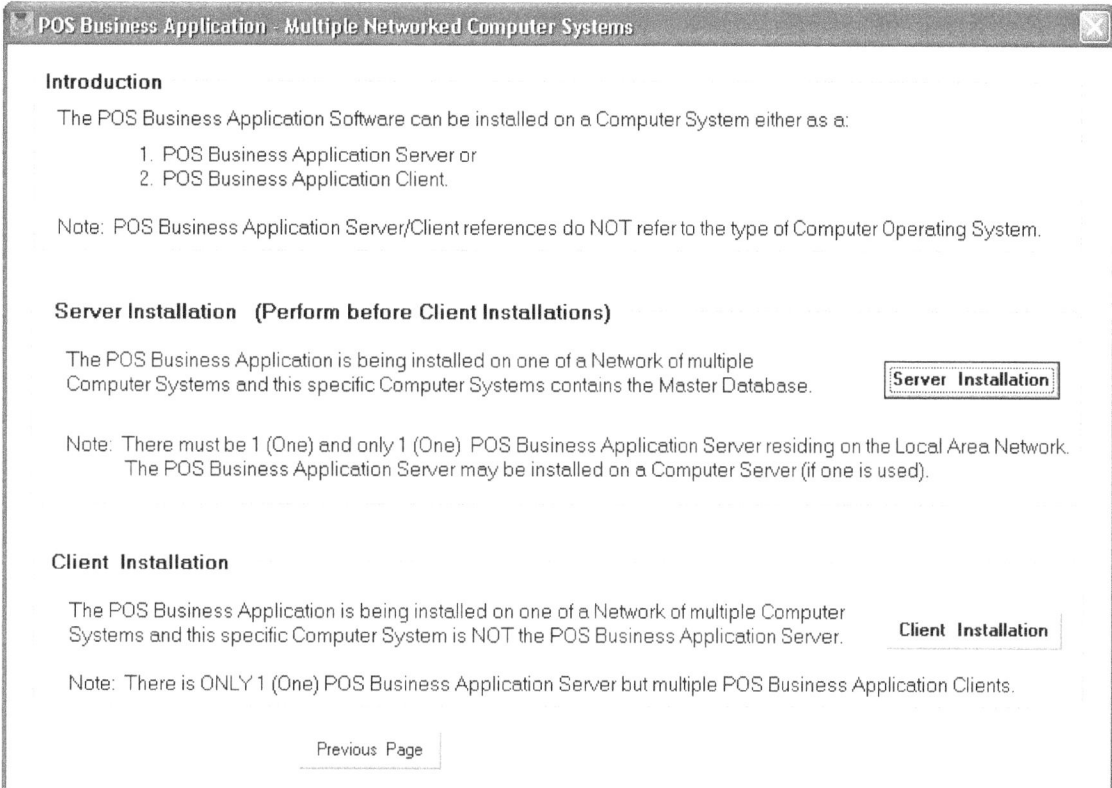

When a network of multiple computers are used, one computer system is designated to be the Server and used to store the central databases and backup files. All the remaining computer systems are designated as clients.

POS Business Application   Installation

2.3.2.1 Server Installation

Pressing the [Server Installation] button displays the following screen:

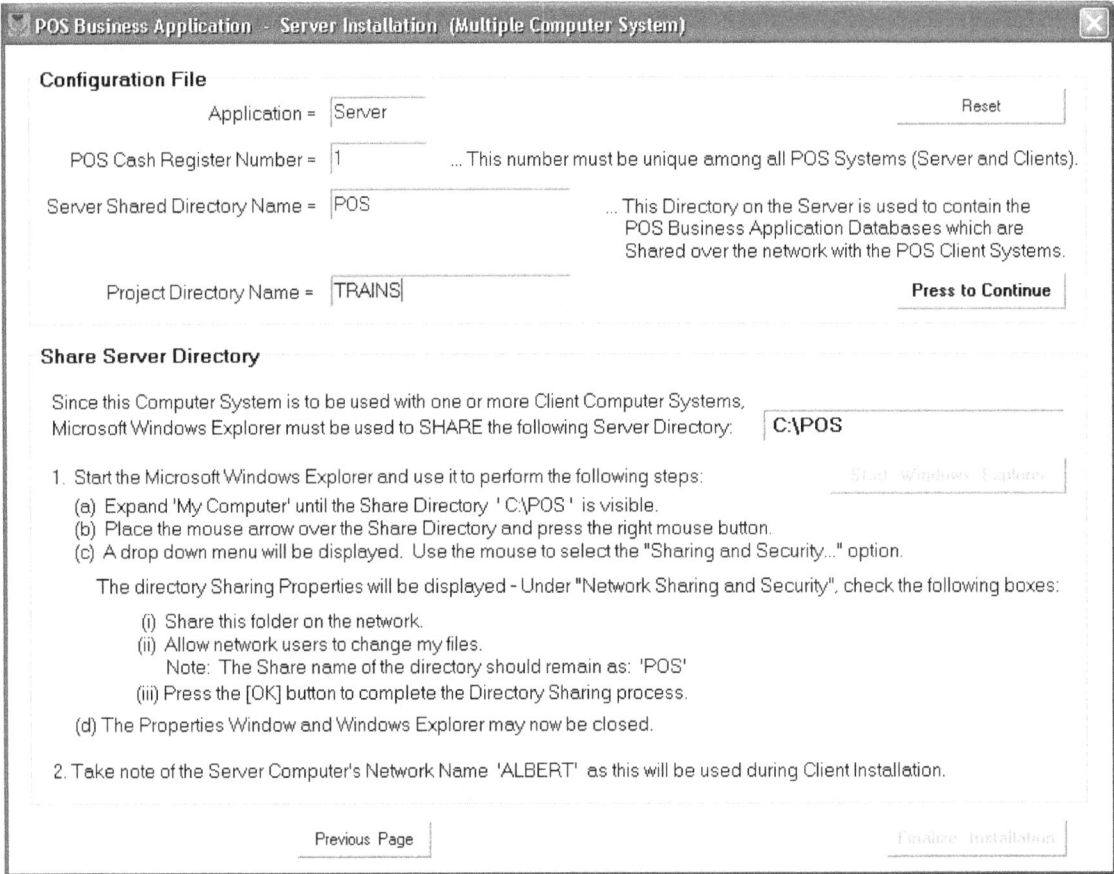

This screen displays the following information:

1. The Application Type
2. The POS Cash Register Number
3. The Server Shared Directory Name
4. The Project Directory Name.

Note: If an incorrect Server/Client installation type was selected, the user may press the [Previous Page] button to return to the previous screen.

2.3.2.1.1 The Application Type

The Application Type is set to 'Server' indicating that this application is currently being configured as a POS Business Application Server. This value may not be changed

POS Business Application — Installation

2.3.2.1.2 The POS Cash Register Number

The current POS Cash Register Number is displayed. Please select a different POS Register Number for each computer system. Any number in the range of [1..999] may be entered.

2.3.2.1.3 The Server Shared Directory Name

In order to permit client computer systems to have access to the Server databases, it is necessary to create a shared directory on the Server. The steps involved to share this directory will be described later.

2.3.2.1.4 The Project Directory Name

The Project Directory Name identifies the directory which will hold all the accounting databases. When the system is initially configured, a demo project directory name called "TRAINS" is used. The project directory name can be changed later when a new empty database is to be created for the user's company database (See "Select Project Database" in the System Manual).

The [Press to Continue] button is now pressed to verify the configuration parameters and to update the Configuration File.

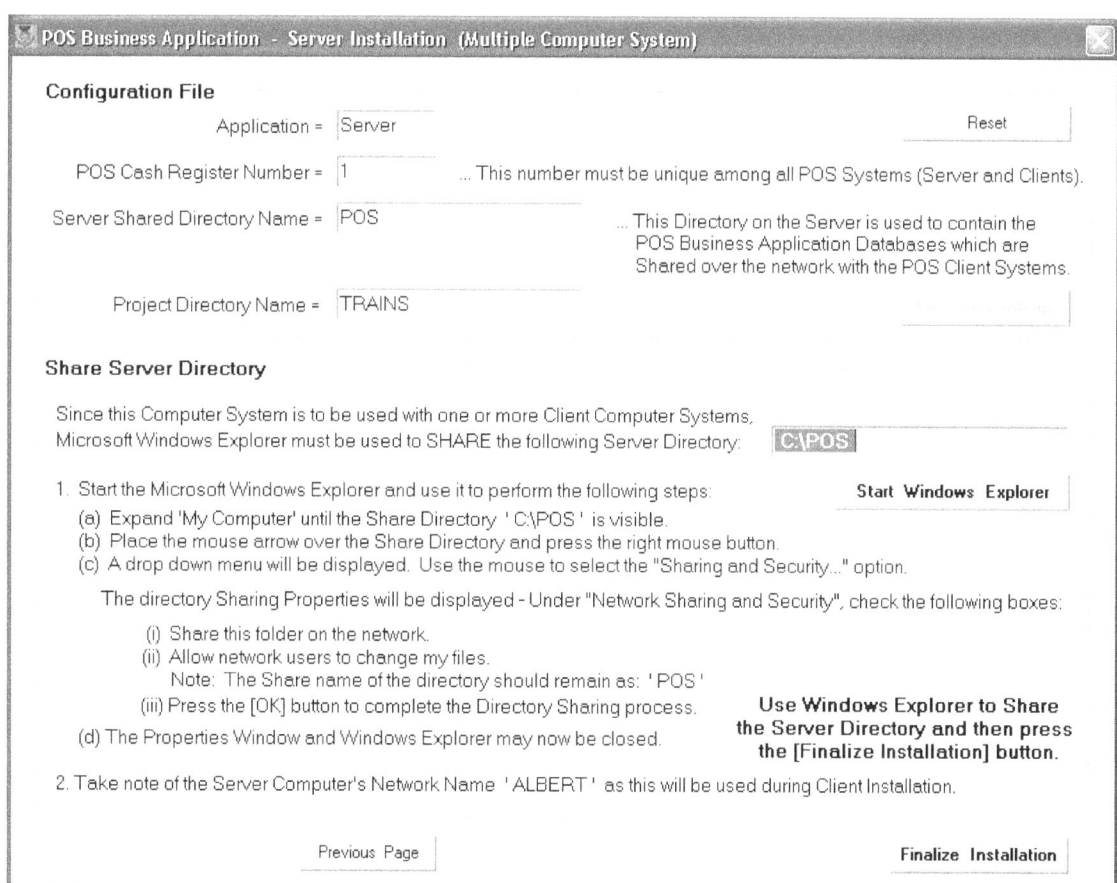

Quantum Blue Technology LLC.

POS Business Application   Installation

The following section will now describe the process which performs the sharing of the shared directory by the POS Business Application Server's Operating System.

2.3.2.1.5 Share Server Directory

The following instructions will now identify how to share the Server "Shared Directory". These instructions are as per Microsoft Windows XP – for other Microsoft Operating Systems, please refer to the associated Microsoft User Manuals.

Note: The Server Shared Directory allows the Client computer systems to access the Server Project Databases.

In the "Share Server Directory" section, displayed on the "Server Installation (Multiple Computer System)" screen, the user is presented with the Server Directory name which is to be shared.

The user is then requested to start Microsoft Windows Explorer. The [Start Windows Explorer] button may be pressed to start this application.

Once Windows Explorer has been started, use it to perform the following steps:

1. Expand the 'My Computer' section until the required shared directory is visible.
2. Place the mouse arrow over the Share Directory name and press the right mouse button.
3. Select the 'Sharing and Security…' option from the displayed drop down menu.

Under the Network Sharing and Security section, check the following boxes:

a) Share this folder on the network
b) Allow network users to change my files

POS Business Application   Installation

The following screen is displayed by the Microsoft Windows Operating System:

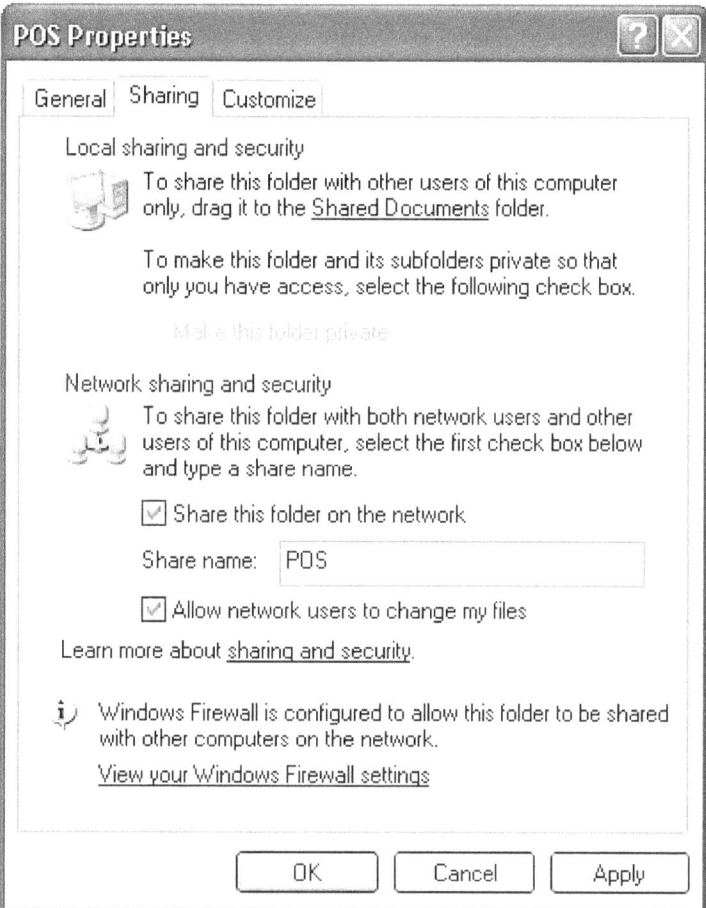

Note: The Share Name of the directory should remain as the Server Shared Directory Name described earlier.

The Properties Window and the Windows Explorer Window may now be closed.

Note: Please take note of the Server Computer's Network Name as this will be used during Client Installation.

2.3.2.1.6 *Finalize Installation*

The [Finalize Installation] button may now be pressed to accept the data fields and to automatically update the POS Business Application Configuration File.

The POS Business Application program will be automatically restarted and the various database directories and databases will be automatically created.

2.3.2.1.7 Demo Database Installation

The user is given notification that the Demo Database will be installed. The Demo Database called "Trains" (providing train toy store inventory data) contains various database files which allows the user to immediately try various aspects of the POS Business Application.

Once the Demo Database has been successfully installed, the user is then informed regarding how to log into the system. The Supervisor password has been set to "super" and all the general user names have the same password "user" – do not include the quotation marks when entering these passwords; passwords are also case sensitive. These user names and passwords are associated with the Demo Database.

Some of the pre-defined user names and passwords that exist in the Demo Database are:

User Name	Password
Supervisor	super
Steve	user
Colin	user

When the System User Login Screen is displayed, the operator may login using any one of these user names and passwords.

Note: The Supervisor User Name permits full access to all system features whereas the other user names provide various limited access. Please refer to the "System" Operator's Manual in order to be aware of the implications of changing these features.

Note: Once the user is logged on, the system may now be used.

2.3.2.1.8 Edit POSBA Configuration File

The POS Business Application uses the POS Configuration file to determine various operating criteria (eg. whether to run as a Server or as a Client). The previously described configuration process automatically changes the configuration file. If the user wishes to manually change these configuration parameters (or change additional parameters) the configuration file may be edited by a standard text editor. If the configuration file is changed, the POS Business Application must be restarted for the new values to take effect.

The POS Configuration file (called "POS_Configuration.ini") resides in the destination folder which was selected when the POS Business Application was installed.

This folder is usually the location: c:\Program Files\QuantumBlueTechnology\POSBA

The POS Configuration file may be edited by using the WordPad text editor which is supplied with the Microsoft Windows Operating System. Please refer to the Microsoft Windows documentation regarding the operating instructions for the WordPad editor.

POS Business Application   Installation

2.3.2.1.9 POSBA Server Configuration File Example

A Typical Server POS Business Application Configuration file is as follows:

```
; File: POS_Configuration.ini
;
; This file identifies the various POS initialization variables.
;
; Note: Each POS Register must have a unique POS Register number.
;
; NOTE: THESE SETTINGS ARE ONLY READ AT SYSTEM STARTUP!!!
;

[System]
Application       = Server           ; Server, Client
Sound             = Off              ; On, Off


[Drives]
Server = C:                          ; Drive letter + colon (eg. C:)
Server_Name              = Orion     ; The Network Name of the Server
Server_Shared_Directory  = POS       ; The shared directory on the Server

Local_drive_low_limit    = 5.0       ; Gigabytes   (Will be implemented in a future release)
Server_drive_low_limit   = 5.0       ; Gigabytes   (Will be implemented in a future release)


[Directory]
Project                  = "Trains"


[Options]
Register  = 1                        ; Number (This number must be unique!!!)


[General]
Currency_Symbol          = $         ; Currency Symbol, $, L, R, etc.
Minimize_Screens         = Off       ; On, Off - Only for Main Screen at present
Fixed_Forms              = None      ; All, None, POS
Display_Network_Messages = On        ; On, Off

Auto_POS                 = Off       ; On, Off
Auto_Shutdown            = Off       ; On, Off - Only used by Clients (future release)
Exit_Block               = Off       ; On, Off - Only used by Clients


[Programs]
PDF_Reader = "C:\Program Files\Adobe\Acrobat 5.0\Reader\AcroRd32.exe"
```

POS Business Application   Installation

2.3.2.2 Client Installation

To configure the POS Business Application as a Multiple Computer System Client, please press the Multiple Networked Computer Systems screen's [Client Installation] button as seen below:

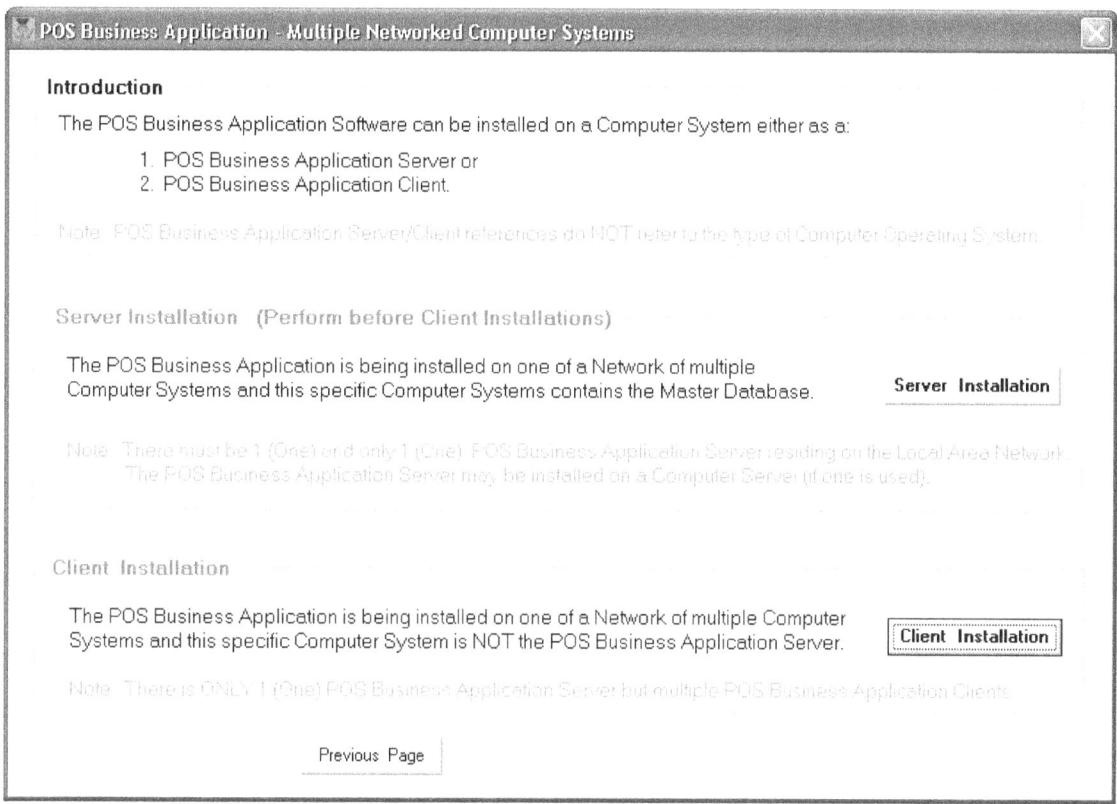

POS Business Application — Installation

The POS Business Application - Client Installation screen will be displayed:

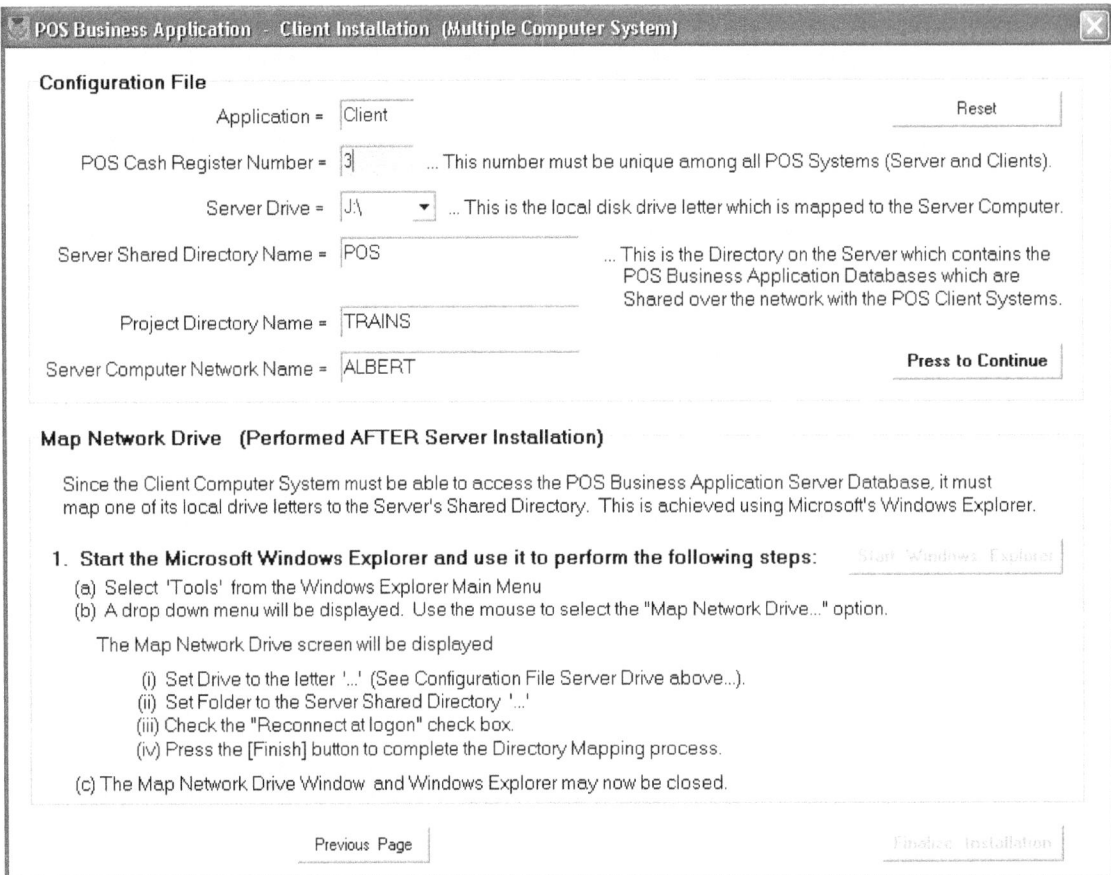

This screen displays the following information:

1. The Application Type
2. The POS Cash Register Number
3. The Server Drive
4. The Server Shared Directory Name
5. The Project Directory Name
6. The Server Computer Network Name

Note: If an incorrect Server/Client installation type was selected, the user may press the [Previous Page] button to return to the previous screen.

2.3.2.2.1 The Application Type

The Application Type is set to 'Client' indicating that this application is currently being configured as a POS Business Application Client. This value may not be changed

POS Business Application　　　　　　　　　　Installation

2.3.2.2.2 The POS Cash Register Number

The current POS Cash Register Number is displayed. Please select a different POS Register Number for each computer system. Any number in the range of [1..999] may be entered.

2.3.2.2.3 The Server Drive

The Server Drive is the local computer system's disk drive letter which will be mapped to the shared directory on the Server Computer.

2.3.2.2.4 The Server Shared Directory Name

The Server Shared Directory Name is the Server Directory which is being shared by the Server.

2.3.2.2.5 The Project Directory Name

The Project Directory Name identifies the directory which will hold all the accounting databases. When the system is initially configured, a demo project directory name called "TRAINS" is used. The project directory name can be changed later when a new empty database is to be created for the user's company database (See "Select Project Database" in the System Manual).

2.3.2.2.6 Server Computer Network Name

The Server Computer Network Name must be set to the network name of the POS Business Application Server computer. This name was identified during Server Installation when the POS Business Application software was being configured on the Server computer system.

The [Press to Continue] button is now pressed to verify the configuration parameters and to update the Configuration File.

The Client Network Drive mapping process will now be described.

2.3.2.2.7 Map Network Drive

The following instructions will now identify how to map a Client's unused local drive letter to a shared network directory on the Server. The following instructions are as per Microsoft Windows XP – for other Microsoft Operating Systems, please refer to the associated Microsoft User Manuals.

Note: The Server Shared Directory allows the Client computer systems to access the Server Project Databases.

POS Business Application — Installation

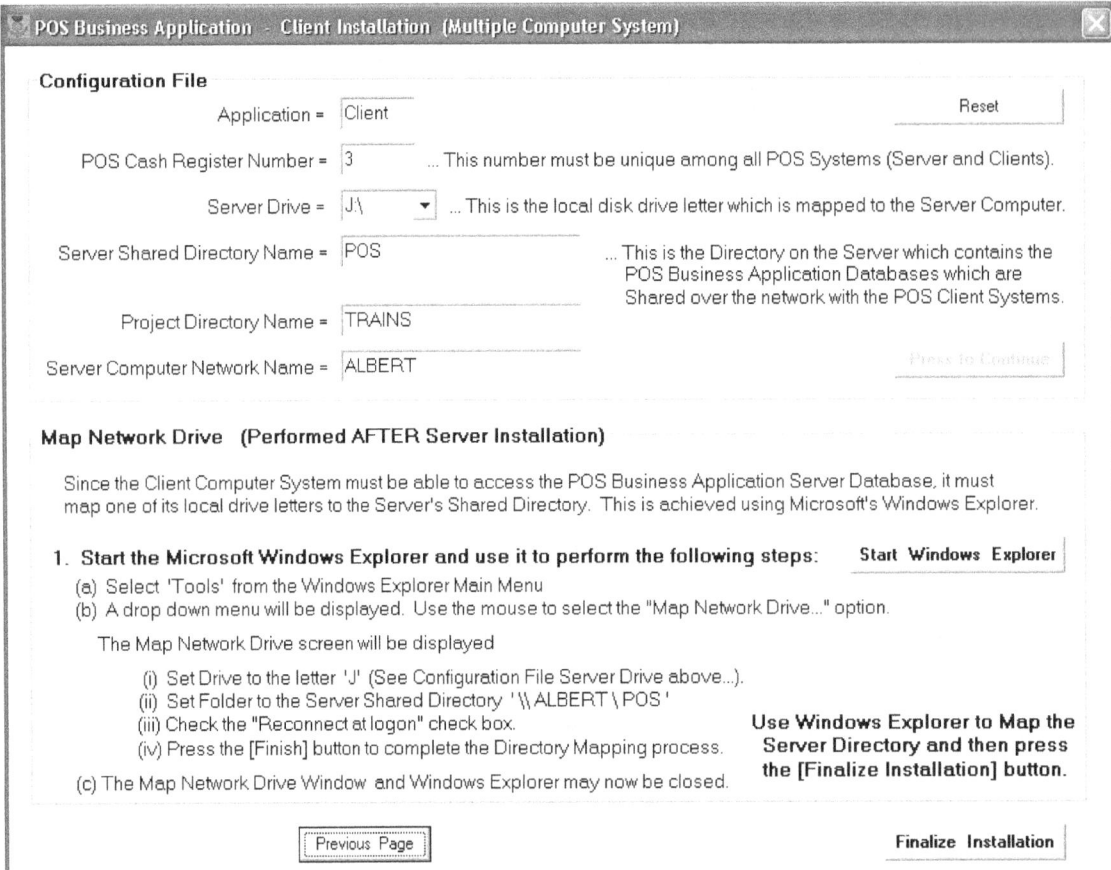

In the "Map Network Drive" section, displayed on the "Client Installation" screen shown above, the user is presented with a set of instructions which detail how to map a local drive to a network folder.

The user is first requested to start Microsoft Windows Explorer.
The [Start Windows Explorer] button may be pressed to start this application.

Once Windows Explorer has been started, use it to perform the following steps:

1. Select 'Tools' from the Windows Explorer Main Menu.
2. Select the 'Map Network Drive…' option from the displayed drop down menu.

POS Business Application   Installation

The following screen is displayed by the Microsoft Windows Operating System:

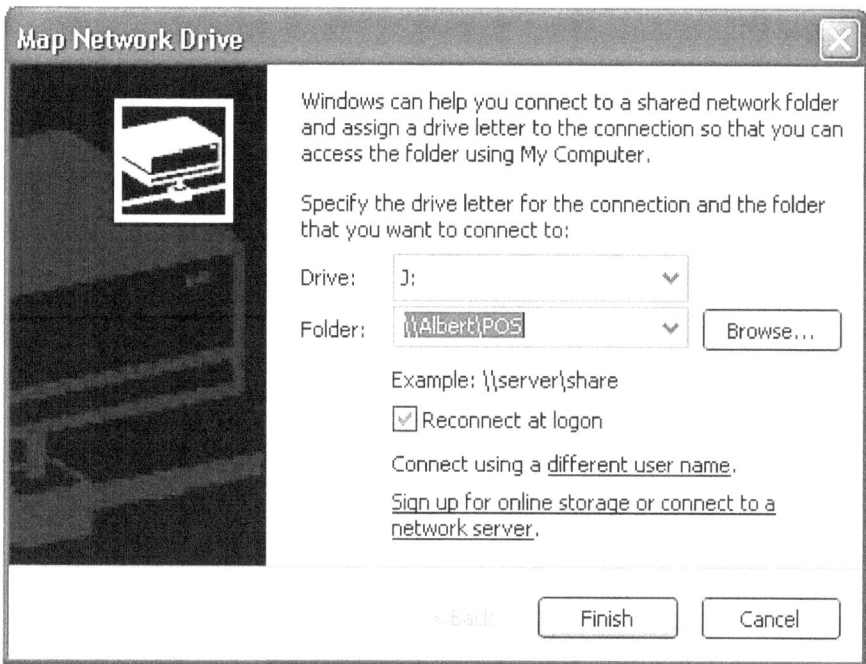

The Map Network Drive screen will now be displayed:

  a) Set Drive to the identified Server Drive letter.
  b) Set Folder to the identified Server Shared Directory
  c) Check the "Reconnect at logon" check box
  d) Press the [Finish] button to complete the Directory Mapping process.

Note: The Server Sharing process must be performed prior to mapping a network drive in order to ensure that the shared directory already exists.

The Map Network Drive Window and the Windows Explorer Window may now be closed.

2.3.2.2.8 Finalize Installation

The [Finalize Installation] button may now be pressed to accept the data fields and to automatically update the POS Business Application Configuration File.

The POS Business Application program will be automatically restarted and the various database directories and databases will be automatically created.

POS Business Application Installation

2.3.2.2.9 Edit POSBA Configuration File

The POS Business Application uses the POS Configuration file to determine various operating criteria (eg. whether to run as a Server or as a Client). The previously described configuration process automatically changes the configuration file. If the user wishes to manually change these configuration parameters (or change additional parameters) the configuration file may be edited by a standard text editor. If the configuration file is changed, the POS Business Application must be restarted for the new values to take effect.

The POS Configuration file (called "POS_Configuration.ini") resides in the destination folder which was selected when the POS Business Application was installed.

This folder is usually the location: c:\Program Files\QuantumBlueTechnology\POSBA

The POS Configuration file may be edited by using the WordPad text editor which is supplied with the Microsoft Windows Operating System. Please refer to the Microsoft Windows documentation regarding the operating instructions for the WordPad editor.

POS Business Application — Installation

2.3.2.2.10 POSBA Client Configuration File Example

A Typical Client POS Business Application Configuration file is as follows:

```
; File: POS_Configuration.ini
;
; This file identifies the various POS initialization variables.
;
; Note: Each POS Register must have a unique POS Register number.
;
; NOTE: THESE SETTINGS ARE ONLY READ AT SYSTEM STARTUP!!!
;

[System]
Application             = Client         ; Server, Client
Sound                   = Off            ; On, Off


[Drives]

Server = Z:                              ; Drive letter + colon (eg. C:)
Server_Name             = Orion          ; The Network Name of the Server
Server_Shared_Directory = POS            ; The shared directory on the Server

Local_drive_low_limit   = 5.0            ; Gigabytes  (Will be implemented in a future release)
Server_drive_low_limit  = 5.0            ; Gigabytes  (Will be implemented in a future release)


[Directory]
Project                 = "Trains"


[Options]
Register   = 1                           ; Number (This number must be unique!!!)


[General]
Currency_Symbol         = $              ; Currency Symbol, $, L, R, etc.
Minimize_Screens        = Off            ; On, Off - Only for Main Screen at present
Fixed_Forms             = None           ; All, None, POS
Display_Network_Messages = On            ; On, Off

Auto_POS                = Off            ; On, Off
Auto_Shutdown           = Off            ; On, Off - Only used by Clients (future release)
Exit_Block              = Off            ; On, Off - Only used by Clients


[Programs]
PDF_Reader = "C:\Program Files\Adobe\Acrobat 5.0\Reader\AcroRd32.exe"
```

3 Appendix A

3.1 System Configuration File

The System Configuration File is used to configure the basic operation of the POS Business Application. Each computer system has its own POS Business Application Configuration INI file which is located in the application program's installation directory.

The name of the System Configuration file is: "POS_Configuration.ini".

The System Configuration file may be edited by a text editor (for example, Microsoft's WordPad text editor). The text may be in upper or lower case letters. When a variable contains a space (for example, the Accounts Payable directory name), the name must be surrounded by quotation marks (ie. "Accounts Payable"). Any text following a semi-colon is regarded as a comment.

The System Configuration File has the following sections (where each section is identified by a name which is surrounded by rectangular brackets, eg. [System]):

1. System
2. Drives
3. Directories
4. Options
5. General
6. Programs

3.1.1 System Section

The System Section provides the following information

1. Application
2. Sound

3.1.1.1 Application

The Application variable is used to define whether the POS Business Application is executing either as a Server or as a Client.

The Application variable may take one of the following values:

1. Server
2. Client

POS Business Application   Installation

3.1.1.2 Sound

The POS Business Application may provide specific sound messages during operation. This feature may be enabled or disabled by the Sound variable.

The Sound variable may take one of the following values:

1. On
2. Off

3.1.2 Drives Section

The Drive Section provides the following information

1. Server
2. Server Name
3. Server Shared Directory
4. Local Drive Low Limit
5. Server Drive Low Limit

3.1.2.1 Server

This variable depends upon whether the computer system is being used as a POS Business Application Server or as a POS Business Application Client.

3.1.2.1.1 POS Business Application Server

The Server variable indicates which local drive is to be used to access the POS Business Application Server shared directory.

The POS Business Application Server computer system's operating system would be configured to share this specific directory allowing POS Business Application Clients read/write access to the database files it contains.

For example:

The POS Business Application Server may use a directory called C:\POS for its databases. This directory is configured to be shared allowing other computer systems read/write access.

Since this directory is on the C: drive, the Server variable would then be set as follows:

>   Server = C:

POS Business Application   Installation

3.1.2.1.2 POS Business Application Client

The Server variable indicates which local drive is to be used to access the POS Business Application Server directories.

The POS Business Application Client computer system's operating system would be configured to map this local drive letter to the remote shared Server directory. This mapping would be enabled to occur each time the Client computer system is powered on.

For example:

The POS Business Application Client may map an unused drive letter (say "Z") to be associated with the directory shared by the server (say the directory is called "POS").

The Client computer system would be configured to perform this mapping each time it is powered up.

The Server variable would then be set as follows:

    Server = Z:

3.1.2.2 Server Name

The Server_Name variable is used to identify the network name of the computer which is being used as the server.

If the network name of the computer system being used as the POS Business Application Server was caller "Orion" then the Server Name variable would be set as follows:

    Server_Name = Orion

3.1.2.3 Server Shared Directory

The Server_Shared_Directory variable is used to identify the name of the directory which is being shared on the computer being used as the server.

If the server computer is sharing a drive called "POS" then the Server Shared Directory variable would be set as follows:

    Server_Shared_Directory = POS

POS Business Application   Installation

3.1.2.4 Local Drive Low Limit

The Local_drive_low_limit variable is used to identify the minimum available amount of local disk drive space required by the POS Business Application. When the minimum available local disk space drops below this specified amount the user will be notified.

If the low limit was to be 5 Gigabytes then the Local_drive_low_limit variable would be set as follows:

     Local_drive_low_limit = 5.0

Note: This will be implemented in a future release.

3.1.2.5 Server Drive Low Limit

The Server_drive_low_limit variable is used to identify the minimum available amount of server disk drive space required by the POS Business Application. When the minimum available server disk space drops below this specified amount the user will be notified.

If the low limit was to be 5 Gigabytes then the Server_drive_low_limit variable would be set as follows:

     Server_drive_low_limit = 5.0

Note: This will be implemented in a future release.

3.1.3 Directories Section

This section identifies the various directory names used by both the Server and the Client computer systems.

A project directory identifies the relevant company master directory.

For Example:

```
Project = "Trains"
```

If a new company database is to be created, the project directory can be set accordingly.

For Example:

```
Project = "Model Railway Shop2"
```

POS Business Application　　　　　　　　Installation

Note: If any variable parameter is set to a value which is comprised of two or more words, the words must be surrounded by quotation marks as shown above.

3.1.4　Options Section

The Options Section provides the following information:

1. Register

3.1.4.1　Register

The Register variable is used to identify the Register number to be used by this Point-Of-Sale Terminal. The POS Business Application permits a range of [1 .. 999] registers.

Please Note: Each Point-Of-Sale Register number must be unique.

POS Business Application — Installation

3.1.5 General Section

The General Section provides the following information:

1. Currency Symbol
2. Minimize Screens
3. Fixed Forms
4. Display Network Messages
5. Auto POS
6. Auto Shutdown
7. Exit Block

3.1.5.1 Currency Symbol

The currency symbol variable is used to identify the money symbol in use for this region. For example, in countries which use the dollar symbol, the currency symbol would be set as follows:

    Currency_Symbol = $

3.1.5.2 Minimize Screens

The Minimize Screens variable is used to permit the POS Business Application Main Screen to be minimized or the be left permanently maximized.

If the Main Screen is permitted to be minimized then the Minimize_Screens variable may be set as follows:

    Minimize_Screens = On

If the Main Screen is to be kept in its maximized state then the Minimize_Screens variable should be set to its inactive position as follows:

    Minimize_Screens = Off

POS Business Application   Installation

3.1.5.3 Fixed Forms

The Fixed_Forms variable is used to control the fixing of certain POS Business Application Screens. When an application screen is fixed then it may not be moved on the screen. A fixed application (for example, the Point-Of-Sale screen) prevents the user from easily changing to other Windows programs and keeps the computer system dedicated as a Point-Of-Sale Terminal.

The available options are:

1. All   - All screen forms are fixed
2. None - No screen forms are fixed
3. POS   - Only the Point-Of-Sale screen form is fixed

If all screens are to be fixed, then the Fixed_Forms variable should be set as follows:

    Fixed_Forms = All

If no screens are to be fixed, then the Fixed_Forms variable should be set as follows:

    Fixed_Forms = None

If only the POS screen is to be fixed, then the Fixed_Forms variable should be set as follows:

    Fixed_Forms = POS

3.1.5.4 Display Network Messages

The Display_Network_Messages variable is used to indicate if network messages are to be displayed to the user. Network messages indicate when specific databases have been updated and are displayed in the status window at the bottom of the screen.

If network messages are to be displayed then the Display_Network_Messages variable should be set as follows:

    Display_Network_Messages = On

If network messages are seen as a distraction and are to be kept hidden from the user then the Display_Network_Messages variable should be set as follows:

    Display_Network_Messages = Off

3.1.5.5 Auto POS

The Auto POS variable is used to instruct the POS Business Application to immediately display the POS screen once the application is started. This is to restrict counter staff from accessing the Windows environment or other features of the POS Business Application.

If the Auto POS feature is to be used, then the variable should be set as follows:

    Auto_POS = On

If the Auto POS feature is not to be used, then the variable should be set as follows:

    Auto_POS = Off

3.1.5.6 Auto Shutdown

The Auto_Shutdown variable is used to indicate if the POS Business Application is to power down the computer system when the application is terminated. This feature is only available to POS Business Application Clients.

If the POS Business Application is to power down the computer system when the application is terminated then the Auto_Shutdown variable should be set as follows:

    Auto_Shutdown = On

If the POS Business Application is not to power down the computer system when the application is terminated then the Auto_Shutdown variable should be set as follows:

    Auto_Shutdown = Off

Note: This will be implemented in a future release.

3.1.5.7 Exit Block

The Exit_Block variable is used to allow or to prevent non-authorized users (see the section on System Access) from exiting the POS Business Application.

If an un-authorized user is not permitted to exit the POS Business Application then the Exit-Block variable should be set as follows:

    Exit_Block = On

If an un-authorized user is permitted to exit the POS Business Application then the Exit-Block variable should be set as follows:

    Exit_Block = Off

3.1.6 Programs Section

The General Section provides the following information:

1. Path to the PDF reader program.

3.1.6.1 PDF Reader

The PDF Reader variable is used to fully identify the directory path to the PDF Reader program.

For example:

    PDF_Reader = "C:\Program Files\Adobe\Acrobat 5.0\Reader\AcroRd32.exe"

POS Business Application   Installation

3.2 Microsoft Vista Operating System Installation

3.2.1 Directory Sharing

When the POS Business Application is installed on a computer system which utilizes the Microsoft Vista Operating System, the application's database directory may be shared with other computer systems in one of two ways:

1. As a Protected Shared Directory
2. As an Un-Protected Shared Directory

3.2.1.1 Protected Shared Directory

Using protected shared directories will provide the most protection to POS Business Application databases since only permitted computer system users will be permitted access.

To configure the POS Business Application database directory as a protected shared directory, the server must be provided with the identification of each user (a name and a password) who is permitted access. When the POS Business Application directory is shared, each required users is added to the access list. The "co-owner" access option must also be selected in order to allow the user to write to and read from the system database files.

To implement this, proceed as follows:

1. Access the Vista "Network and Sharing Center"
2. Turn ON password protected sharing
3. Share the POS Business Application database directory (eg "C:\POS") with each permitted user and set their corresponding share option to "Co-owner"

Please refer to the Microsoft documentation for more details.

3.2.1.2 Un-Protected Shared Directory

Using un-protected shared directories allows any computer system access to the shared directory. This should not be a problem for a small business using a protected (ie. firewalled) Local Area Network (LAN) and is certainly the easiest approach. If more security is required later, the shared directory may be changed to protected sharing.

To implement this, proceed as follows:

1. Access the Vista "Network and Sharing Center"
2. Turn OFF password protected sharing
3. Share the POS Business Application database directory (eg "C:\POS") with "Everyone" and set the share option to "Co-owner"

Please refer to the Microsoft documentation for more details.

3.2.2 Compatibility Mode

The Point-Of-Sale Business Application performs various system operations which may be blocked by the Microsoft Vista Operating System. In order to ensure that the Point-Of-Sale Business Application executes with the correct operating system privileges, it is necessary to execute the application using a specific compatibility mode.

This is easily achieved by setting the Point-Of-Sale Business Application compatibility options. The Point-Of-Sale Business Application compatibility options must be set on each Vista computer system which has the application installed.

There are two ways of accomplishing this:

1. Setting the POS Business Application desktop icon properties field
2. Using the Microsoft Vista Program Compatibility Wizard

3.2.2.1 POS Business Application desktop icon

The POS Business Application is usually installed with a desktop icon. If this is not the case please refer to the required Microsoft documentation for the relevant Operating System and create a desktop icon for the POS Business Application.

To change the POS Business Application compatibility mode proceed as follows:

1. Right click on the POS Business Application desktop icon
2. Select the "Properties" field
3. Under "Compatibility Mode" select the option to run this program in compatibility mode for "Windows XP (Service Pack 2)".

When the POS Business Application is subsequently executed by clicking on its associated desktop icon, the application will then be correctly executed in Windows XP mode.

POS Business Application   Installation

3.2.2.2   Microsoft Vista Program Compatibility Wizard

To do this please proceed as follows:

First select the **Control Panel** from the Vista **Start** Menu

Select the **Control Panel Home** to display the Vista view (ie. Not the classic view)
Select **Programs**

Locate the **Programs and Features** title and
Select **Use an older program with this version of Windows**

The **Program Compatibility Wizard** will be started.

    Welcome to the Program Compatibility Wizard   Press [Next >]

    How do you want to locate the program that you would like to run with compatibility settings

        Select **I want to choose from a list of programs**   Press [Next >]

    A list of programs installed on this computer will be displayed

        Select the **Point-Of-Sale Business Application** program   Press [Next >]

    Select a compatibility mode for the program

        Select **Microsoft Windows XP (Service Pack 2)**   Press [Next >]

    Select display settings for the program

        Do not select any display setting options   Press [Next >]

    Does the program require administrator privileges?

        Select **Run this program as an administrator**   Press [Next >]

    <u>Note</u>:   At this point, ensure that the Point-Of-Sale Business Application is not currently executing.

POS Business Application   Installation

Test your compatibility settings   Press [Next >]

At this stage the user is permitted to test that the Point-Of-Sale Business Application is executing correctly and will be started automatically.

<u>Note</u>: **The Vista Operating System may ask your permission to run the Point-Of-Sale Business Application program.**

Select [Allow]

The Point-Of-Sale Business Application program should start running. Let it complete its initialization process and then terminate the Point-Of-Sale Business Application program.

Now it is time to complete the Compatibility Wizard

Did the program work correctly?

Select **Yes, Set this program to always use these compatibility settings**
                                                                                                                              Press [Next >]

Program Compatibility Data
Would you like to send this information to Microsoft – This is not required., so

Select **No**   Press [Next >]

Completing the Program Compatibility Wizard
You have successfully adjusted the compatibility setting for this program

                                                                                                    Press [Finish]

<u>Note</u>: The above Point-Of-Sale Business Application compatibility options must be set on each Vista computer system which has the application installed.

Operator's Manual

Systems

Project: Point-Of-Sale Business Application
Date: April 14th 2008
Revision: 2.1.7
Company: Quantum Blue Technology LLC.

Copyright Notice

Copyright ©2005, 2006, 2007, 2008 Quantum Blue Technology LLC. – All rights reserved worldwide. This document is proprietary to **Quantum Blue Technology LLC.** And may contain information that is to be maintained as Trade Secret. It is intended for use only by **Quantum Blue Technology LLC.** Employees and its' contractors, customer employees, and authorized personnel. It may not be copied, translated, or transcribed in whole or in part without the express permission of the copyright holder **Quantum Blue Technology LLC.**

Quantum Blue Technology LLC
1424 Welsh Way, Ramona
California 92065
U.S.A.

Phone: USA (858) 837-2160
Email: info@QuantumBlueTechnology.com
Web: www.QuantumBlueTechnology.com

Please Note:

Due to ongoing design and development, **Quantum Blue Technology LLC.** May, at any time, and without notification, amend and update either this document and/or the associated "POS Business Application" software package.

Change History

Date	Version	Author	Reason for Change
1/5/06	1.0.0	Steve McClure	Initial Draft.
4/21/06	1.1.0	Steve McClure	Added more detail.
4/26/06	1.2.0	Steve McClure	Started Error Message Section.
9/4/06	2.0.0	Steve McClure	First Pre-Release.
11/9/06	2.1.0	Steve McClure	Second Pre-Release.
11/20/06	2.1.1	Steve McClure	Minor updates.
12/15/06	2.1.2	Steve McClure	Added more Import Database details.
12/18/06	2.1.3	Steve McClure	Added Transaction Source Database.
1/8/07	2.1.4	Steve McClure	Minor Updates.
1/29/07	2.1.5	Steve McClure	Term Code Updated.
1/7/08	2.1.6	Steve McClure	General updates.
4/14/08	2.1.7	Steve McClure	Added Vista OS Information.

Table of Contents

1 SCOPE 1
    1.1 GENERAL 1
        1.1.1 Operating System *1*
        1.1.2 Hardware Requirements *1*
    1.2 SERVER / CLIENT STATIONS 2
        1.2.1 Server Station *2*
            1.2.1.1 License 3
        1.2.2 Client Station *3*
            1.2.2.1 License 3
    1.3 OVERVIEW 4
    1.4 ABBREVIATIONS 5
    1.5 END-USER LICENSE AGREEMENT (EULA) 5

2 POS BUSINESS APPLICATION 6
    2.1 SINGLE OR MULTIPLE NETWORKED COMPUTER SYSTEMS (CLIENT/SERVER) 6
    2.2 DISTRIBUTED ENCRYPTED NETWORK DATABASE 6
    2.3 POINT-OF-SALE (POS) USER INTERFACE 8
    2.4 INVENTORY CONTROL 10
    2.5 ACCOUNTS RECEIVABLE MODULE 11
    2.6 DATABASE IMPORT / EXPORT 11

3 SYSTEM MENU 12
    3.1 SYSTEM 12
        3.1.1 Software Installation *12*
        3.1.2 Select POS Register *13*
        3.1.3 Select Project Database *13*
    3.2 LICENSE 15
        3.2.1 Enter License Key *15*
        3.2.2 Reset Network License Registration *16*
        3.2.3 Display Network License Registrations *16*
    3.3 USER MENU 17
        3.3.1 Login/Logout Menu *17*
        3.3.2 Change Password Menu *18*
        3.3.3 Identify Users Menu *19*
        3.3.4 Specific User Options *20*
        3.3.5 System Menus *21*
            3.3.5.1 Identify Users 21
            3.3.5.2 Point Of Sale Menu 21
                3.3.5.2.1 POS Start/Close Business 21
                3.3.5.2.2 POS Account Override 21
                3.3.5.2.3 POS Transaction Edit 21
            3.3.5.3 Inventory Menu 21

3.3.5.4		Accounts Menu	22
3.3.5.5		Payroll Menu	22
3.3.6	*New User Password*		*22*
3.3.7	*Supervisor Password*		*22*

3.4 DATABASE MENU 23
- *3.4.1   File Conversion Utility 23*
- *3.4.2   Import Database 25*
  - 3.4.2.1   Initialize POS Business Application Database 26
  - 3.4.2.2   Specify Import File 26
  - 3.4.2.3   Specify Import Configuration File.. 26
  - 3.4.2.4   Import Functions 28
  - 3.4.2.5   Import Log 29
  - 3.4.2.6   Finalize Database 29
- *3.4.3   Export Database 29*
- *3.4.4   Backup Database 30*
- *3.4.5   Restore Database 31*
  - 3.4.5.1   Restore Database from File 31
  - 3.4.5.2   Restore Database from Directory... 32

3.5 OPTIONS MENU.. 33
- *3.5.1   Receipt Number 33*
- *3.5.2   Invoice Number 34*
- *3.5.3   Quote Number 34*
- *3.5.4   Source Document Number 35*
- *3.5.5   Credit Card Codes 35*
  - 3.5.5.1   Imported Databases 36
- *3.5.6   Tax Codes 37*
  - 3.5.6.1   Imported Databases 38
- *3.5.7   Sale Types 39*
  - 3.5.7.1   Imported Databases 40
- *3.5.8   Term Codes 41*
  - 3.5.8.1   Imported Databases 42
- *3.5.9   Transaction Codes 43*
  - 3.5.9.1   Imported Databases 45
- *3.5.10 Transaction Sources.. 46*
  - 3.5.10.1   Imported Databases 47
- *3.5.11 System Wide Options... 48*
  - 3.5.11.1   Company Options 50
    - 3.5.11.1.1   Full Company Address 50
    - 3.5.11.1.2   Cash Receipt Company Address.. 51
    - 3.5.11.1.3   Contact Information 51
    - 3.5.11.1.4   Accounting Information 51
    - 3.5.11.1.5   Internet Information 51
  - 3.5.11.2   System Options 52
    - 3.5.11.2.1   Server Logon User Profile 52
    - 3.5.11.2.2   Internet License Key Server Address 52
  - 3.5.11.3   Inventory Options 53

		3.5.11.4	POS Options	53

- 3.5.11.4.1 General Options 54
  - 3.5.11.4.1.1 Check Purchase Authorizations 54
  - 3.5.11.4.1.2 Credit Card Purchase Authorizations 55
  - 3.5.11.4.1.3 Start of Business Register Balance 55
  - 3.5.11.4.1.4 Purchase Discounts 55
  - 3.5.11.4.1.5 Customer Details 56
  - 3.5.11.4.1.6 Quotes 56
  - 3.5.11.4.1.7 Fees 56
  - 3.5.11.4.1.8 Miscellaneous 56
- 3.5.11.4.2 Cash Receipt Options 57
- 3.5.11.4.3 Account Receipt Options 58
- 3.5.11.4.4 Quote Receipt Options 60

- *3.5.12 Printer Selection* *62*
  - 3.5.12.1 Register Printer 63
  - 3.5.12.2 Account Printer 64
  - 3.5.12.3 Report Printer 64
- *3.5.13 Cash Register Drawer* *65*
- 3.6 SOFTWARE UPDATE 66
- 3.7 EXIT MENU 66

4 HELP 67

- 4.1 CALCULATOR 67
- 4.2 CALENDAR 67
- 4.3 ABOUT 67

5 APPENDIX 68

- 5.1 DATABASE BACKUP PROCEDURE 68
- 5.2 COMPARISON OF WINDOWS OPERATING SYSTEMS 68
  - *5.2.1 Windows Vista* *68*
  - *5.2.2 Windows XP* *69*
    - 5.2.2.1 Windows XP Home Edition 69
    - 5.2.2.2 Windows XP Professional Edition 69
  - *5.2.3 Windows 2000 (or later versions)* *70*
  - *5.2.4 Windows 2000 Server (or later versions)* *70*
- 5.3 WINDOWS FILE SYSTEM 70
- 5.4 AUXILIARY EQUIPMENT 70
  - *5.4.1 Bar Code Scanner* *71*
  - *5.4.2 Printers* *71*
- 5.5 ERROR MESSAGES 71
  - *5.5.1 Printer Not Available* *72*
  - *5.5.2 Server Not Available* *72*

POS Business Application   Systems

1 Scope

This document is the Systems Manual for the Point-Of-Sale Business Application. This manual describes the various user configurable system options.

1.1 General

The Point-Of-Sale (POS) Business Application is designed for the small business and provides networking capabilities not normally available to general Point-Of-Sale systems.

The principal features which set this POS Business Application Software apart from other POS accounting software systems are the following:

- Ease of Use
- Distributed Encrypted Databases
- Quicker Data Access via Calendar Indexed Databases
- Re-Posting of POS Sales transactions if database recovery is required
- Safe Non-Destructive Database Backup and Restore Operations

Please refer to the Overview document for a more detailed description of these features.

1.1.1 Operating System

The POS Business Application software executes on a standard IBM Personal Computer System (or compatible) which executes one of the following operating systems:

1. Windows Vista
2. Windows XP (Professional or Home Editions, or later versions)
3. Windows 2000 (or later versions)
4. Windows 2000 Server (or later versions)

Note: The POS Business Application may operate correctly on previous versions of Windows, however, at this time it has not been verified.

1.1.2 Hardware Requirements

The following minimum IBM PC compatible computer features are required:

- Pentium III 1GHz
- 512MB RAM
- LAN Network Interface
- Video Monitor (800 x 600 minimum)
- Mouse
- Keyboard

The POS Business Application program interface screens have been designed to fit on a monitor set to 800 x 600 pixel resolution. This permits the image to fill the entire screen thereby allowing the text to be easily readable by both the customer and the counter staff.

Note: A DVD R/W device would be recommended for storing Server Database Backups.

1.2 Server / Client Stations

The POS Business Application executes as either a:

1. Server Station
2. Client Station

Note: The term "Server" and "Client" refers to the type of POS Business Application installation and not to the type of operating system executing on the computer.

Note: The POS Business Application computer software may be installed on a computer system as either a Server Application or as a Client Application. The same software program is used for both these types of installations.

1.2.1 Server Station

In a single computer environment, the computer will be configured as a POS Business Application Server.

In a multiple networked computer environment, one computer will be configured as a POS Business Application Server and the remaining computers will be configured as POS Business Application Clients.

The computer system which is configured to be the POS Business Application Server contain the central databases. These databases are shared over the network with the POS Business Application Client computers. The Server Station is used to perform database import and export operations, as well as database backup and restore operations.

The POS Business Application Server can execute the following modules:

1. Inventory Module
2. Point-Of-Sale Module
3. Accounts Receivable Module

Note: Other modules are in the process of being developed.

POS Business Application   Systems

1.2.1.1 License

The POS Business Application (POSBA) may be installed on one or more networked computer systems. Of these computer systems, one is designated the POS Business Application "Server" since it holds the primary databases. Up to 99 POS Business Application "Client" networked computer systems may be associated with this Server system.

The POS Business Application license is a single fixed price license. This license permits the user to install the POS Business Application software on a POSBA Server computer system and also on up to 99 networked POSBA Client computer systems all for one fixed price.

The POS Business Application license is installed on the POSBA Server system.

1.2.2 Client Station

In a single computer environment, the computer will be configured as a POS Business Application Server.

In a multiple networked computer environment, one computer will be configured as a POS Business Application Server and the remaining computers will be configured as POS Business Application Clients.

The computer systems which are configured to be the POS Business Application Clients contain copies of various Server databases. The Client Stations constantly monitor the Server databases and download new copies of required databases whenever they have detected that the databases have been updated.

Note: The POS Business Application may utilize up to 99 client stations.

1.2.2.1 License

Each Client Station accesses the license stored on the POSBA Server system. No additional client license need be purchased.

POS Business Application   Systems

1.3 Overview

When the POS Business Application is started, the main screen will be displayed as shown below:

The main screen provides the following information:

1. The Company Name

   The top line indicates the authorized user of the POS Business Application software.

2. The Main Menus

   The main menu identifies the various POS Business Application modules available to the user. If a menu label is in bold letters then that specific module is available to the user currently logged onto the POS Business Application system.

3. System Status

The System Status is located at the bottom of the display. It identifies the current system date and time, the user currently logged on (if any), an information message area and Server availability.

Server Availability is indicated as follows:

    a) Local   - Client is operating in local mode (ie. Server is not available)
    b) Server   - Client can communicate with the Server
    c) SERVER - This computer system is the Server

1.4 Abbreviations

CSV	Comma Separated Variable
EULA	End-Users License Agreement
PC	Personal Computer
POS	Point-Of-Sale
UPS	Uninterruptible Power Supply

1.5 End-User License Agreement (EULA)

Please refer to the Installation Manual for a complete description of the End-User License Agreement.

POS Business Application

2 POS Business Application

The POS Business Application consists of a single computer program which has been designed to operate either in Server or Client mode. The program utilizes a system configuration file which identifies the mode of operation as well as specifying various system options. For more information regarding the system configuration file please refer to the Installation Manual.

The POS Business Application has the following main features:

1. Distributed Encrypted Network Databases
2. System User Password Control
3. Single or Multiple Networked Computer Systems (Server & Client Stations)
4. Point-Of-Sale (POS) Terminal
5. Inventory Control Module
6. Accounts Receivable Module
7. Database Import and Export
8. Database Backup and Restore

Note: Additional features are currently under development.

2.1 Single or Multiple Networked Computer Systems (Client/Server)

The POS Business Application may operate either on a single IBM PC compatible computer system or on multiple networked IBM PC compatible computers. Each computer system uses the Microsoft Windows Operating System.

The principal location of the various POS Business Application databases is on the computer system designated as the Server. If a single computer system is used then that computer would be designated the Server.

When a networked set of several computers are used then one computer system is designated to be the Server and the remaining computer systems would be designated as Clients. In such an environment, each Client constantly monitors the various Server's databases and when a Client determines that a particular Server database has been updated, it automatically copies this database to its local file system.

2.2 Distributed Encrypted Network Database

The main restriction with many Point-Of-Sale systems is their reliance on both the network and the Server computer system. These POS systems locate their central database on the server computer and the client computer systems must access this database via the network in order to perform any Point-Of-Sale operations.

POS Business Application — Systems

A major cause for concern with users of such systems is with regard to what would happen if the network or the server were to fail. If either of these failures were to occur then the client computer systems would not be able to access the central database and would therefore not be able to perform Point-Of-Sale transactions. In this situation, the counter staff would then be required to make hand written sales receipts and refer to previously printed (and perhaps outdated) price lists. This method of operation is tedious, slow and can easily generate errors.

Later, when the Server and/or network are once more operational, the handwritten sale transactions have to be manually entered into the accounting system – another time consuming operation which is also fraught with possible errors

This POS Business Application system, however, is designed to minimize these conditions. It uses a distributed encrypted database and is therefore not totally reliant on the network nor on the Server. Although our Server contains the central database, any changes to this database are passed on to database copies which reside on each Client computer system. If the Server or the network were to subsequently fail, each POS Business Application Client computer system would still contain copies of the latest relevant inventory and accounts receivable databases and may still be used to perform Point-Of-Sale transactions with the current inventory stock part numbers and prices.

Of course, it stands to reason that during the period that the Server/Network is non-operational, a specific Client terminal only has a copy of each database and can not therefore determine what sales transactions have occurred on other Client POS terminals. This being the case, inventory information like the number of items in stock may not be accurate, however, in most situations this is not a problem since a customer is generally only purchasing items which actually exist and which they themselves have taken from a store shelf. This inconvenience is somewhat offset by the fact that POS sales transactions are basically unaffected and may still continue as normal

Once the Server/Network are once more operational, the transaction sales data collected by each POS terminal may then be posted to the Server thereby updating the central database. The updated databases are then downloaded to the various client systems and the correct inventory stock quantities displayed.

All Server and Client databases are encrypted to provide basic system security. For higher level security, the file system encryption features of Windows XP Professional may be utilized.

POS Business Application — Systems

2.3 Point-Of-Sale (POS) User Interface

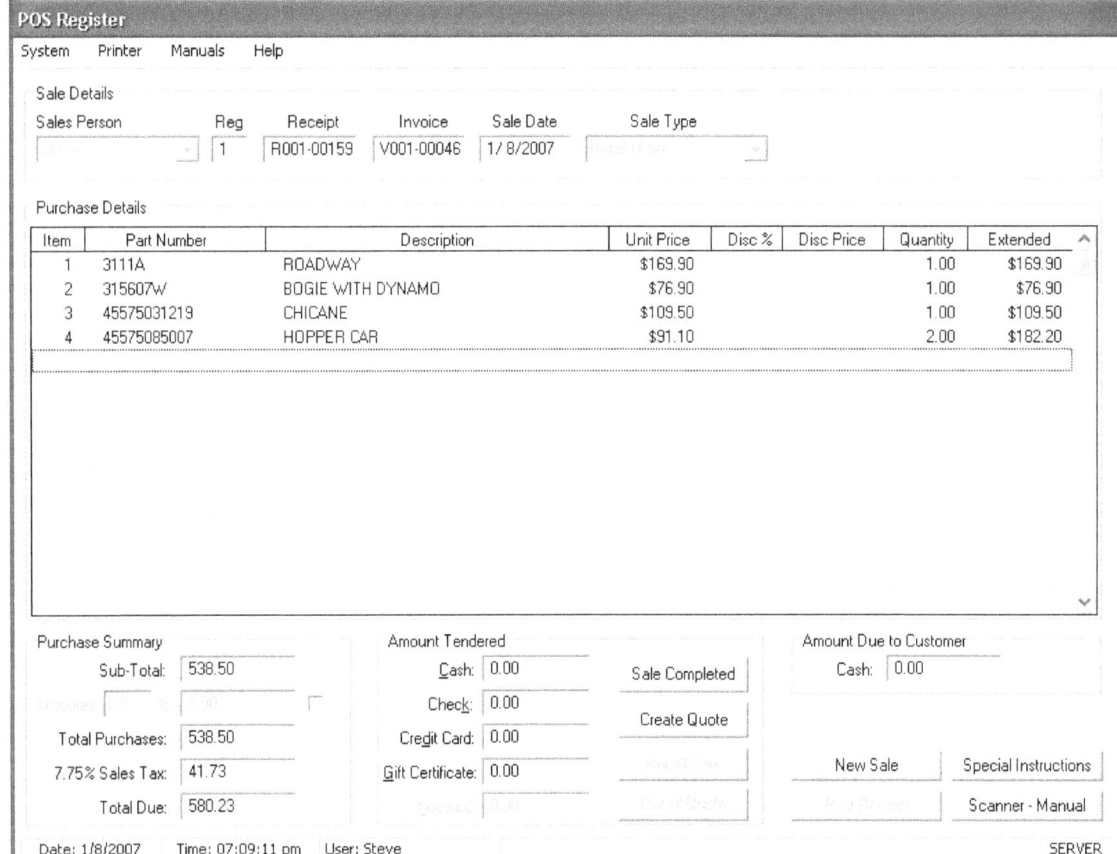

The POS Terminal permits the user to perform cash or account sale transactions as well as creating quote statements. Cash or account sale transactions are recorded and transferred to the Server at the end of the business day. The POS Terminal permits the use of a bar code scanner during sales line item entry. Only one listing of each purchased product is displayed on the screen and on the receipt.

When an additional, previously entered product is input, the previously entered product quantity is adjusted accordingly. This helps to ensure that the correct number of items are charged to the customer.

If the network or Server were to suddenly fail, all Client POS Terminals would still continue to operate, thereby allowing the current sale to be completed and also allowing subsequent sales to be performed.

The user may identify which system printers are to be used for reports, account statements and till slips.
An ESC/POS till slip printer interface is also provided.

POS Business Application — Systems

The following POS Terminal features are available:

1. Price breaks for quantity purchases
2. Transaction line item price modification (specify price or discount percentage)
3. Overall discount for items not previously discounted
4. Indicate special handling instructions (ie. delivery information appended to receipt)

Sales data is stored in a hierarchical directory file structure which permits fast and efficient access to database records. Any number of sales transactions may be stored without adversely affecting the system performance. Previous Sales may be accessed and viewed. Quotes may be created and printed. Quotes may be converted into a sale without the need to re-enter purchase information.

The following POS Reports are provided:

1. Register Summary Report
2. Register Full Report (identify sales transactions)
3. Register Year Report (spreadsheet providing register totals for each day of the year)
4. Sales Tax Report

POS Business Application   Systems

2.4   Inventory Control

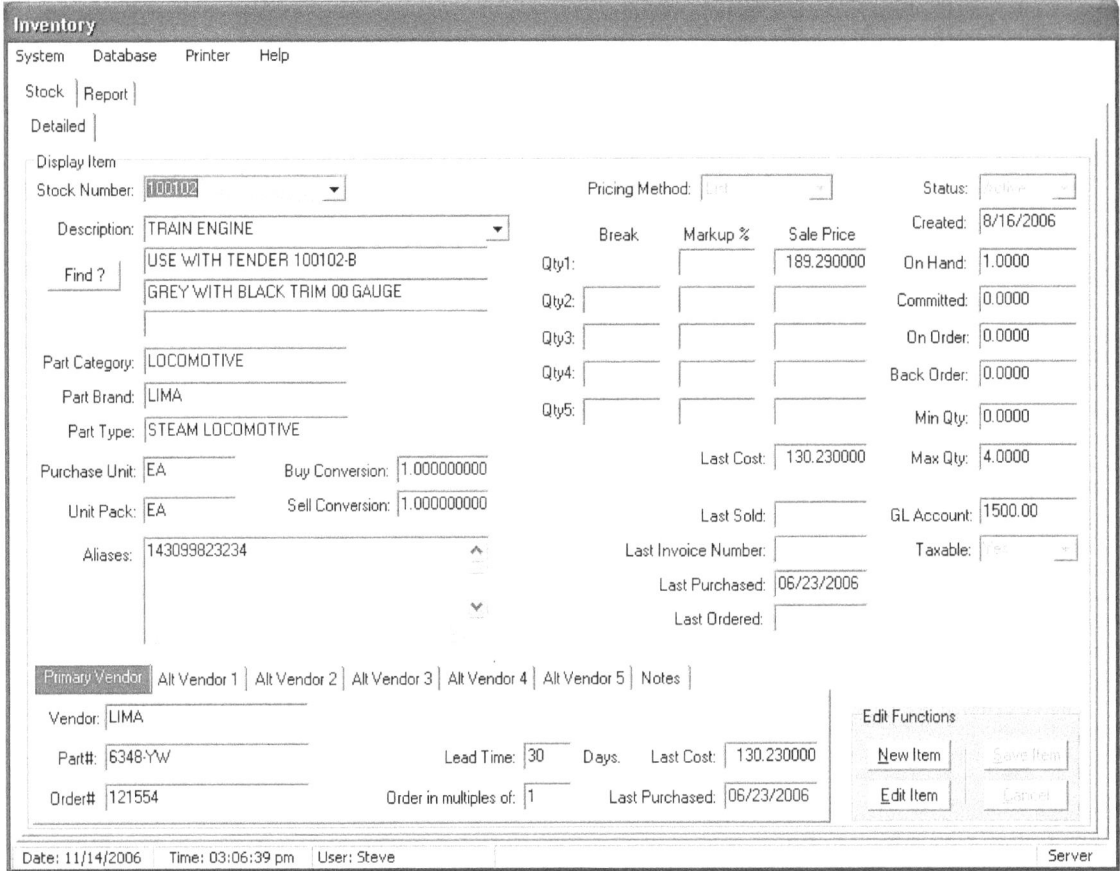

The Inventory Control module allows the user to edit and/or view the various inventory items. Inventory items are identified by a stock number and by one or more aliases. Each inventory item can have a four line description and can be associated as belonging to a specific category, brand and type. List and Markup pricing methods permit the item sale price to be defined as either a fixed price or as a percentage markup based on the last cost. Quantity price breaks may also be defined. Primary and alternate vendor information may be stored with the inventory item as an aid when ordering additional inventory. The Report section allows a specific report to be selected and generated. Report Parameters may be specified to extract specific groups of inventory items. Multiple nested sorts may be performed to allow the report to be ordered as required.

The following reports are provided which may be viewed and/or printed as required:

1. Quick Stock List Report
2. Price Book Report
3. Under and Over Stock Reports
4. Stock Value Report
5. Stocktake Worksheet Report
6. Stock Labels (with Bar Code 39 Generation)

2.5 Accounts Receivable Module

The Accounts Receivable module permits the user to identify various customers who may purchase items on credit. The customer's name and address, credit limit, purchase terms and tax code may be specified. Customer Job Names and authorization information may also be defined – this information may be viewed during a POS sale and is used to identify which customer employee may purchase against which specific job. Various charge, account, credit and aging statistics are collected and may be viewed. A Transaction / Payment history can be viewed and Payments / Adjustments can be applied to the account.

The following Accounts Receivable reports are available:

1. Customer Summary Report
2. Customer Full Report
3. Address Labels
4. Aged Analysis Report
5. Statements Report

2.6 Database Import / Export

The Database Import Section allows existing data from a different accounting system to be imported into the POS Business Application. Imported data must be in Comma Separated Variable (CSV) format. A conversion utility has also been provided to convert dBASE files to CSV format. The Database Import feature permits the user to specify the name/location of specific CSV variables to be imported as well as their destination position within the new database structure. Multiple databases can be combined during the import process into a single destination database.

The Database Export Section permits exportation of POS Business Application database data to CSV files.

3   System Menu

The System Menu provides the following sub-menu options:

1. System
2. License
3. User
4. Database
5. Options
6. Software Update
7. Exit

> **Note:** These options are available when the Supervisor has logged on. The standard user may not have all these options displayed.

3.1   System

When the System menu is selected, the user can select from the following sub-menu:

1. Software Installation
2. Select POS Register
3. Select Project Database

3.1.1   Software Installation

When the Software Installation menu is selected a message will be displayed which indicates that the POS Business Application software has already been installed. The user may proceed to re-install the software or can cancel the installation.

If the software installation is selected then the various system installation screens will be displayed and the user can select the Server/Client system options. Please refer to the Installation Manual for a complete description of these installation screens and the various options which may be selected.

POS Business Application — Systems

3.1.2 Select POS Register

This menu option is used to allow the user to change this computer system's register number. The register number value resides in the configuration file and may be changed either by this menu option or by manually editing the configuration file – Please refer to the Installation manual for details regarding the configuration file.

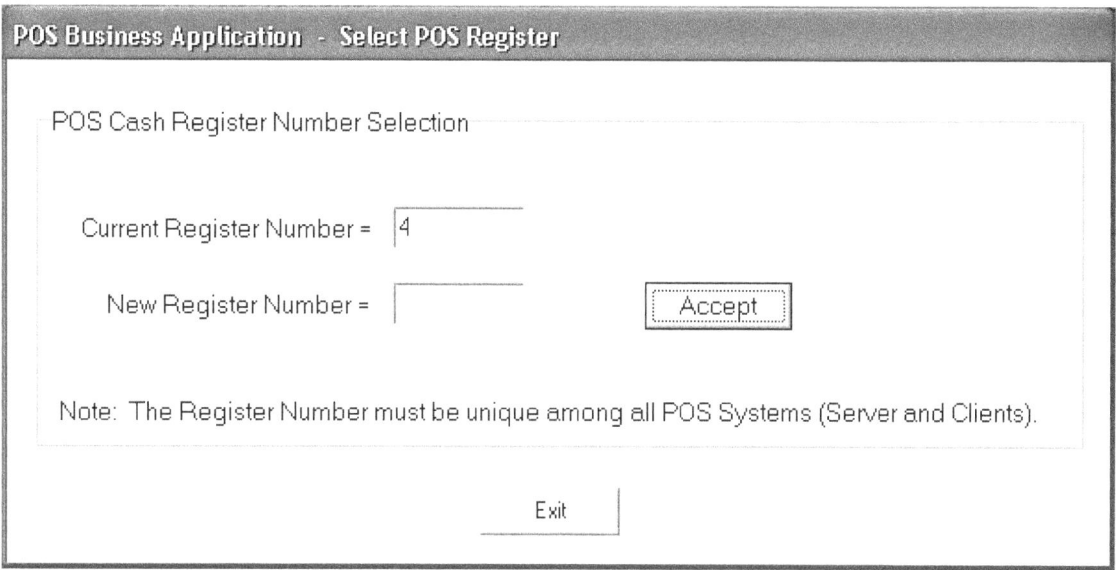

When the "Select POS Register" menu option is first selected, a screen will be displayed which indicates the current register number and allows the entry of a new register number value.
To change the current register number, simply enter the new register number and press the [Accept] button. The configuration file will be updated and the program restarted.

If the current register number does not need to be changed, press the [Exit] button to cancel the operation.

3.1.3 Select Project Database

This menu option is used to allow the user to change this computer system's project database. The project database is used to contain all the database files pertaining to a specific project (ie. company). If the POS Business Application software was installed with the DEMO database, then the Current Project Name would be set to "DEMO". If the user is now wanting to start building a database for a real company then the current project name would be changed to the company name, for example: Model Train Shop

The project name resides in the configuration file and may be changed either by this menu option or by manually editing the configuration file – Please refer to the Installation manual for details regarding the configuration file.

POS Business Application   Systems

When the "Select Project Database" menu option is first selected, a screen will be displayed which indicates the current project name and allows the entry of a new project name.

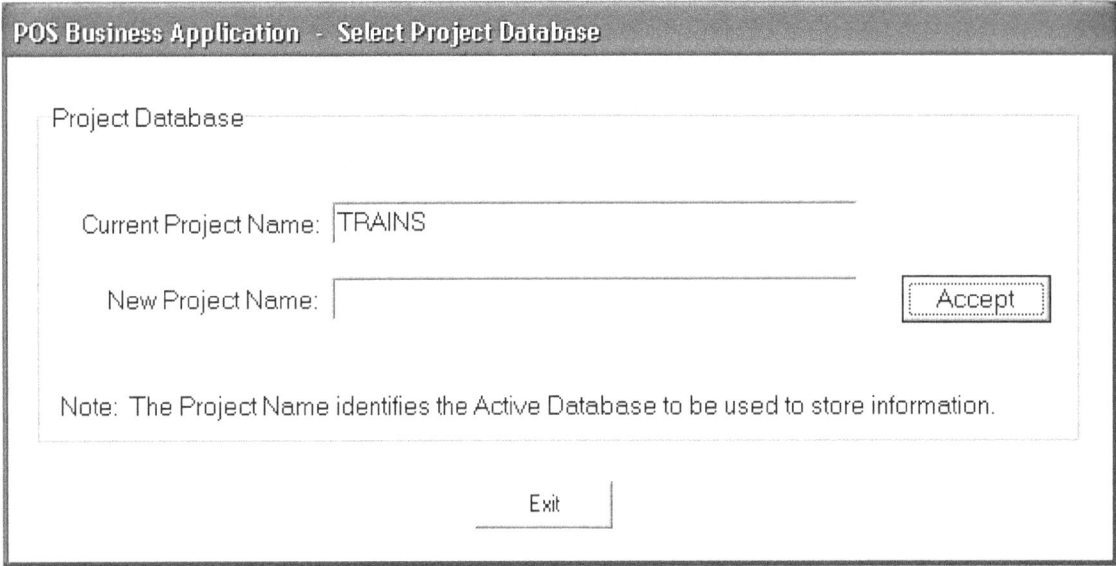

To change the current project name, simply enter the new project name and press the [Accept] button. The configuration file will be updated and the program restarted.

If the current project name does not need to be changed, press the [Exit] button to cancel the operation.

Please Note: Since each Server and Client computer systems have their own unique configuration file, they must each be individually configured to use the required project name.

POS Business Application   Systems

3.2 License

When the License menu is selected, the following sub-menu is displayed:

1. Enter License Key
2. Reset Network License Registration
3. Display Network License Registrations

3.2.1 Enter License Key

The "Enter License Key" sub-menu displays a screen which allows the user to enter a license key into the system. License Keys are used to change a demo version of the POS Business Application to a fully functional purchased version. License keys are also used to select the various POS Business Application features which have been purchased.

When the license key has been entered and the [Accept] key pressed, the license type and licensed parameters will be displayed on the screen. If an invalid license has been entered an error message is displayed.

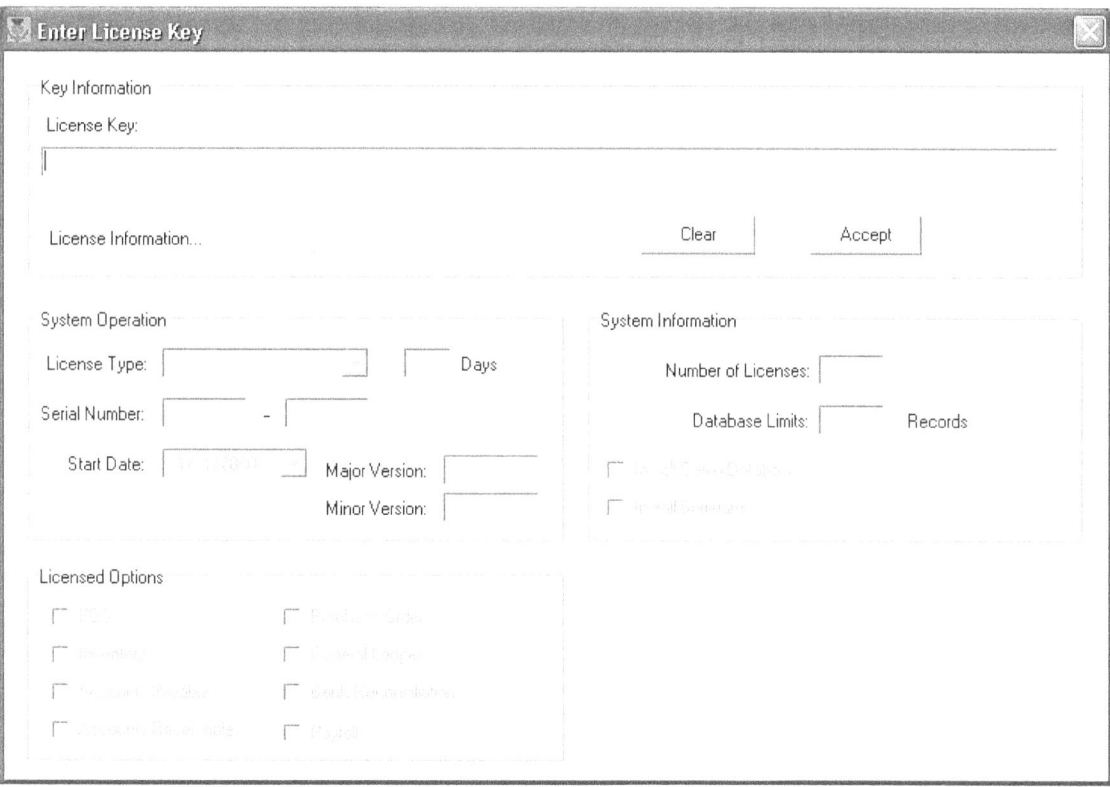

Note: When a license key is entered on the server it is automatically copied to all the client systems and then installed.

POS Business Application   Systems

3.2.2 Reset Network License Registration

When the POS Business Application software starts executing, it proceeds to register itself with a central database located on the server. This task is used to identify which POS Register numbers have been used and to ensure that the same POS Register number is used only once.

The "Reset Network License Registration" menu is used to reset the registration database and to force all computer systems to re-register.

3.2.3 Display Network License Registrations

When the "Display Network License Registrations" menu is selected, a screen is displayed which will show all registered applications. Each applications network computer name and POS Register number are displayed. The number of registered applications and the maximum number of licenses is also displayed.

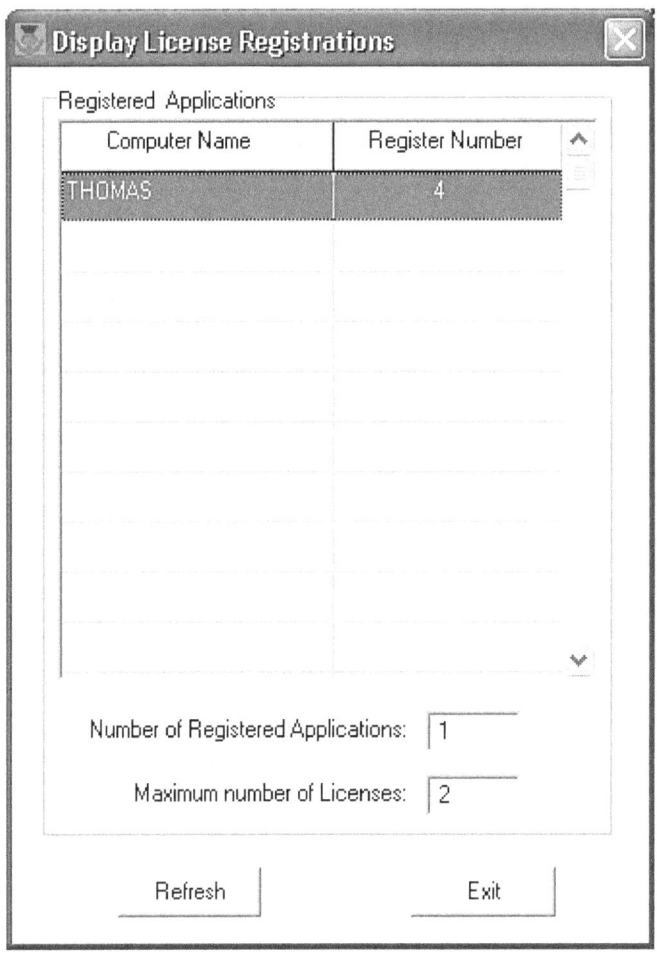

POS Business Application   Systems

3.3 User Menu

When the User Menu has been selected the following sub-menu will be displayed:

1. Login/Logout
2. Change Password
3. Identify Users

3.3.1 Login/Logout Menu

If no user is currently logged onto the POS Business Application then the "Login" menu option will be displayed.

If a user is currently logged onto the POS Business Application then the "Logout" menu option will be displayed. Pressing "Logout" will cause the current user to be logged out of the POS Business Application. To log onto the application, select the "Login" menu option and the System User Login dialog box will be displayed.

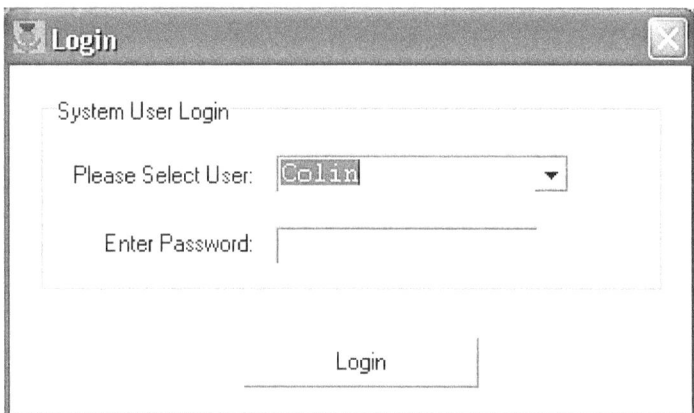

The user can then select their name from the User drop-down box, enters their password and then presses the [Login] button.

If a correct password has been entered, the user will be logged into the POS Business Application. The System Status will display the logged on user name and the main menu options available to the user will be displayed in bold letter. Menu options displayed in grayed-out letters are not available to the user.

If an incorrect password has been entered then the System Status message area will display the error "Invalid User Password". Initially the system only contains a single Supervisor user.

POS Business Application   Systems

3.3.2 Change Password Menu

If a logged in user wishes to change their password, the "Change Password" menu option may be selected. The System Users Database will then be locked and the Change Password dialog box displayed.

The user may then enter their current password and then enter and confirm their new password. Pressing the [Accept] button will cause the new password to be assigned to this user. Pressing the [Cancel] button will cancel the operation leaving the original password unchanged.

When changing a password, the user performing the change is provided sole access to the Server's System Users Database. This prevents any other user from performing a password change or an Identify User operation at that time – such a user would be notified that the System Users Database is currently locked by the user currently performing the password change.

Updated Server System User Databases are downloaded to Clients thereby making the databases available to the Clients if the Server or the Network were to subsequently fail. This implies that under such failure conditions, the users may still log in to a Client system (ie. operating in Local mode).

However, if the Client is already operating in Local mode and a password change is made then the new password would only be available on that specific Client computer system. When the Server/Network operation has been restored, the password change must be repeated in order for the Server System User database to be updated and subsequently broadcast to all Clients. Only then would the new password be available on all computer systems.

POS Business Application   Systems

<u>Note</u>:   When the Client is operating in Local mode (ie. the Server/Network has failed) the user is permitted to change the local copy of the System Users Database in order to permit continued operation of the system. When Server/Network operation has been restored, the user must immediately re-apply the password changes in order for the entire system to be brought up to date.

3.3.3   Identify Users Menu

The "Identify Users" menu option is selected if a logged in user wishes to add a new user, remove an existing user, or to change a user's current access. The Server's System Users Database will then be locked and the Identify Users dialog box displayed.

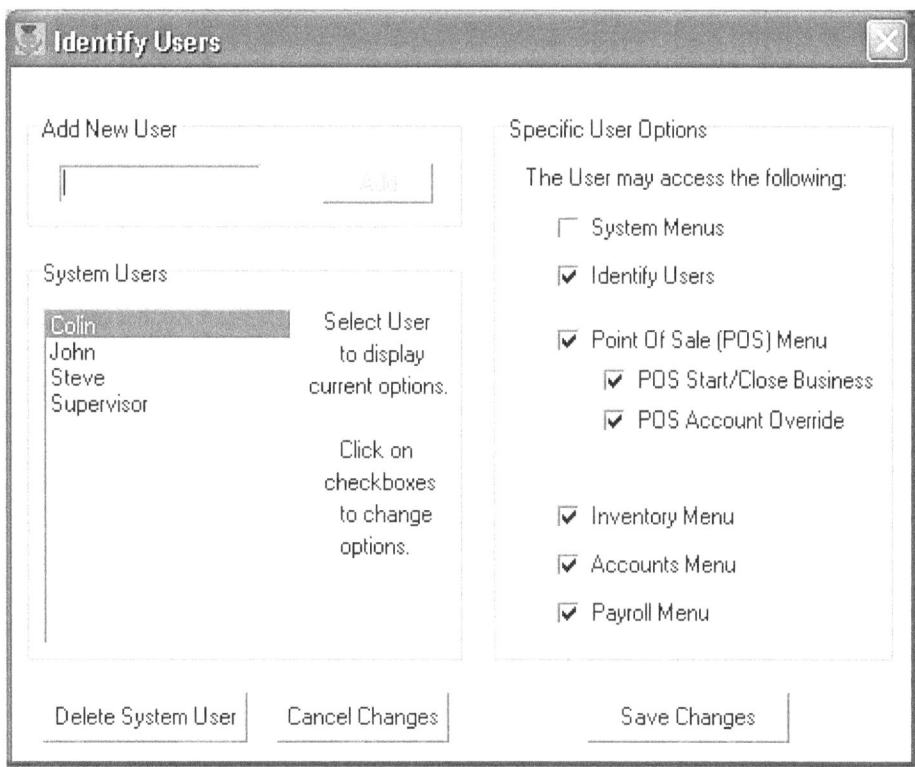

New users may then be added to the system, user access can be modified to allow or prevent access to various POS Business Application modules or options, or old users may be removed from the system. Pressing the [Save Changes] button will cause the modified information to be saved to the System Users Database. Pressing the [Cancel Changes] button will cancel the operation leaving the original System Users Database unchanged.

When performing the "Identify Users" function, the user performing the change is provided sole access to the Server's System Users Database. This prevents any other user from performing a password change or an Identify User change at that time – such a user would be notified that the System Users Database is currently locked by the user currently performing the Identify User operation.

POS Business Application

Updated Server System User Databases are downloaded to Clients thereby making the databases available to the Clients if the Server or the Network fails. This implies that under such failure conditions, the users may still log in to a Client system (ie. operating in Local mode) and access the relevant POS Business Application modules.

However, if the Client is operating in Local mode and an Identify User change is made then the modified user information would only be available on that specific Client computer system. When the Server/Network operation has been restored, the Identify User change must be repeated in order for the Server System User database to be updated and subsequently broadcast to all Clients. Only then would the new User be available to log on to any of the computer systems.

Note: When the Client is operating in Local mode (ie. the Server/Network has failed) the user is permitted to change the local copy of the System Users Database in order to permit continued operation of the system. When Server/Network operation has been restored, the user must immediately re-apply the Identify User changes in order for the entire system to be brought up to date.

3.3.4 Specific User Options

Each user may be given access to the following options:

1. System Menus
2. Identify Users
3. Point Of Sale Menu
    a. POS Start/Close Business
    b. POS Account Override
    c. POS Transaction Edit
4. Inventory Menu
5. Accounts Menu
6. Payroll Menu

If a specific user option checkbox is selected then the user may freely access that specific feature.

If a specific user option checkbox is not selected then the user may not access that specific feature. In certain situations if the user were to attempt to access such a feature, (eg. POS Account Override to change a sale item price), then a Supervisor Override screen would be displayed. Any person who has access to the required feature may then log in to provide temporary authority for this single operation.

POS Business Application   Systems

3.3.5 System Menus

The System Menus are system critical menus which only specifically authorized users should have access. These include, but are not limited to, the following menus:

1. Database Import
2. Database Export

3.3.5.1 Identify Users

This option allows the specified user the ability to access the Identify Users Menu and add new users, modify user options and remove old users from the system.

3.3.5.2 Point Of Sale Menu

All users, by default, have access to the Point Of Sale Menu. This is to permit all users to have the capability of making sale transactions.

However, only specific users should have the following capabilities:

1. POS Start/Close Business
2. POS Account Override
3. POS Transaction Edit

3.3.5.2.1 POS Start/Close Business

This option allows the user to perform the Start of Business and Close of Business till operations.

3.3.5.2.2 POS Account Override

This option allows the user to override a purchase price or discount for a sale transaction.

3.3.5.2.3 POS Transaction Edit

This option allows the user to edit a Point of Sale transaction.

3.3.5.3 Inventory Menu

This option allows the user to access the Inventory module. This access includes the ability to view and edit the Inventory Database and also print out Inventory reports.

POS Business Application   Systems

3.3.5.4 Accounts Menu

This option allows the user to access the Accounts Menu. The Accounts Menu provides access to the following sub-menus:

1. Accounts Payable
2. Accounts Receivable
3. Bank Reconciliation
4. Purchase Order
5. General Ledger

This access allows the user to view and edit these databases and also print out associated reports.

3.3.5.5 Payroll Menu

This option allows the user to access the Payroll module. This access includes the ability to view and edit the Payroll Database and also print out Payroll reports.

3.3.6 New User Password

When a new user is added to the system, the initial password is set to "user". The new user should log onto the system and change their password as soon as possible.

3.3.7 Supervisor Password

The initial Supervisor password is set to "super". The Supervisor should log onto the system and change this password as soon as possible.

3.4 Database Menu

The Database Menu is only available to users with "System Menus" access.

The Database Menu provides the following sub-menus:

1. File Conversion Utility
2. Import Database
3. Export Database
4. Backup Database
5. Restore Database

3.4.1 File Conversion Utility

The "File Conversion Utility" menu option is selected if the user wishes to convert a dBASE data file to CSV (Comma Separated Variable) format. CSV file format is used when importing databases from other accounting systems into the POS Business Application.

Once the "File Conversion Utility" menu option has been selected, the File Conversion Utility screen will be displayed.

POS Business Application   Systems

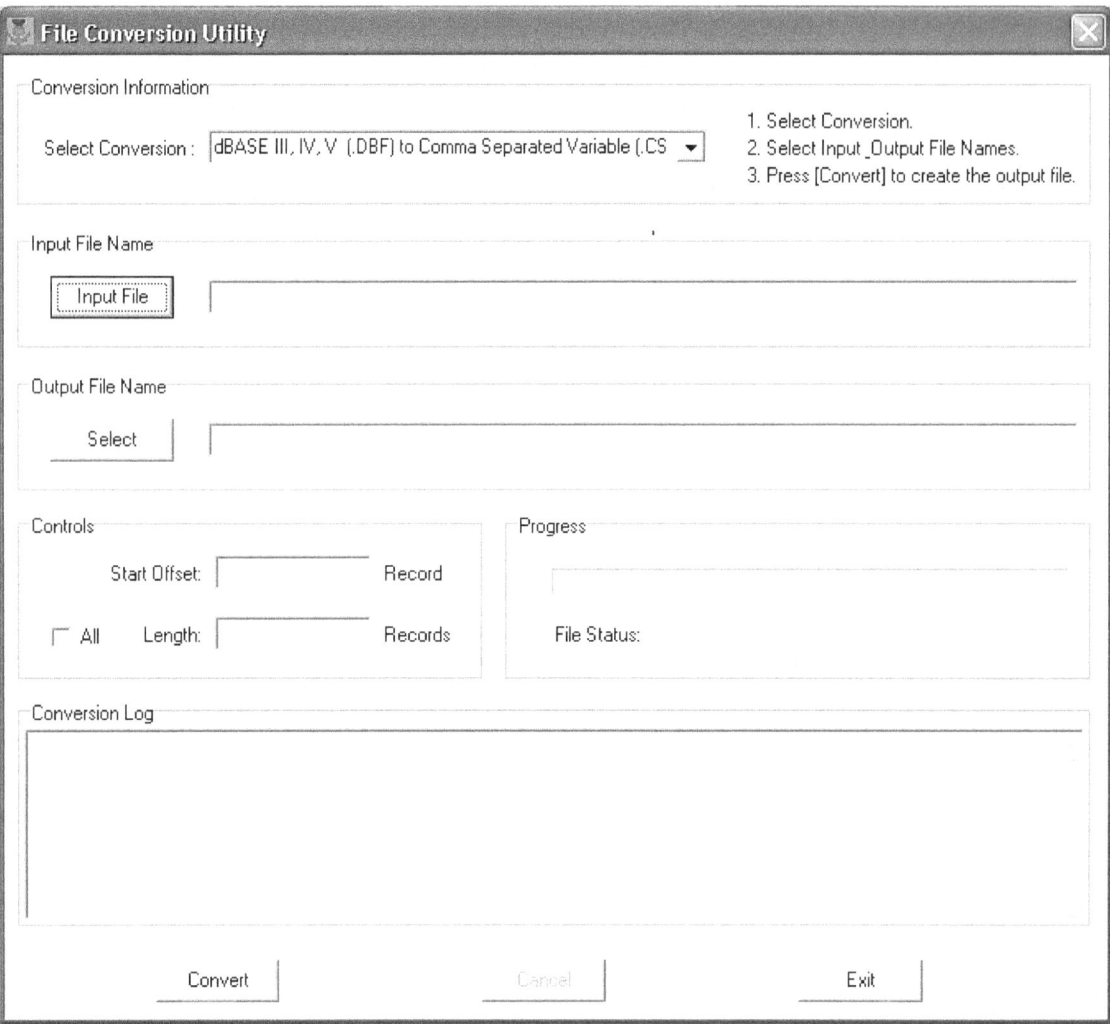

This screen allows the user to select the required conversion, identify the source and destination files and to Convert, Cancel or Exit the conversion process. Progress information is displayed during the conversion process.

POS Business Application   Systems

3.4.2   Import Database

The "Import Database" menu option is selected if the user wishes to create a new POS Business Application database based on information from one or more prior accounting database systems. The accounting system databases being imported must be in CSV file format. The Import Database operation may only be performed on the POS Business Application Server computer system.

When the Import Database menu option is selected, the Import Database screen is displayed.

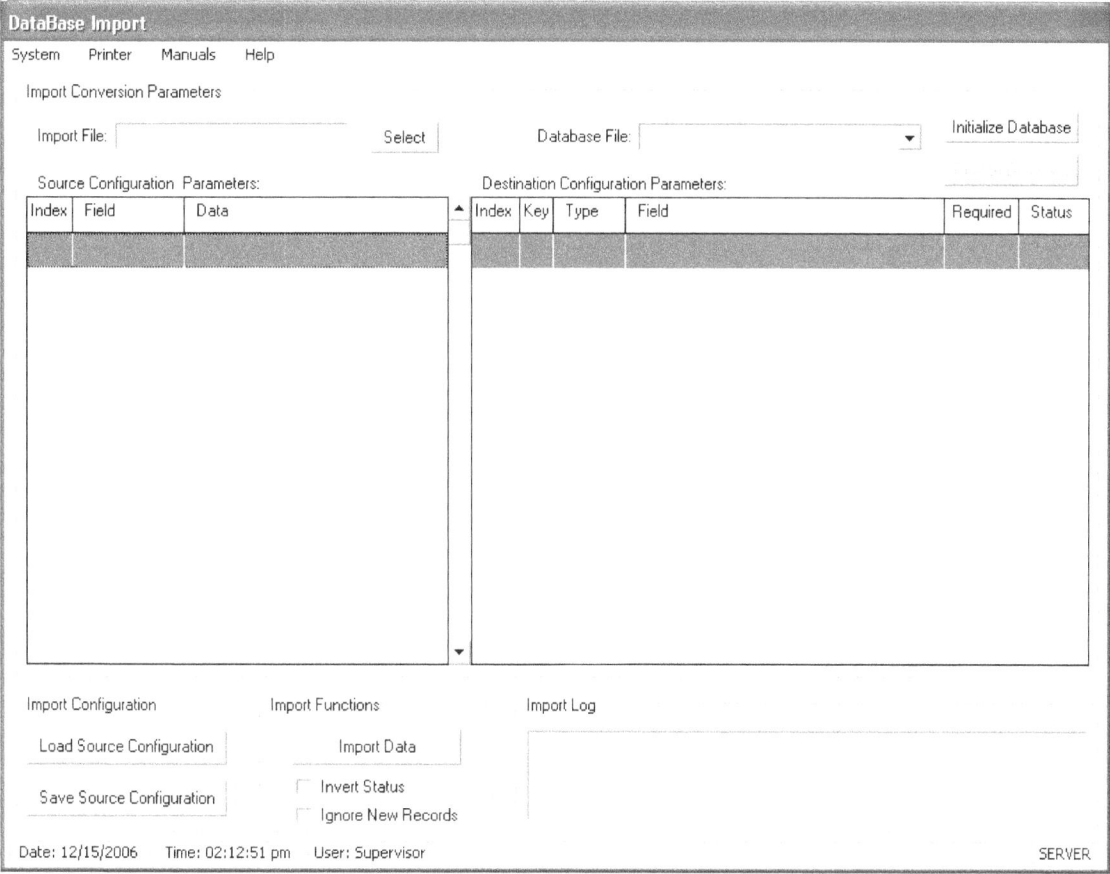

This screen allows the user to:

1. Initialize the appropriate POS Business Application Database
2. Specify the CSV database file to be imported
3. Specify a load source configuration file
4. Perform the Import operation
5. Finalize the Import operation

When creating a specific POS Business Application Database, data may be imported from one or more CSV data files.

POS Business Application   Systems

3.4.2.1 Initialize POS Business Application Database

The POS Business Application Database File is selected from the Drop Down menu. One of the following database files may be selected:

1. Accounts Receivable
2. Accounts Receivable History
3. Inventory
4. Inventory History
5. POS Sale History Register
6. POS Sale History Transaction

Once the specific database file has been selected, the various database fields will be displayed in the Destination Configuration Parameters table.

The [Initialize Database] button may be pressed in order to clear the currently selected POS Business Application database to its initial state.

3.4.2.2 Specify Import File

The Import File [Select] button is pressed to access the computer file system in order to select the appropriate import file. This is a CSV file which contains some or all of the data to be imported.

Once the import file has been selected, the import file name will be displayed.

3.4.2.3 Specify Import Configuration File

The Import Source Configuration File may be loaded from the computer file system by pressing the [Load Source Configuration] button. This configuration file identifies the various import file CSV field names, index positions or constants which are to be associated with and stored in the specified POS Business Application Database.

On a new POS Business Application, the Import Source Configuration File will need to be created by the user. The Import File is a CSV file and its first record usually contains a list of field names. When the Import File is selected these field names are obtained. The user specifies which source configuration parameter is to be associated with which destination configuration parameter by double clicking the mouse on a specific source configuration parameter line. This action causes the Import Source Database Field dialog box to be displayed:

POS Business Application   Systems

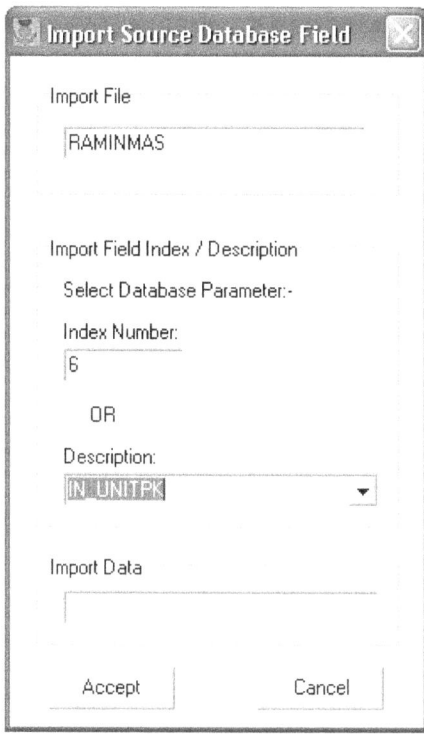
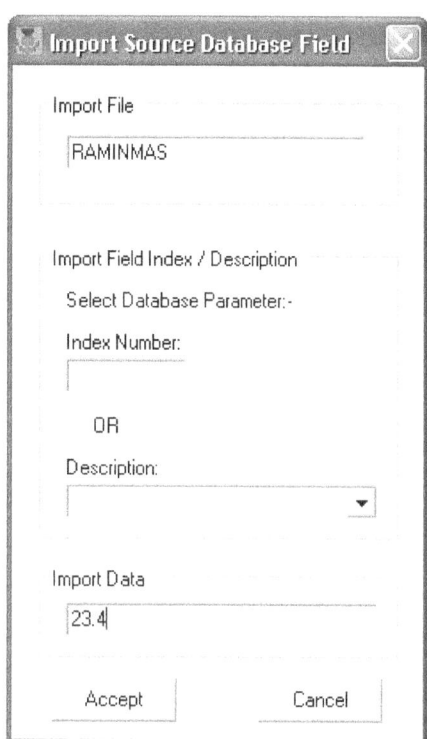

This dialog box permits the user to enter a specific index number, select a specific field description name (above left example), or enter a specific constant (above right example) to be imported for this specific POS Business Application Database field. Once the import field information has been entered, the [Accept] key is pressed to store the entry in the Source Configuration Parameter table. If the [Cancel] key is pressed then any specified import field information will be ignored. Once all the relevant Source Configuration Parameters have been specified, the Source Configuration Parameters may be saved for future use by pressing the [Save Source Configuration] button.

If the mouse is over a source configuration parameter line and the right mouse button is pressed, an edit pop-up menu is displayed which allows the user to swap parameter lines, insert or delete parameters, clear a parameter or clear all parameters.

POS Business Application   Systems

The following screen example indicates various source configuration field data which is to be imported into the Inventory Database:

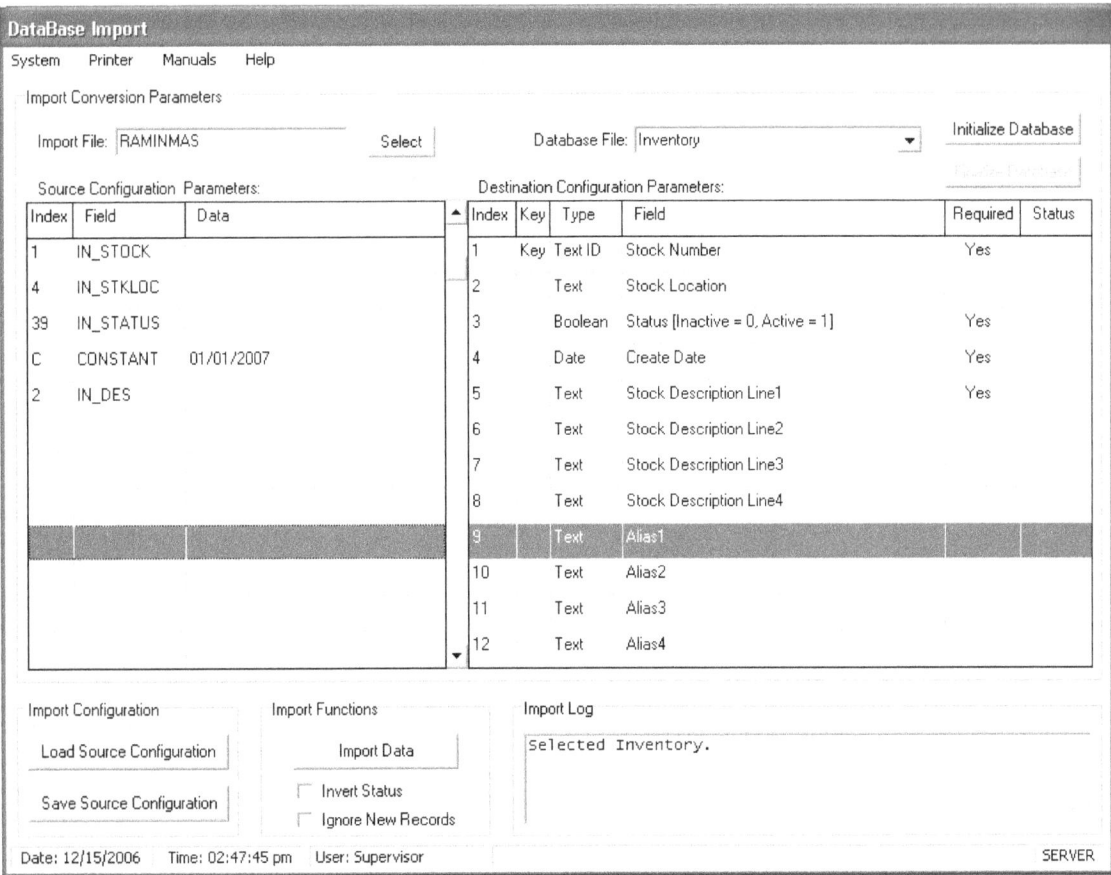

3.4.2.4 Import Functions

If, when importing status information, it may be required that the logic value be inverted (ie. the import file identified an Active status by the value '0' whereas the POS Business Application identifies Active status by the value '1'). This inversion is achieved by selecting the "Invert Status" check box.

Also, it might occur that a specific secondary import file may contain additional record entries not found in a specific master import file. These additional entries may be ignored by selecting the "Ignore New Records" check box.

The [Import Data] button may then be pressed to start the import process.

If subsequent data files are to be imported into the currently selected POS Business Application Database, this is achieved by selecting a new Import File, loading or specifying new source configuration parameters and once more pressing the [Import Data] button. This process may be repeated as often as necessary.

POS Business Application   Systems

3.4.2.5 Import Log

As the import process is executing, a status bar is displayed to show the progress. When the import process is complete, the import log is displayed. Double Clicking (using the mouse) on the Import Log will display a larger log screen. The user can then verify the status of the import operation.

3.4.2.6 Finalize Database

Once all the relevant data has been imported to a specific POS Business Application database, the database is finalized by pressing the [Finalize Database] button. The finalization process scans the imported database and creates the necessary index tables which allow the database to be accessed.

<u>Note</u>: An imported database may only be finalized if data for all the required fields has been imported.

3.4.3 Export Database

If a POS Business Application Database is to be exported as a CSV file, this is performed by selecting the "Export Database" menu option.

When selected, the Database Export screen will be displayed. The POS Business Application Database file to be exported is selected from the associated drop-down list. The Export File is then selected by pressing the [Select] button and either selecting an existing file name or specifying a new file name to be used for the export file.

The [Export Data] button is pressed to perform the export process. A CSV file will be created which has the relevant field name definitions stored in the first record. A progress bar will indicate the export operations progress. Pressing the [Cancel] button will cancel the Export Database operation. Pressing the [Exit] button will exit the Export Database screen.

POS Business Application   Systems

3.4.4 Backup Database

The "Backup Database" menu is used to display the Backup Database screen. The POS Business Application Database Backup operation allows the various databases to be converted to a single backup file for transfer to removable media (eg. removable hard drive, DVD-ROM, etc.). The system generated backup file name includes the current date and time and is therefore easily identified as shown below:

    For example: `POS_Database_Backup 2006-11-03 11-15-21.BAK`

Each database backup operation will create a new unique backup file and will never overwrite any previous backup file.

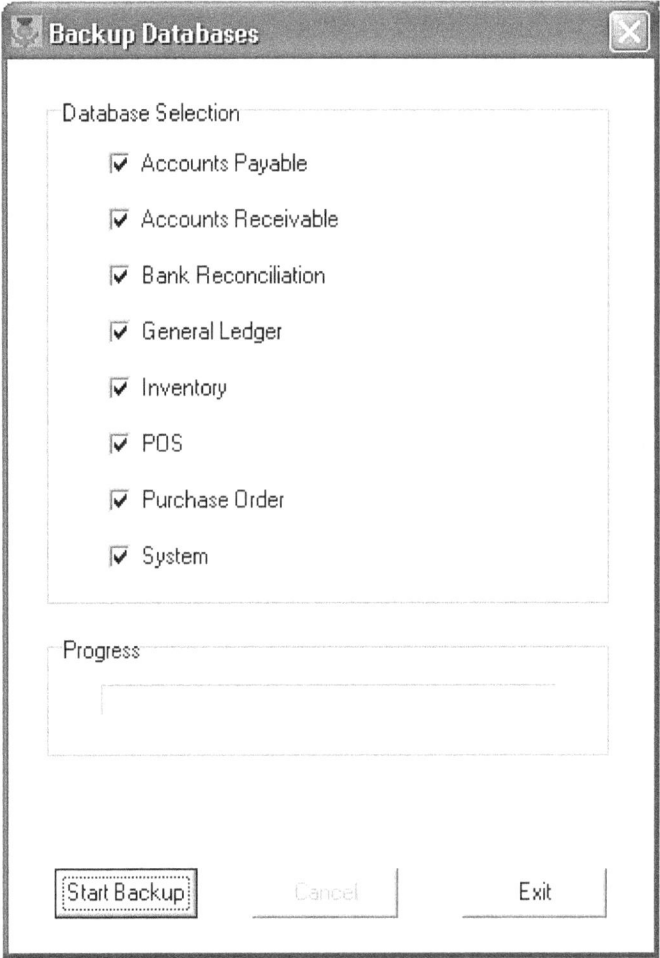

The database backup is started by pressing the [Start Backup] button.
The backup process may be cancelled by pressing the [Cancel] button.
Pressing the [Exit] button will exit the Backup Databases screen.

Note: Please refer to the Appendix for a description of a suitable backup procedure.

POS Business Application   Systems

3.4.5 Restore Database

The "Restore Database" menu displays the following sub-menus:

1. Restore Database from File
2. Restore Database from Directory

The POS Business Application Database Restore operation can take a specified backup file and expand it to create the required system directories and databases. Prior to performing the Database Restoration, the previously existing database directory will be renamed and will therefore not be overwritten during this process.

The Database Restore operation also has the capability of restoring from a previous database directory.

The default Database Backup and Database Restore operations do not erase or modify any existing database files, therefore the user is never faced with the situation where the system database could be overwritten due to operator error. If the user wishes to overwrite the active database directory during a restore operation, an override option is provided.

3.4.5.1 Restore Database from File

When the "Restore Database from File" menu is pressed, the Restore Database (from Backup File) screen is displayed.

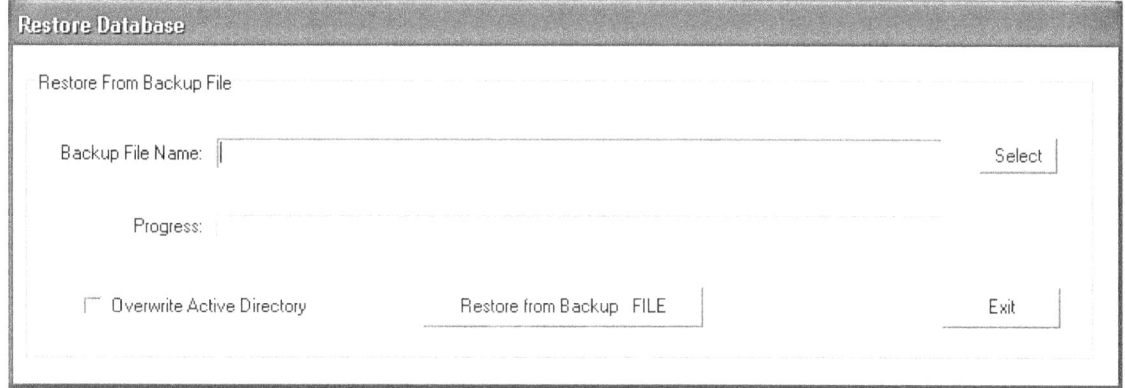

This screen restores backup files which were created by the POS Business Application "Backup Database" option described earlier.

The [Select] button is used to access the computer file system and to select the relevant backup file to be restored.

POS Business Application   Systems

The [Restore from Backup File] button is pressed to start the restoration process. During the restoration process, the currently active database directory is renamed and a new active directory created with the restored databases.

On occasion an error message may be displayed indicating that the active directory may not be renamed since the Windows Operating System has reported that it is currently in use. Under such conditions, please ensure that no other program is currently accessing the active directory. If required, the "Overwrite Active Directory" option may be selected to proceed without renaming the active directory. The active database directory will simply be overwritten with the restored databases and may not be recovered.

The [Exit] button may be pressed to exit the Restore Database screen.

3.4.5.2 Restore Database from Directory

When the "Restore Database from Directory" menu is pressed, the Restore Database (from Backup Directory) screen is displayed.

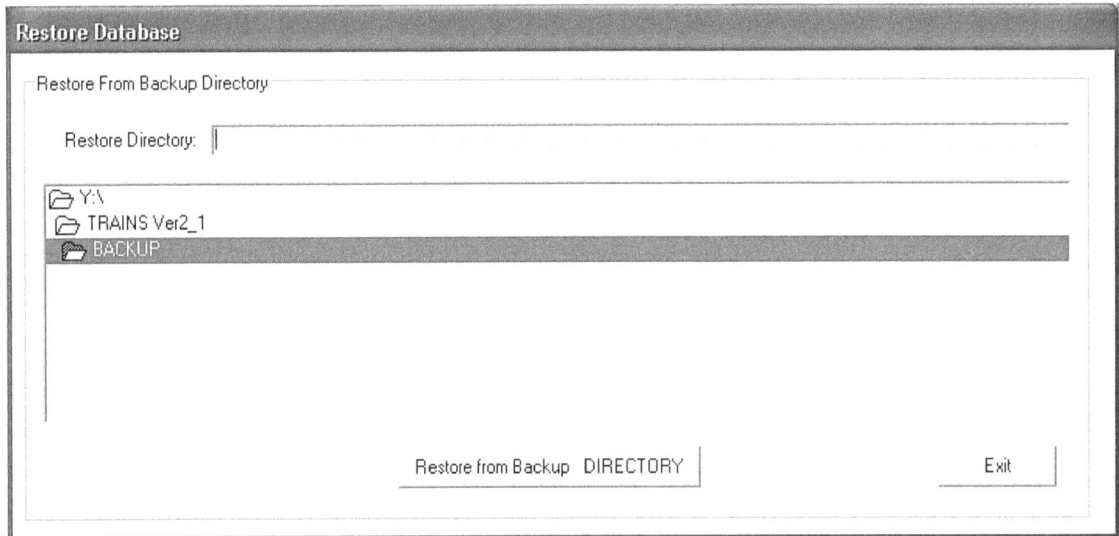

This screen restores a previously backed up directory back to active status.

First select the database directory which is to be restored. Database directories are named as follows:
        DATABASE BACKUP 2006-11-09 17-47-33

This database was created at 5:47pm on the 9th of Nov 2006.

Once the relevant database backup has been found, double click on the directory name to select it. The full directory name will be seen in the Restore Directory field.

Press the [Restore from Backup DIRECTORY] button to start the restoration process.
The [Exit] button may be pressed to exit the Restore Database screen.

POS Business Application   Systems

3.5 Options Menu

This menu option is only available to users with System Menu access (eg. Supervisor). When this menu option has been selected, the following sub-menu will be displayed:

1. Receipt Number
2. Invoice Number
3. Quote Number
4. Source Document Number
5. Credit Card Codes
6. Tax Codes
7. Sale Types
8. Term Codes
9. Transaction Codes
10. System Wide Options
11. Printer Selection
12. Cash Register Drawer

3.5.1 Receipt Number

When the Receipt Number menu is selected, a dialog box is displayed which allows the user to select the next receipt number to be used.

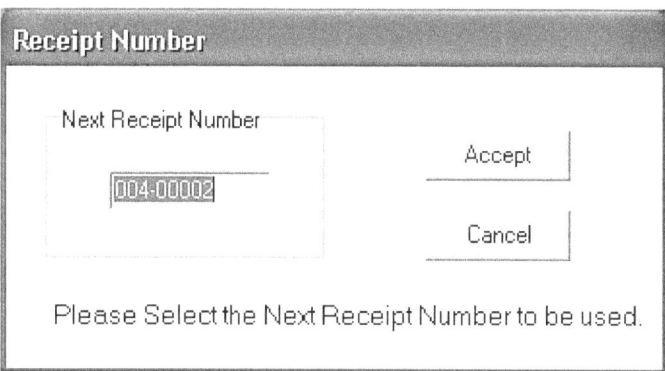

Each computer system contains its own Receipt Number database.

3.5.2 Invoice Number

When the Invoice Number menu is selected, a dialog box is displayed which allows the user to select the next invoice number to be used.

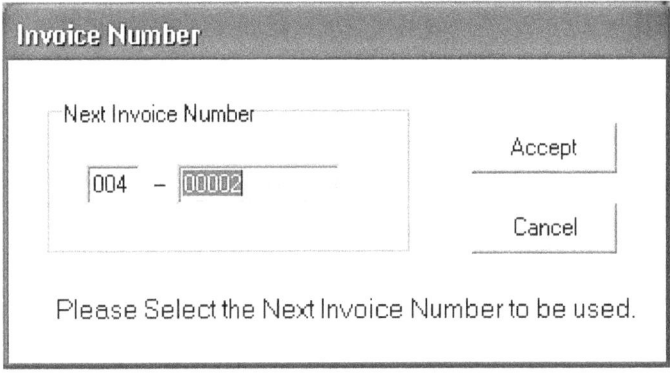

Each computer system contains its own Invoice Number database.

3.5.3 Quote Number

When the Quote Number menu is selected, a dialog box is displayed which allows the user to select the next quote number to be used.

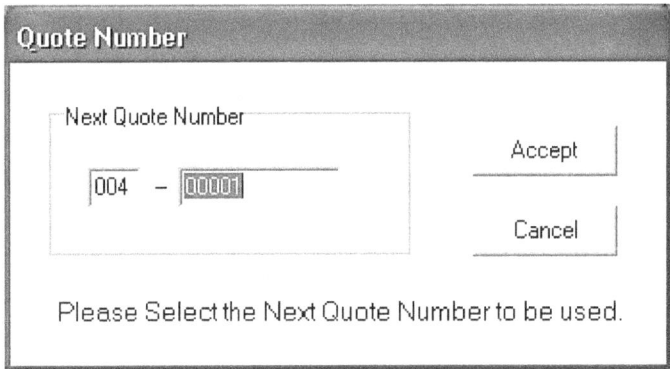

Each computer system contains its own Quote Number database.

POS Business Application — Systems

3.5.4 Source Document Number

When the Source Document Number menu is selected, a dialog box is displayed which allows the user to select the next source document number to be used.

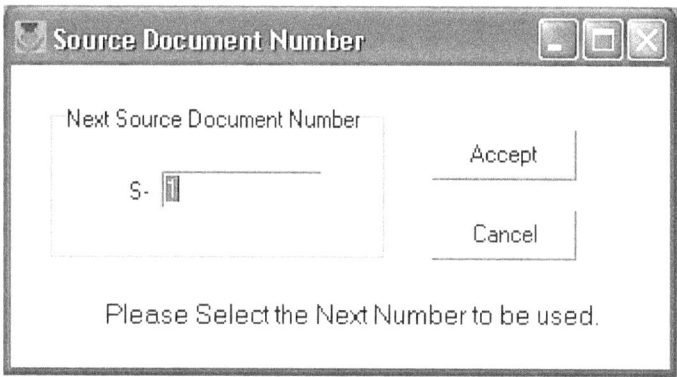

Each computer system contains its own source document number database.

3.5.5 Credit Card Codes

When the Credit Card menu is selected, the user is presented with the Credit Card Code Editor screen.

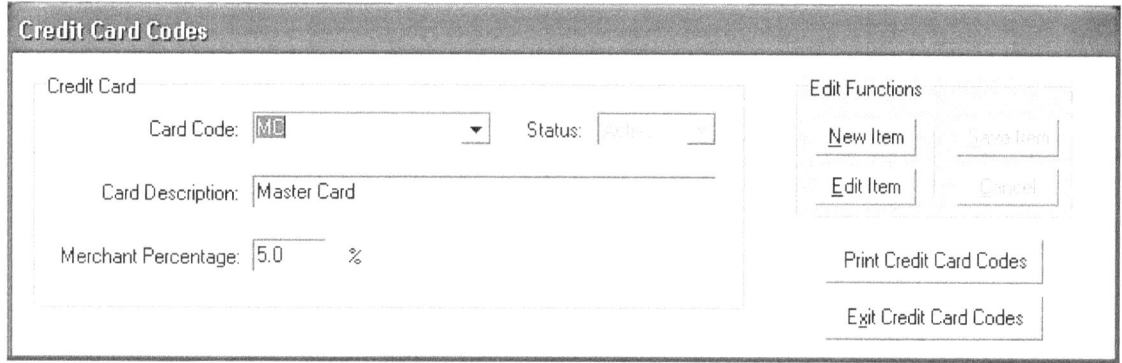

New credit card codes may be defined and existing credit card code options may be changed. The Edit Functions provides four function keys. Use the [New Item] button to enter a new credit card code. The [Edit Item] button is used to edit the currently displayed card code. When editing the database, the new information is saved to the database by pressing the [Save Item] button. Pressing the [Cancel] button will cancel the edit and the database will remain unchanged.

When changing Credit Card Code information, the user performing the change is provided sole access to the Credit Card Code Database on the Server. This prevents any other user from performing a Credit Card Code change at that time – such a user would be notified that the Credit Card Code Database is currently locked by the user currently performing the Credit Card Code change.

Updated Credit Card Code Databases are downloaded to Clients thereby making the databases available to the Clients if the Server or the Network were to subsequently fail. This implies that under such failure conditions, the users may still access their local copy of this database during POS operation.

Credit Card Codes may be entered as follows (do not enter the quotation marks):

1. Press the Edit Functions [New Item] button to create a new credit card code.

2. The Credit Card Code ID may be set to "AMEX" to indicate American Express.

3. The Status is set to Active to indicate that this credit card code may be used in the system. If set to Inactive, the credit card code is disabled.

4. The Card Description is set to some descriptive text to be associated with AMEX, for example, "American Express".

5. The Merchant Percentage would be set to the relevant percentage.

6. Press the Edit Functions [Save Item] button to save the new credit card code.

The credit card code ID "AMEX" has now been defined and may now be associated with sales information.

Note: When the Client is operating in Local mode (ie. the Server/Network has failed) the user is not permitted to change the Credit Card Code Database.

3.5.5.1 Imported Databases

If a database import is performed which brings in pre-existing data from a prior accounting system, the user must ensure that the credit card codes specified in the imported database are also defined in the POS Business Application's Credit Card Code Database.

Credit Card codes are used in the following imported databases:

- Accounts Receivable
- POS Sale History Register Database

For example, if an imported database used a credit card code called "BANKCC", then the Credit Card Code Editor screen in the previous section must be used to define this card code along with the card description and merchant percentage parameters associated with this credit card code.

3.5.6 Tax Codes

When the Tax Codes menu is selected, the user is presented with the Tax Codes Editor screen.

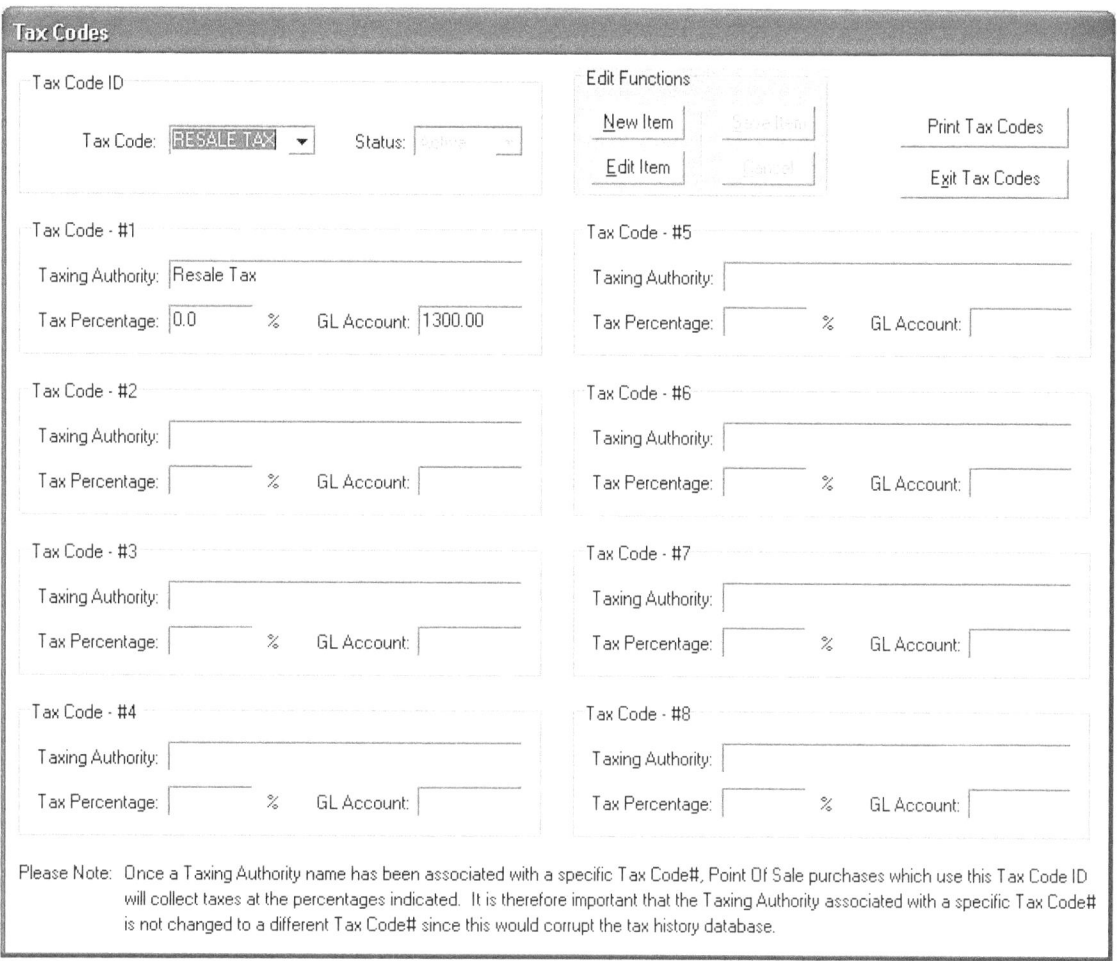

New Tax Codes may be defined and existing tax codes may be changed. A tax code can define up to 8 separate sub-tax codes (eg. city tax, state tax, county tax, etc.). The Edit Functions provides four function keys. Use the [New Item] button to enter a new tax code. The [Edit Item] button is used to edit the currently displayed tax code. When editing the database, the new information is saved to the database by pressing the [Save Item] button. Pressing the [Cancel] button will cancel the edit and the database will remain unchanged.

When changing Tax Code information, the user performing the change is provided sole access to the Tax Code Database on the Server. This prevents any other user from performing a Tax Code change at that time – such a user would be notified that the Tax Code Database is currently locked by the user currently performing the Tax Code change. Updated Tax Code Databases are downloaded to Clients thereby making the databases available to the Clients if the Server or the Network were to subsequently fail. This implies that under such failure conditions, the users may still access their local copy of this database during POS operation.

Tax Codes are used to specify the sales tax to be applied to a specific sale. For example, in San Diego, California, the local tax code is 7.75%. This may be entered as follows (do not enter the quotation marks):

1. Press the Edit Functions [New Item] button to create a new tax code.

2. The Tax Code ID may be set to "CASD" to indicate California, San Diego.

3. The Status is set to Active to indicate that this tax code may be used in the system. If set to Inactive, the tax code is disabled.

4. The Tax Code #1 Taxing Authority is set to some descriptive text to be associated with CASD, for example, "San Diego, California (Sales Tax)".

5. The Tax Percentage would be set to "7.75". The GL Account is for future use.

6. Press the Edit Functions [Save Item] button to save the new tax code.

The tax code ID "CASD" has now been defined and may now be associated with an accounts receivable customer or with a particular sales type.

Note: Tax Codes may be created but not deleted. Deleting a tax code is not permitted since any historical data which referenced that tax code would then be invalid.

Note: When the Client is operating in Local mode (ie. the Server/Network has failed) the user is not permitted to change the Tax Code Database.

3.5.6.1 Imported Databases

If a database import is performed which brings in pre-existing data from a prior accounting system, the user must ensure that the tax codes specified in the imported database are also defined in the POS Business Application's Tax Code Database.

Tax codes are used in the following imported databases:

- Accounts Receivable
- POS Sale History Register Database
- POS Sale History Transaction Database

For example, if an imported database used a tax code called "CATX", then the Tax Codes Editor screen in the previous section must be used to define this code along with the various taxing authorities, tax percentages and GL accounts associated with this tax code.

POS Business Application   Systems

3.5.7 Sale Types

When the Sale Types menu is selected, the user is presented with the Sale Types Editor screen.

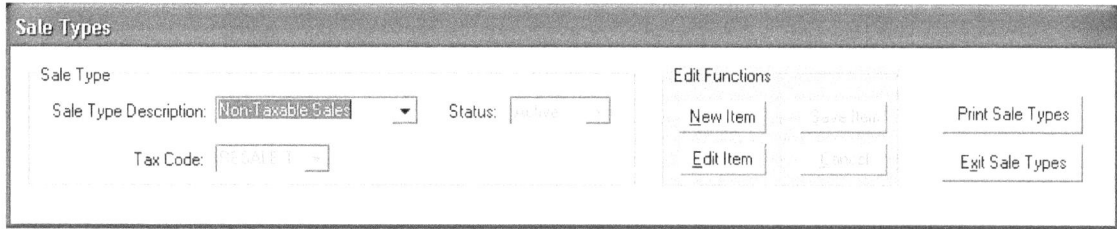

New Sale Types may be defined and existing sale types may be changed. Sale types are used in the Point-Of-Sale to identify the type of sale being performed. The Edit Functions provides four function keys. Use the [New Item] button to enter a new sales type description. The [Edit Item] button is used to edit the currently displayed sales type description. When editing the database, the new information is saved to the database by pressing the [Save Item] button. Pressing the [Cancel] button will cancel the edit and the database will remain unchanged.

When changing Sale Type information, the user performing the change is provided sole access to the Sale Type Database on the Server. This prevents any other user from performing a Sale Type change at that time – such a user would be notified that the Sale Type Database is currently locked by the user currently performing the Sale Type change. Updated Sale Type Databases are downloaded to Clients thereby making the databases available to the Clients if the Server or the Network were to subsequently fail. This implies that under such failure conditions, the users may still access their local copy of this database during POS operation.

Sale Types are used by the POS Terminal to identify what sales tax is to be applied to a specific sale. For example, in San Diego, California, the local tax code is 7.75%. This was set up earlier as a tax code called "CASD". The sale type is associated with this tax code as follows (do not enter the quotation marks):

1. Press the Edit Functions [New Item] button to create a new sale type description.

2. The Sale Type Description may be set to "Retail (Taxable)" to indicate a taxable retail sale. Sale Types are sorted and displayed in ascending order. Prefix a sale type with a number (eg. "1 – Retail (Tax)") to displayed it at the top of the list.

3. The Status is set to Active to indicate that this sale type may be used in the system. If set to Inactive, the sale type is disabled.

4. The Tax Code is set to a previously defined tax code – for example, "CASD".

5. Press the Edit Functions [Save Item] button to save the new sale type.

The sale type description "Retail (Taxable)" has now been defined and may now be displayed in the Sale Type list on the POS Terminal. When used, the current CASD tax value (in this case, 7.75%) will be associated with this particular sale.

Note: Sale Types may be created but not deleted. Deleting a sale type is not permitted since any historical data which referenced that sale type would then be invalid.

Note: When the Client is operating in Local mode (ie. the Server/Network has failed) the user is not permitted to change the Sale Type Database.

3.5.7.1 Imported Databases

If a database import is performed which brings in pre-existing data from a prior accounting system, the user must ensure that the sale type codes specified in the imported database are also defined in the POS Business Application's Sale Types Database.

Sale Type codes are used in the following imported database:

- POS Sale History Transaction Database

For example, if an imported database used a sales type code called "Retail", then the Sales Types Code Editor screen in the previous section must be used to define this code (ie. Sales Type Description parameter) along with the associated tax code.

POS Business Application — Systems

3.5.8 Term Codes

When the Term Codes menu is selected, the user is presented with the Term Codes Editor screen.

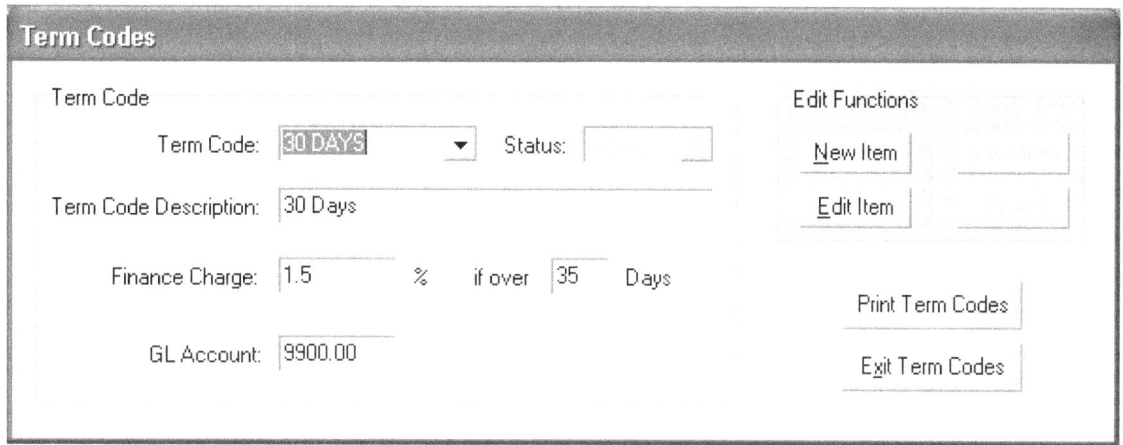

New Term Codes may be defined and existing term codes may be changed. Term Codes are used by the Accounts Receivable module to specify if finance charges or discounts are to be applied to the account purchase. If an account purchase has not been paid in a particular period of time then a finance charge may be applied. If an account purchase was paid within a period of time then a discount credit may be applied.

The Edit Functions provides four function keys. Use the [New Item] button to enter a new Term Code. The [Edit Item] button is used to edit the currently displayed term code. When editing the database, the new information is saved to the database by pressing the [Save Item] button. Pressing the [Cancel] button will cancel the edit and the database will remain unchanged.

When changing Term Code information, the user performing the change is provided sole access to the Term Code Database on the Server. This prevents any other user from performing a Term Code change at that time – such a user would be notified that the Term Code Database is currently locked by the user currently performing the Term Code change. Updated Term Code Databases are downloaded to Clients thereby making the databases available to the Clients if the Server or the Network were to subsequently fail. This implies that under such failure conditions, the users may still access their local copy of this database during POS operation.

Term Codes are used by the POS Terminal to identify what term code is to be applied to a specific sale. For example (do not enter the quotation marks):

1. Press the Edit Functions [New Item] button to create a new Term Code.

2. The Term Code may be set to "30" to indicate a net 30 days sale.

3. The Status is set to Active to indicate that this term code may be used in the system. If set to Inactive, the term code is disabled from future use.

4. The Term Code Description is used to describe the term code – for example, "Net 30 Days".

5. The Finance charge percentage is entered, eg. "1.5".

6. The "if over" day limit is specified, eg "40". The customer will only be charged a 1.5% finance charge if the purchase was not paid within 40 days.

7. The GL Account field is for future use. Use the default value, "1200.00".

8. Press the Edit Functions [Save Item] button to save the new sale type.

The Term Code "30" has now been defined and may now be associated with a specific customer account (See the Accounts Receivable Term Code field).

Note: Term Codes may be created but not deleted. Deleting a term code is not permitted since any historical data which referenced that term code would then be invalid.

Note: When the Client is operating in Local mode (ie. the Server/Network has failed) the user is not permitted to change the Term Code Database.

3.5.8.1 Imported Databases

If a database import is performed which brings in pre-existing data from a prior accounting system, the user must ensure that the term codes specified in the imported database are also defined in the POS Business Application's Term Codes Database.

Term codes are used in the following imported databases:

- Accounts Receivable
- Accounts Receivable History Database
- POS Sale History Register Database

For example, if an imported database used a term code called "30DAYS", then the Term Codes Editor screen in the previous section must be used to define this code along with the various other parameters associated with this terms code.

POS Business Application   Systems

3.5.9 Transaction Codes

When the Transaction Codes menu is selected, the user is presented with the Transaction Codes Editor screen.

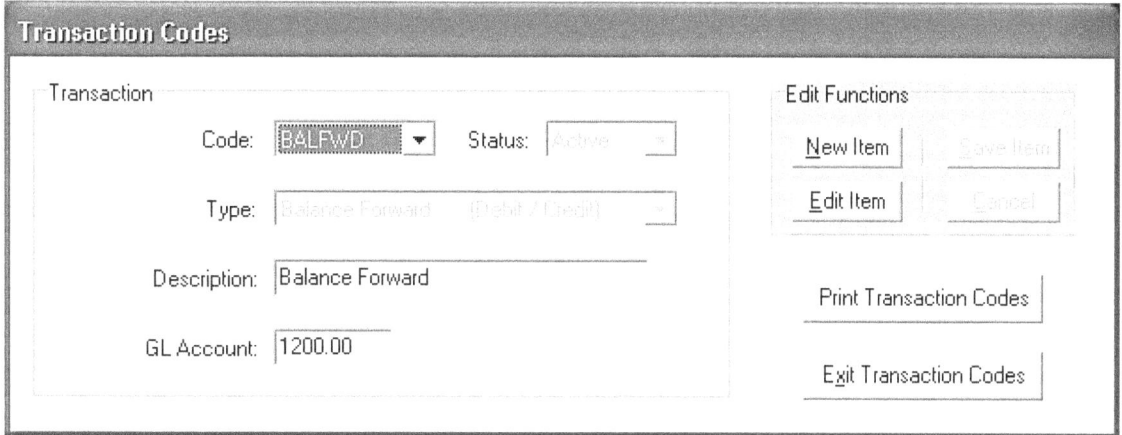

New Transaction Codes may be defined and existing transaction codes may be changed. Transaction Codes are used throughout the POS Business Application to identify whether a transaction is a credit or a debit.

The Following types of transactions are provided:

- Balance Forward
- POS Invoice
- Customer Charge
- Customer Credit
- Payment Received
- Payment Adjustment
- Unapplied Payment
- Unapplied Credit
- Finance Charge

Balance Forward
A balance forward transaction may be a credit (eg. -10.56) or a debit (+10.56).

POS Invoice
A Point-Of-Sale Invoice transaction may be a credit (eg. –10.56) or a debit (+10.56).

Customer Charge
A Customer Charge transaction is always a debit (eg. +10.56).

Customer Credit
A Customer Credit transaction is always a credit (eg. +10.56).

POS Business Application   Systems

Payment Received
A Payment Received transaction is always a credit (eg. +10.56).

Payment Adjustment
A Payment Adjustment transaction is always a debit (eg. +10.56).

Unapplied Payment
An Unapplied Payment transaction is always a credit (eg. +10.56).

Unapplied Credit
An Unapplied Credit transaction is always a credit (eg. +10.56).

Finance Charge
A Finance Charge transaction is always a debit (eg. +10.56).

The Edit Functions provides four function keys. Use the [New Item] button to enter a new Transaction Code. The [Edit Item] button is used to edit the currently displayed Transaction Code. When editing the database, the new information is saved to the database by pressing the [Save Item] button. Pressing the [Cancel] button will cancel the edit and the database will remain unchanged.

When changing Transaction Code information, the user performing the change is provided sole access to the Transaction Code Database on the Server. This prevents any other user from performing a Transaction Code change at that time – such a user would be notified that the Transaction Code Database is currently locked by the user currently performing the Transaction Code change. Updated Transaction Code Databases are downloaded to Clients thereby making the databases available to the Clients if the Server or the Network were to subsequently fail. This implies that under such failure conditions, the users may still access their local copy of this database during POS operation.

Transaction Codes are used by the POS Business Application to identify how a transaction is to be processed. It is necessary to provide at least one transaction code for each transaction type. If a different accounting package database is being imported to the POS Business Application then the user may create transaction codes as used in the existing database. This would permit imported Accounts Receivable history data to be correctly displayed and subsequently processed.

For example (do not enter the quotation marks):

1. Press the Edit Functions [New Item] button to create a new Transaction Code.

2. The Transaction Code is set to "0" to indicate a Balance Forward transaction.

3. The Status is set to Active to indicate that this transaction code may be used in the system. If set to Inactive, the transaction code is disabled from future use.

4. The Transaction Code is set to "Balance Forward (Debit/Credit)".

5. The Description is set to "Balance Forward".

6. The GL Account is for future use and may be set to the default value of 1200.00

7. Press the Edit Functions [Save Item] button to save the new sale type. The Transaction Code "0" has now been defined and may now be used when processing a specific customer account history records.

Note: Transaction Codes may be created but not deleted. Deleting a transaction code is not permitted since any historical data which referenced it would then be invalid.

Note: When the Client is operating in Local mode (ie. the Server/Network has failed) the user is not permitted to change the Transaction Code Database.

3.5.9.1 Imported Databases

If a database import is performed which brings in pre-existing data from a prior accounting system, the user must ensure that the transaction codes specified in the imported database are also defined in the POS Business Application's Transaction Codes Database.

Transaction codes are used in the following imported databases:

- Accounts Receivable History Database

For example, if an imported database used a transaction code called "POSINV", then the Transaction Codes Editor screen in the previous section must be used to define this code along with the various other parameters associated with this transaction code.

POS Business Application — Systems

3.5.10 Transaction Sources

When the Transaction Sources menu is selected, the user is presented with the Transaction Sources Editor screen.

New Transaction Sources may be defined and existing transaction sources may be changed. Transaction Sources are used in the system to identify where specific transactions originated. The Edit Functions provides four function keys. Use the [New Item] button to enter a new transaction source. The [Edit Item] button is used to edit the currently displayed transaction source. When editing the database, the new information is saved to the database by pressing the [Save Item] button. Pressing the [Cancel] button will cancel the edit and the database will remain unchanged.

When changing Transaction Source information, the user performing the change is provided sole access to the Transaction Source Database on the Server. This prevents any other user from performing a Transaction Source change at that time – such a user would be notified that the Transaction Source Database is currently locked by the user currently performing the Transaction Source change. Updated Transaction Source Databases are downloaded to Clients thereby making the databases available to the Clients if the Server or the Network were to subsequently fail. This implies that under such failure conditions, the users may still access their local copy of this database during POS operation.

Transaction Sources are entered into the system as follows:

1. Press the Edit Functions [New Item] button to create a new transaction source.

2. Enter the new Transaction Source, "POS" in this example.

3. The Status is set to Active to indicate that this transaction source may be used in the system. If set to Inactive, the transaction source is disabled.

4. The Transaction Source Type is set to one of the previously defined source types – for example, "Point-Of-Sale".

5. Enter a description for this specific transaction source.

6. Press the Edit Functions [Save Item] button to save the new transaction source.

The transaction source "POS" has now been defined and may now be used in the system.

Note: Transaction Sources may be created but not deleted. Deleting a transaction source is not permitted since any historical data which referenced that transaction source would then be invalid.

Note: When the Client is operating in Local mode (ie. the Server/Network has failed) the user is not permitted to change the Transaction Source Database.

3.5.10.1 Imported Databases

If a database import is performed which brings in pre-existing data from a prior accounting system, the user must ensure that the transaction sources specified in the imported database are also defined in the POS Business Application's Transaction Sources Database.

Transaction Sources are used in the following imported database:

- Inventory History Database

For example, if an imported database used a transaction source called "POS", then the Transaction Sources Code Editor screen in the previous section must be used to define this code along with its other associated parameters.

POS Business Application   Systems

3.5.11 System Wide Options

When the System Wide Options menu is selected, the user is presented with the System Wide Options screen.

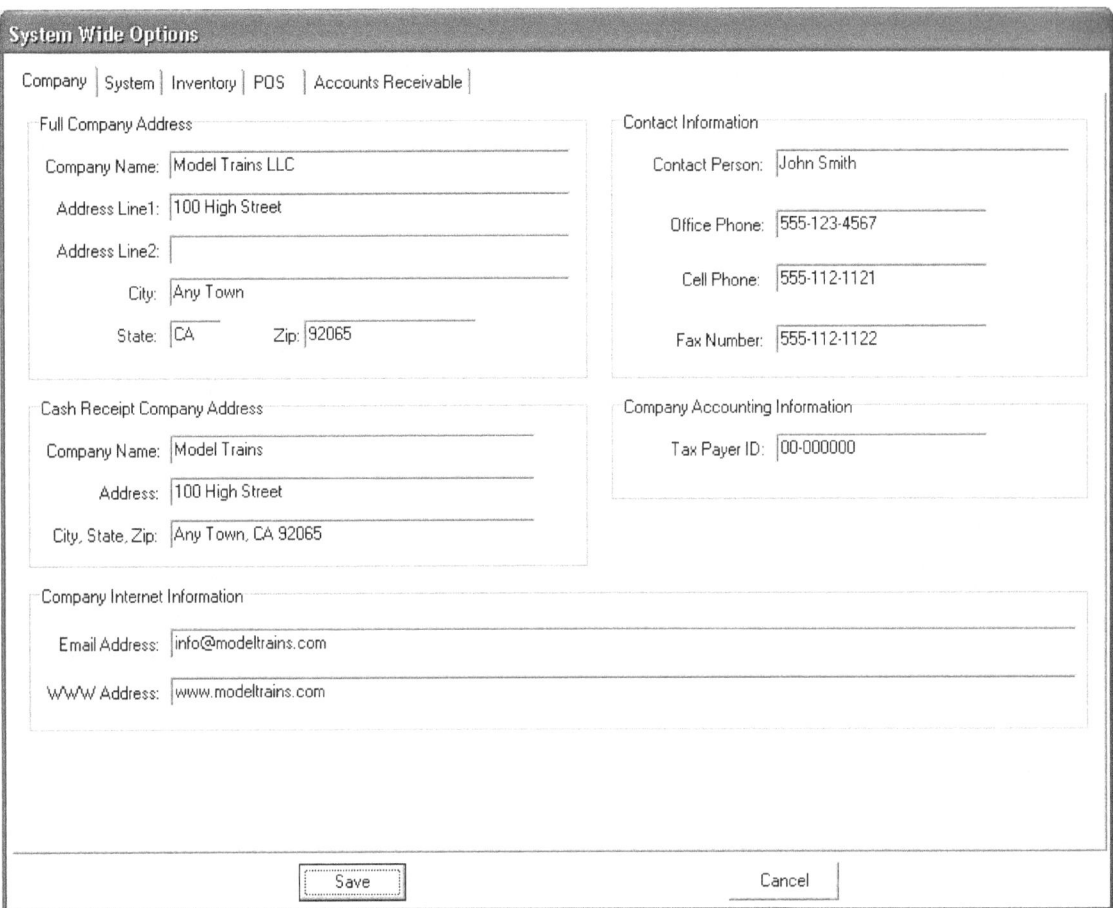

When changing System Wide Options, the user performing the change is provided sole access to the System Wide Options Database on the Server. This prevents any other user from performing a System Wide Option change at that time – such a user would be notified that the System Wide Options Database is currently locked by the user currently performing the System Wide Option change.

Updated System Wide Options Databases are downloaded to Clients thereby making the databases available to the Clients if the Server or the Network were to subsequently fail. This implies that under such failure conditions, the users may still access their local copy of this database during POS operation.

However, if the Client is already operating in Local mode and a System Wide Option change is made then the new System Wide Option would only be available on that specific Client computer system. When the Server/Network operation has been restored, the System Wide Option change must be repeated in order for the Server System Wide

Options database to be updated and subsequently broadcast to all Clients. Only then would the new System Wide Option information be available to all computer systems.

Note: When the Client is operating in Local mode (ie. the Server/Network has failed) the user is permitted to change the local copy of the System Wide Options Database in order to permit continued operation of the system. When Server/Network operation has been restored, the user must immediately re-apply the System Wide Option changes in order for the entire system to be brought up to date.

The System Wide Options screen allows the user to change the following:

1. Company Options
2. System Options
3. Inventory Options
4. POS Options
5. Accounts Receivable Options

3.5.11.1 Company Options

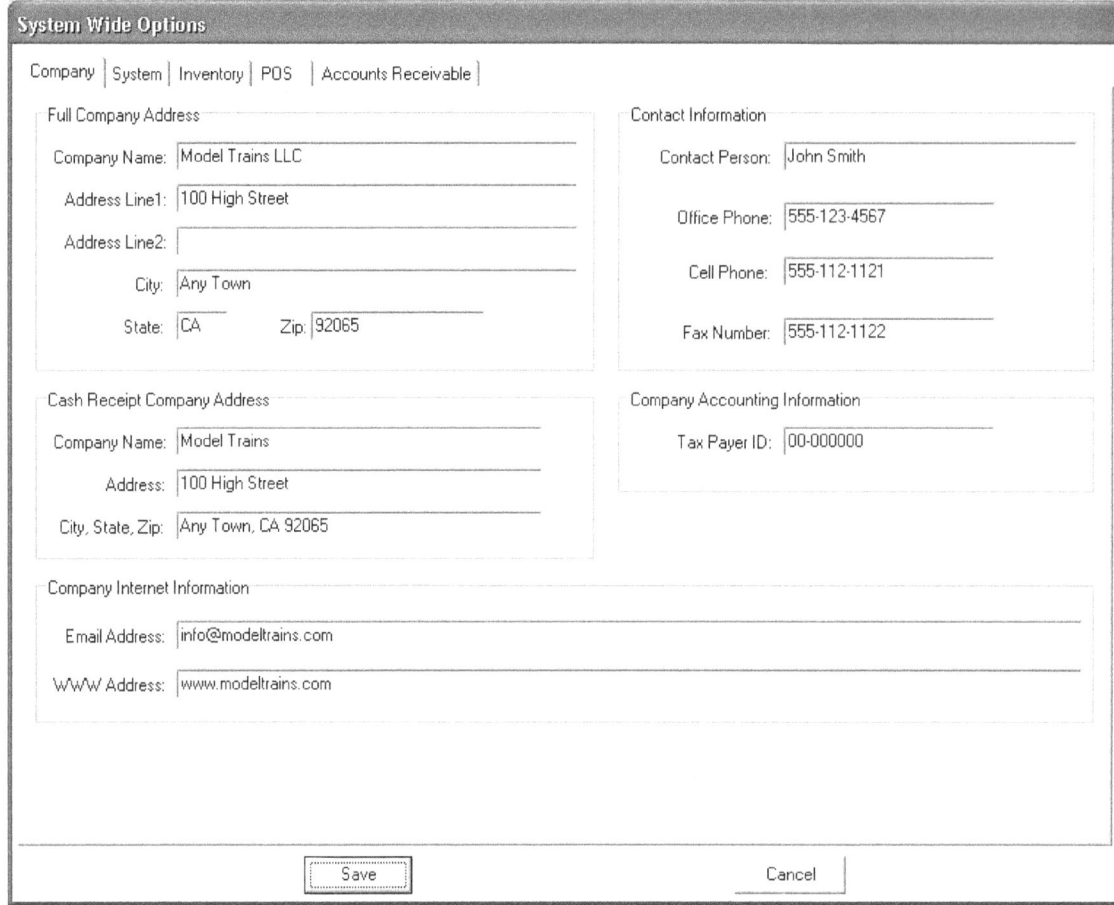

The Company Options screen allows the entry of the following information:

1. Full Company Address
2. Cash Receipt Company Address
3. Contact Information
4. Accounting Information
5. Internet Information

3.5.11.1.1 Full Company Address

The Full Company Address group allows the entry of the following information:

- Company Name
- Company Address Lines 1 and 2
- City, State and Zip Code

The Company Name and address is used in various reports as well as on the account and quote statements.

3.5.11.1.2 Cash Receipt Company Address

The Cash Receipt Company Address group allows the entry of the following information:

- Company Name
- Company Address
- City, State and Zip Code

The Cash Receipt company address is the address which is to be printed on the cash till slips.

3.5.11.1.3 Contact Information

The Contact Information group allows the entry of the following information:

- Contact Person
- Office Phone
- Cell Phone
- Fax Number

Contact information may be printed on the cash till slip and the account and quote statements.

3.5.11.1.4 Accounting Information

The Company Accounting Information group allows the entry of the following information:

- Tax Payer ID

3.5.11.1.5 Internet Information

The Company Internet Information group allows the entry of the following information:

- Email Address
- WWW Address

The Email and WWW addresses may be printed on the cash till slip and the account and quote statements.

POS Business Application   Systems

3.5.11.2 System Options

The System Options screen allows the user to change the following:

1. Server Logon User Profile
2. Internet License Key Server Address

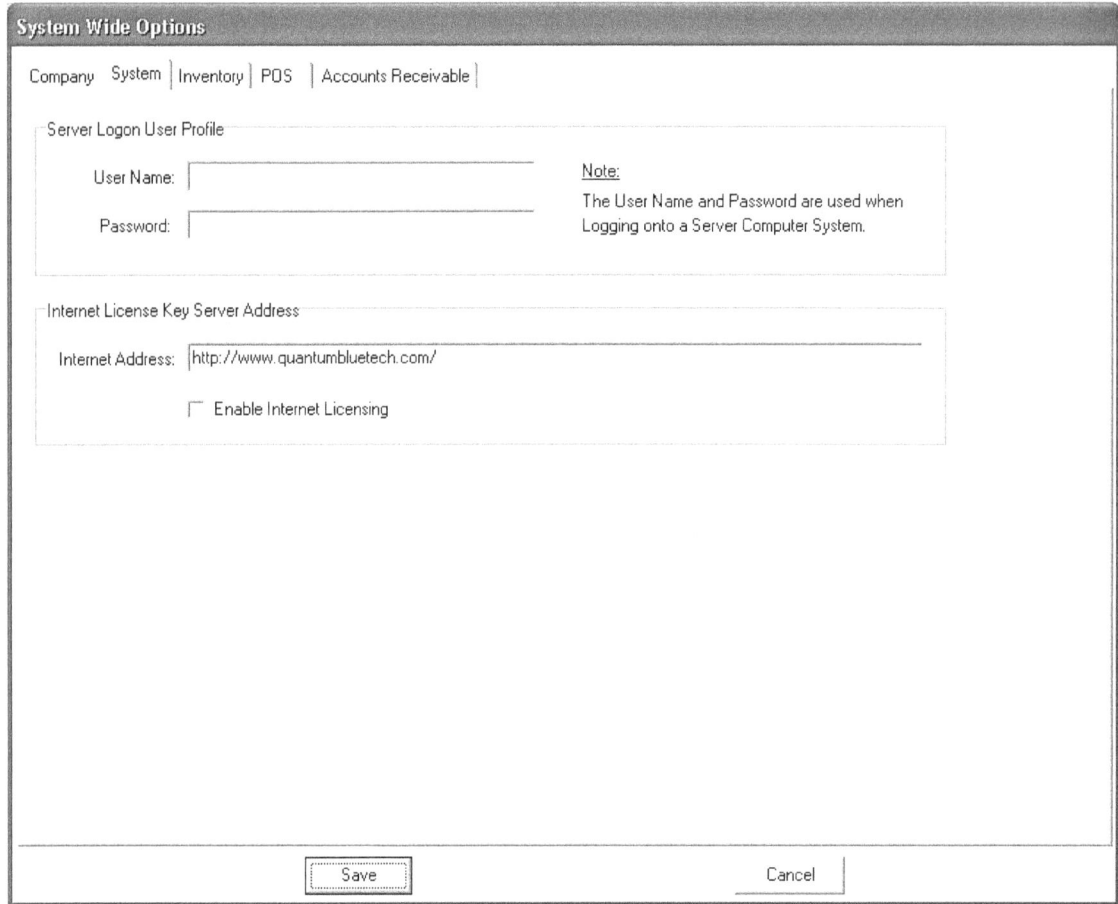

3.5.11.2.1 Server Logon User Profile

The Server Logon User Profile identifies the User Name and associated Password which is required when the system performs the drive mapping operation. This is only required when mapping onto drives protected by a Windows Server Operating System.

3.5.11.2.2 Internet License Key Server Address

This is for future use.

The Internet Address field should be blank.

The "Enable Internet Licensing" checkbox should be disabled (ie. not checked).

POS Business Application   Systems

3.5.11.3 Inventory Options

The General Inventory Options screen allows the specification of:

- The minimum markup percentage – A warning message is displayed during Inventory Edit if the markup percentage entered is less than the minimum markup percentage specified here.

- Stock Location – The usage of the stock location field for the Inventory Module may be turned on or off.

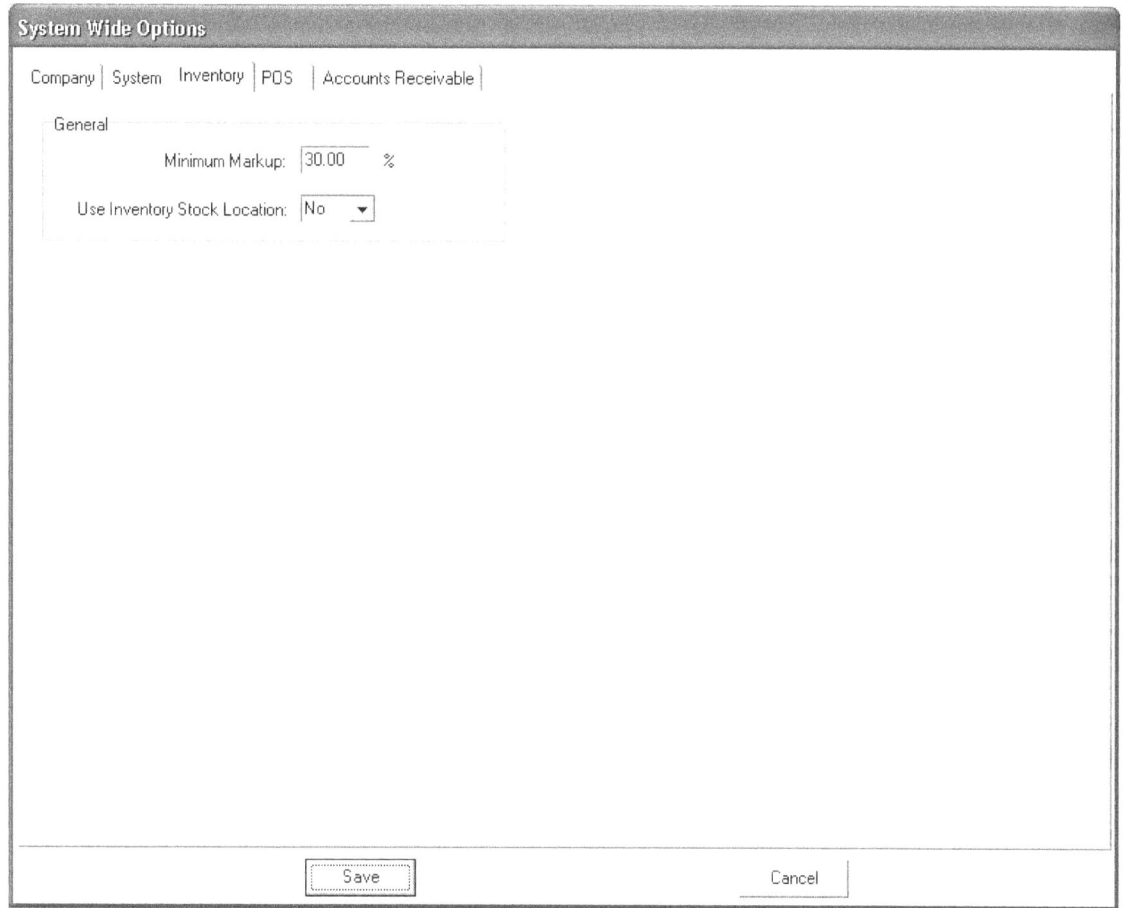

3.5.11.4 POS Options

When this option is selected the user may select between the following:

1. General Options
2. Cash Receipt Options
3. Account Receipt Options
4. Quote Receipt Options

POS Business Application   Systems

3.5.11.4.1 General Options

When this option has been selected, the General POS Options screen will be displayed.

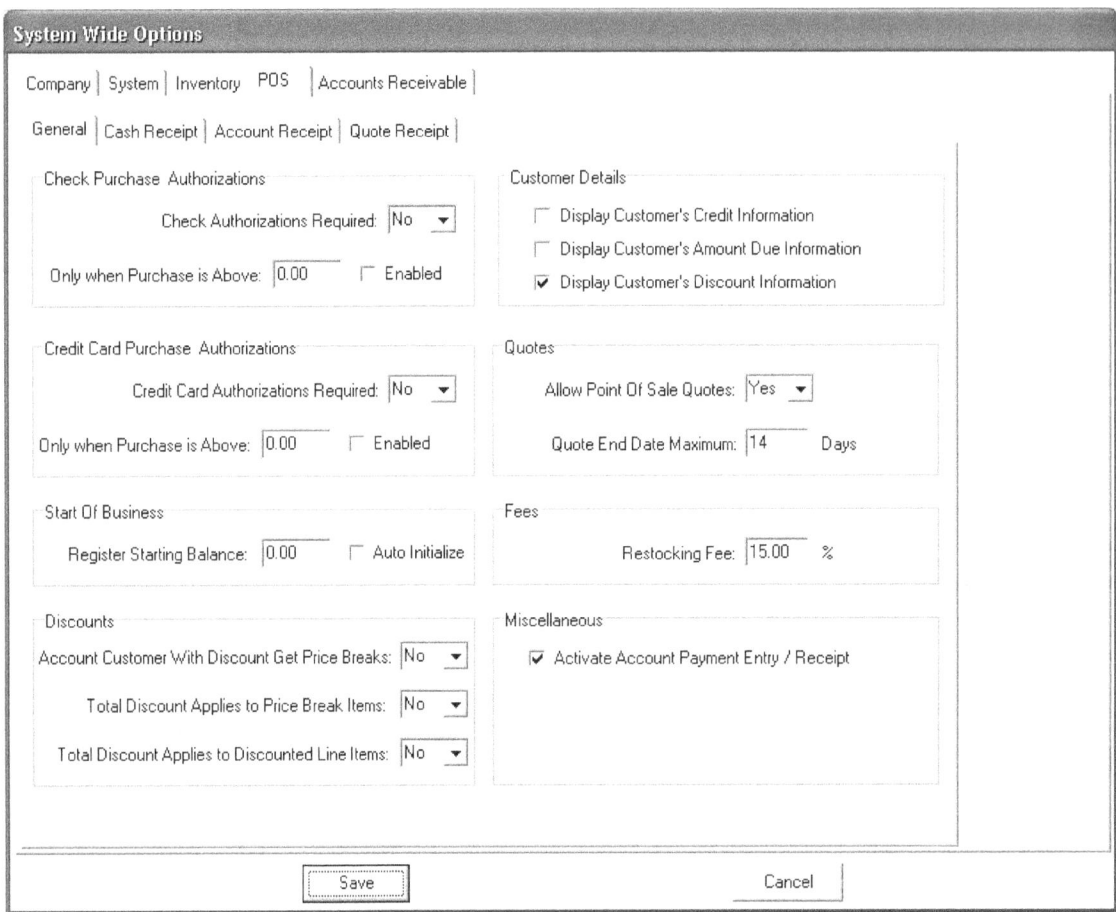

This screen allows the user to specify:

1. Check Purchase Authorizations
2. Credit Card Purchase Authorizations
3. Start of Business Register Balance
4. Purchase Discounts
5. Customer Details
6. Quotes
7. Fees
8. Miscellaneous

3.5.11.4.1.1 Check Purchase Authorizations

The Check Authorizations Required feature may be turned on or off. If the feature is turned on then check authorizations are required for all purchases paid by check. If the feature is turned on, a separate option may be enabled to check for authorization only if the purchase is above a specific amount.

# POS Business Application	Systems

3.5.11.4.1.2 Credit Card Purchase Authorizations

The Credit Card Authorizations Required feature may be turned on or off. If the feature is turned on then credit card authorizations are required for all purchases paid by credit card. If the feature is turned on, a separate option may be enabled to check for authorization only if the purchase is above a specific amount.

3.5.11.4.1.3 Start of Business Register Balance

This field is used to identify the cash register till starting balance.

If the cash register till is always started with, for example, $200 dollars of cash in the drawer, then the transaction register history starting register balance for the current business period can be automatically initialized by setting the Register Starting Balance field to 200.00 and checking the Auto Initialize checkbox.

If the user wishes to override this automatic starting amount, this can be performed in the POS Terminal screen.

If the Auto Initialize feature is turned off then the register starting amount can be specified in the POS Terminal screen.

3.5.11.4.1.4 Purchase Discounts

The following discount options may be selected:

1. Account Customers with Discounts get Price Breaks
2. Total Discount applies to Price Break Items
3. Total Discount applies to Discounted Line Items

Account Customers with Discounts get Price Breaks
This option is used to specify if account customers, who are given discounts on their purchases, are also permitted to get price breaks on quantity items. This option may be turned on or off.

Total Discount applies to Price Break Items
This option is used to specify if the total discount applied to a sale is also to apply to price break items contained in the sale. This option may be turned on or off.

Total Discount applies to Discounted Line Items
This option is used to specify if the total discount applied to a sale is also to apply to discounted line items. This option may be turned on or off.

3.5.11.4.1.5 Customer Details

When a POS Account transaction is in progress, this option is used to display or hide the account credit, account amount due and account discount information.

3.5.11.4.1.6 Quotes

This option is used to specify if the POS Terminal is permitted to create quotes. If quotes are permitted, the maximum number of days before the quote expires may also be specified.

3.5.11.4.1.7 Fees

This option identifies the restocking fee (if applicable). If a fee percentage is specified then any returns will be credited by the amount minus the restocking fee.

3.5.11.4.1.8 Miscellaneous

This option permits the usage of the Account Payment Entry/Receipt feature. This feature allows a payment receipt to be created and printed for account customers who come into the store to make a payment.

3.5.11.4.2 Cash Receipt Options

When this option has been selected, the Cash Receipt Options screen will be displayed.

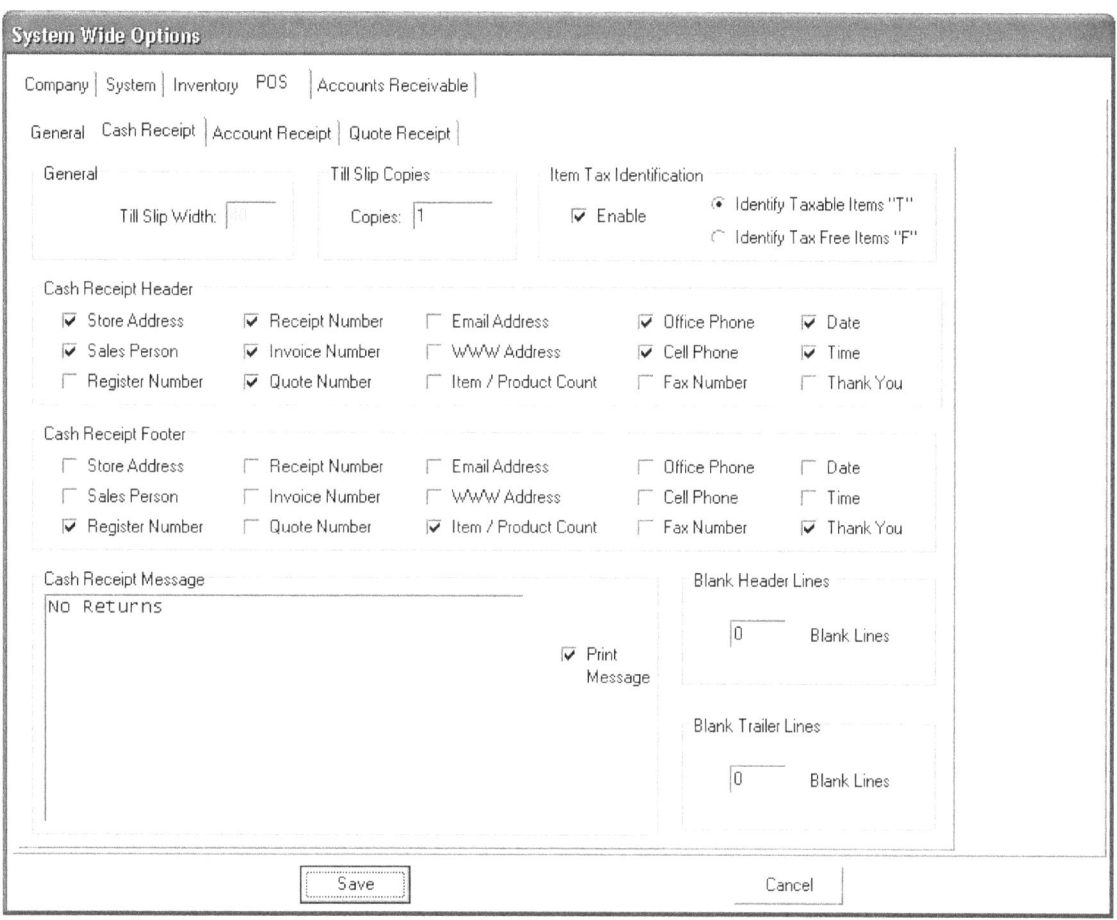

The cash till slip width is set by default to be 40 characters wide. The number of till slip copies that are required to be printed at the completion of each cash sale may be specified. The number of blank header or trailer lines that are to be printed may also be specified.

The Cash Receipt screen also allows the user to identify various information (and their location) to be printed on the cash till slip.

This information includes:

1. Item Tax Identification (ie. a 'T' printed adjacent to taxable line items)

2. Cash receipt header and footer information
    a. Store Address
    b. Sales Person
    c. Register Number
    d. Receipt Number

e. Invoice Number
f. Quote Number
g. Email Address
h. WWW Address
i. Item / Product Count
j. Office Phone
k. Cell Phone
l. Fax Number
m. Date
n. Time
o. Thank You

3. Cash Receipt Message

3.5.11.4.3 Account Receipt Options

When this option has been selected, the Account Receipt Options screen will be displayed.

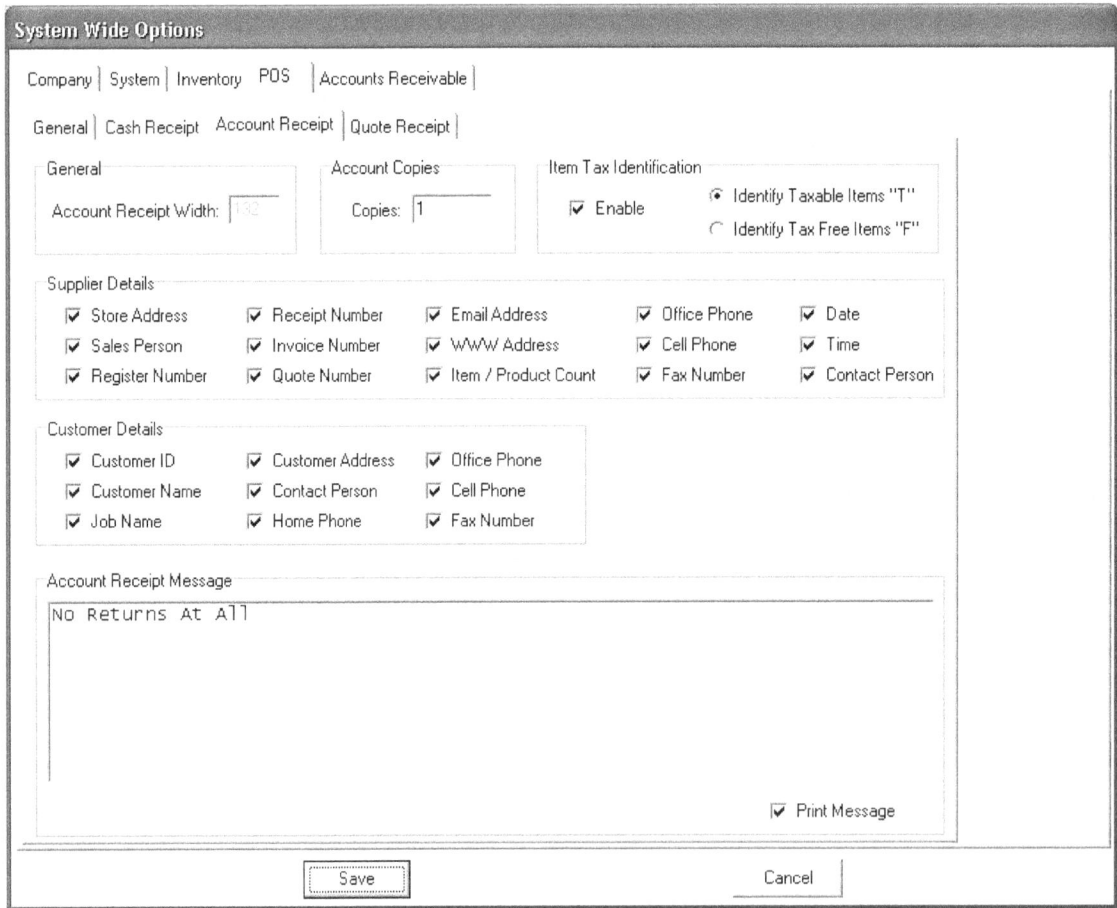

The number of account receipt copies that are required to be printed at the completion of each account sale may be specified.

POS Business Application   Systems

This screen allows the user to identify various information (and their location) to be printed on the account receipt.

This information includes:

1. Item Tax Identification (ie. a 'T' printed adjacent to taxable line items)

2. Supplier Details
    a. Store Address
    b. Sales Person
    c. Register Number
    d. Receipt Number
    e. Invoice Number
    f. Quote Number
    g. Email Address
    h. WWW Address
    i. Item / Product Count
    j. Office Phone
    k. Cell Phone
    l. Fax Number
    m. Date
    n. Time
    o. Contact Person

3. Customer Details
    a. Customer ID
    b. Customer Name
    c. Job Name
    d. Customer Address
    e. Contact Person
    f. Home Phone
    g. Office Phone
    h. Cell Phone
    i. Fax Number

4. Account Receipt Message

3.5.11.4.4 Quote Receipt Options

When this option has been selected, the Quote Receipt Options screen will be displayed.

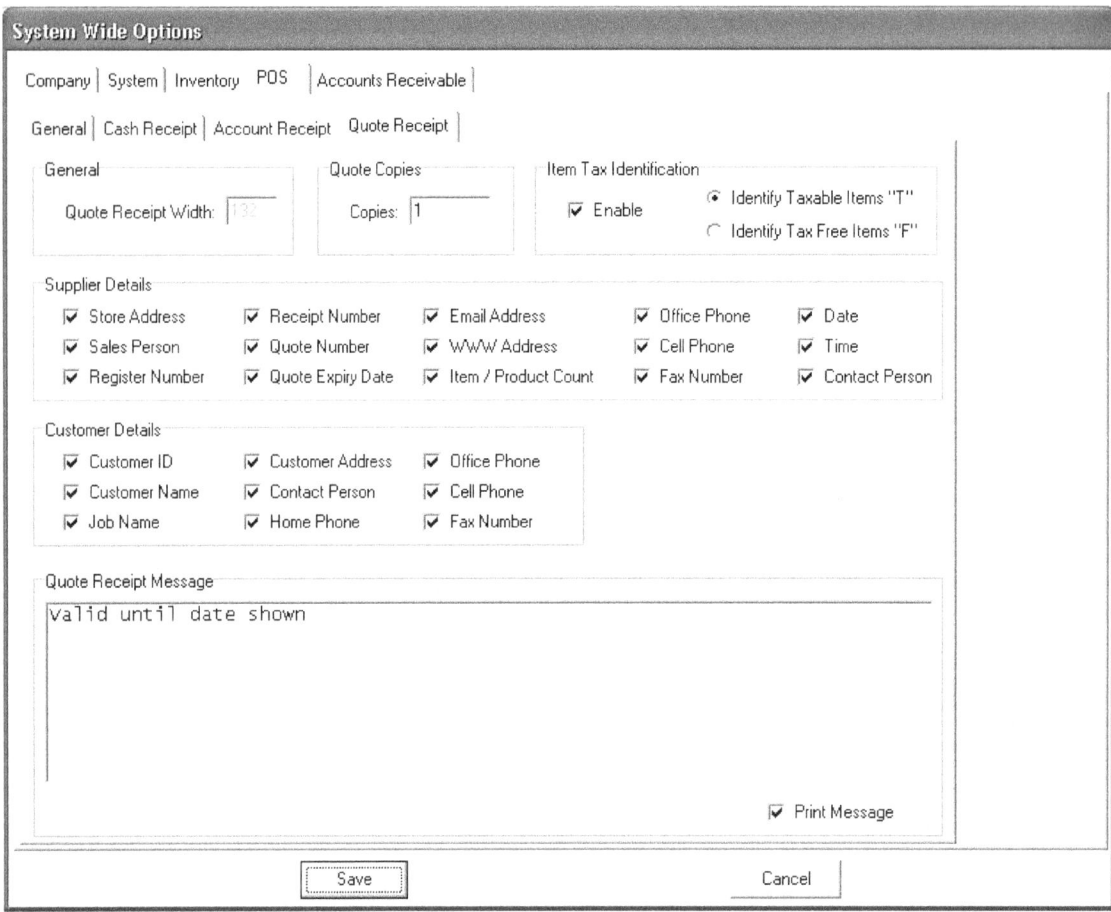

The number of quote copies that are required to be printed at the completion of each quote may be specified.

This screen allows the user to identify various information (and their location) to be printed on the quote receipt.

This information includes:

1. Item Tax Identification (ie. a 'T' printed adjacent to taxable line items)

2. Supplier Details
    a. Store Address
    b. Sales Person
    c. Register Number
    d. Receipt Number
    e. Quote Number
    f. Quote Expiry Date
    g. Email Address
    h. WWW Address
    i. Item / Product Count
    j. Office Phone
    k. Cell Phone
    l. Fax Number
    m. Date
    n. Time
    o. Contact Person

3. Customer Details
    a. Customer ID
    b. Customer Name
    c. Job Name
    d. Customer Address
    e. Contact Person
    f. Home Phone
    g. Office Phone
    h. Cell Phone
    i. Fax Number

4. Quote Receipt Message

3.5.12 Printer Selection

When this option has been selected, the Printer Selection screen will be displayed.

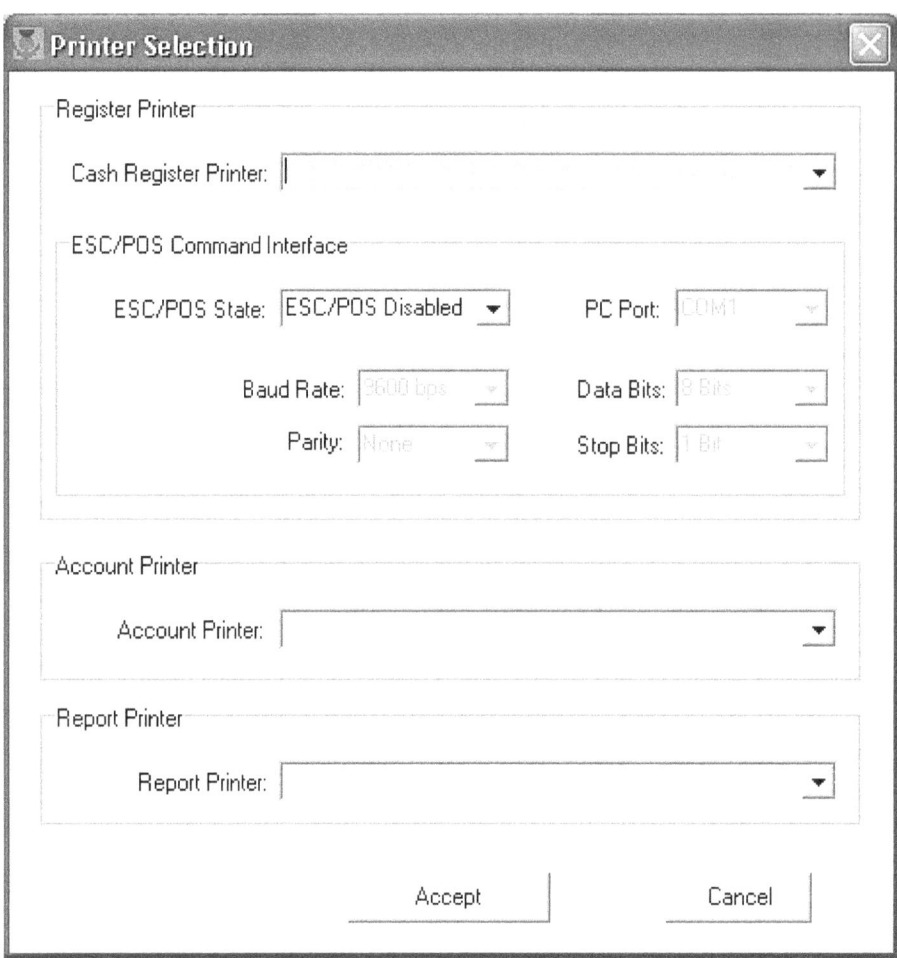

This screen allows the user to identify which computer system printer may be used for specific purposes. Each printer is identified by selecting a specific printer from the drop-down list.

The following printers may be defined:

1. Register Printer
2. Account Printer (also used for Quotes)
3. Report Printer

POS Business Application   **Systems**

3.5.12.1 Register Printer

The till slip printer may use either a Windows Operating System interface driver or the ESC/POS Command Interface. If a Windows Operating System interface driver is used then select the previously installed printer driver by selecting the relevant printer from the Cash Register Printer drop-down list.

If, however, a printer which uses the ESC/POS interface has been installed then select the required operating parameters as follows:

1. Set the ESC/POS State to "ESC/POS Enabled".

2. If a parallel port till slip printer has been installed:
   a. Set PC Port to LPT1 if printer attached to parallel port1.
   b. Set PC Port to LPT2 if printer attached to parallel port2.
   c. Set PC Port to LPT3 if printer attached to parallel port3.

3. else if a serial port till slip printer has been installed:
   a. Set PC Port to COM1 if printer attached to serial port1.
   b. Set PC Port to COM2 if printer attached to serial port2.
   c. Set PC Port to COM3 if printer attached to serial port3.
   d. Set PC Port to COM4 if printer attached to serial port4

   Finally, Set the Baud Rate to the required bit rate speed
   Set the Parity Bit
   Set the number of Data Bits
   Set the number of Stop Bits

3.5.12.2 Account Printer

The account printer uses a Windows Operating System interface driver. Select the previously installed printer driver by selecting the relevant printer from the Account Printer drop-down list.

The Account Printer is also used for printing Quotes.

3.5.12.3 Report Printer

The report printer uses a Windows Operating System interface driver. Select the previously installed printer driver by selecting the relevant printer from the Report Printer drop-down list.

When a report is printed it will be printed on the selected printer.

POS Business Application Systems

3.5.13 Cash Register Drawer

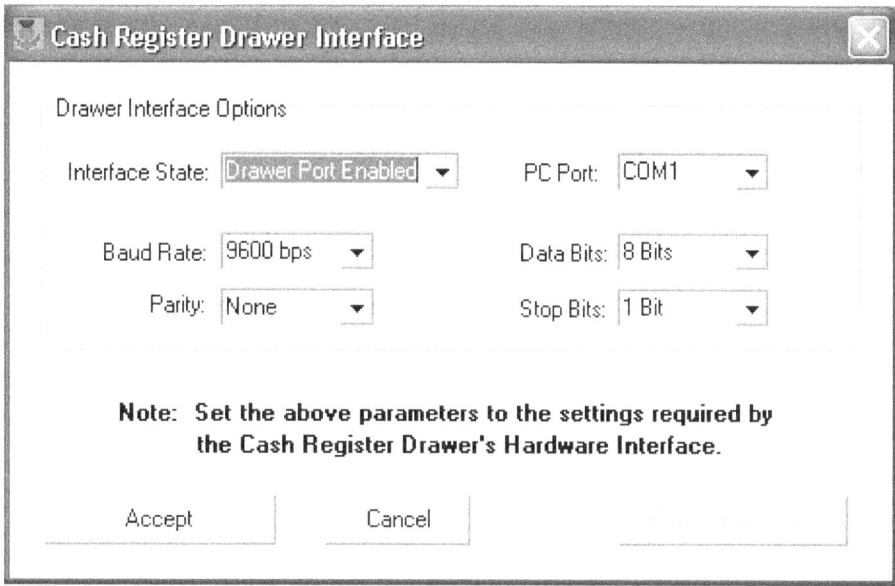

A cash register drawer may be controlled via one of the serial or parallel ports. To activate the cash register drawer interface perform the following:

1. Set the Interface State to "Drawer Port Enabled".
2. Set the PC Port to the serial or parallel port attached to the drawer.

   If a serial port is used, set the serial parameters shown below:

   - Set the Baud Rate to the required bit rate speed
   - Set the Parity Bit
   - Set the number of Data Bits
   - Set the number of Stop Bits

   Press the [Accept] button to activate the selected parameters.

Once the drawer interface has been enabled and the required options accepted, the user may press the [Open Drawer Test] button to verify that the cash register drawer opens correctly.

POS Business Application   Systems

3.6 Software Update

When an updated version of the POS Business Application software is installed on the Server, the Software Update feature is used to copy the updated software program to the client systems.

When the Software Update menu option is selected (on a Client system), the client will then check to see if the Server version has been updated. If this is the case, the user will be asked if the software update is to proceed. Once authorized, the software will be downloaded from the Server to the Client and executed.

If the Software Update menu option is selected on a Server system then a warning message will be displayed.

Note: Each time the Client POS Business Application software is started, it performs an automatic check to determine if the Server contains an updated version of the application. If this is the case, and the user gives authorization to proceed, the new software will be downloaded from the Server to the Client and executed.

3.7 Exit Menu

The exit menu permits the user to terminate the POS Business Application.

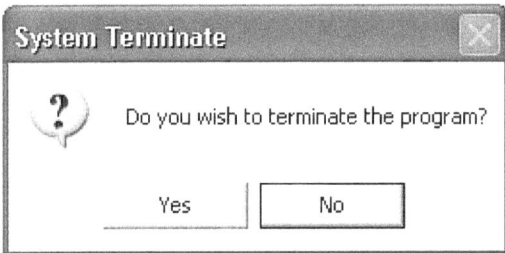

An exit dialog box is displayed with the options of performing the exit or of canceling the exit.

POS Business Application Systems

4 Help

The Help Menu provides the following sub-menus:

1. Calculator
2. Calendar
3. About

4.1 Calculator

When the Calculator menu option is pressed, a calculator screen is displayed. The sales person may use this calculator independently of the POS Business Application. The calculator screen may be closed when finished.

4.2 Calendar

When the Calendar menu option is pressed, a calendar screen is displayed. The calendar screen must be closed in order to continue working with the POS Business Application.

4.3 About

When the About menu option is pressed, an information screen is displayed which provides the following:

1. The software package name "POS Business Application"
2. The version of the POS Business Application software installed
3. The company licensed to use the POS Business Application software package
4. Program maintenance contact information
5. The time and date of when the POS Business Application software was built

POS Business Application — Systems

5 Appendix

5.1 Database Backup Procedure

Backing up the POS Business Application Database is a simple process which should be performed on a daily basis. The Backup process is performed on the server and the generated backup file is placed in the project BACKUP directory.

For example, the backup directory for the Trains Demo Database (using POS Business Application Software Version 2.1) would normally be located as shown below:

> C: \ POS \ TRAINS Ver2_1 \ BACKUP

It is recommended that a DVD R/W or other removable storage medium should be used to store the backup files separate from the Server hard drive. Separate DVD disks should be used for each day of the week.

5.2 Comparison of Windows Operating Systems

The POS Business Application may be run on any one of, or even a mixture of, the following Windows Operating Systems:

1. Windows Vista
2. Windows XP
3. Windows 2000 (or later versions)
4. Windows 2000 Server (or later versions)

Each system provides different features which are discussed in the subsequent sections.

5.2.1 Windows Vista

At this current time, Windows Vista has been recently released and system stability issues are still being determined. The POS Business Application has been successfully tested under a Windows Vista environment.

The only issue to note is that when the POS Business Application is executed under Windows Vista, it must be executed in XP mode. This is to permit the POS Business Application the required authority to execute various operating system functions. Please refer to the POS Business Application Installation Manual for further details.

5.2.2 Windows XP

Windows XP is by far more stable than any of the previous general user Windows Operating Systems (Windows ME, Windows 98, Windows 95 or earlier versions) and is therefore the operating system of choice.

Windows XP comes in two different versions:

1. Windows XP Home Edition
2. Windows XP Professional Edition

5.2.2.1 Windows XP Home Edition

The Windows XP Home Edition is identical to the Professional Edition except principally in the area of file security. If the POS Business Application is being run in an environment where the Business LAN network is strictly local to the business and not attached to any other network or to the Internet then the Home Edition may be quite suitable. In this regard, the POS Business Application performs basic data encryption of its various databases thereby providing a measure of security.

Both the Server and/or Client stations may use the Windows XP Home Edition operating system.

However, if the Business LAN is attached to other networks or to the Internet, or if a more strict data encryption is required then the Windows XP Professional Edition should be utilized.

5.2.2.2 Windows XP Professional Edition

The Windows XP Professional Edition permits a higher level of file security and also permits files to be further protected by data encryption.

Both the Server and/or Client stations may use the Windows XP Professional Edition operating system.

If a high level of file security (ie. Password access) is to be utilized by means of Windows 2000 Server (or later versions) then the Windows XP Professional Edition (or Windows 2000 or later) must be used since the Windows XP Home Edition does not provide Windows 2000 Server access.

5.2.3 Windows 2000 (or later versions)

Windows 2000 (or later) and Windows XP Professional have many similar features and either may be used to run the POS Business Application.

5.2.4 Windows 2000 Server (or later versions)

Windows 2000 Server (or later versions) provides the highest level of security by permitting various directories to be accessible only to specific users. This access is password protected and thereby inhibits access to any casual user. A Windows 2000 (or later) or Windows XP Professional system must be used to gain access to a protected Windows Server file system directory.

Windows Server operating systems also limit the number of client computer stations which may access its protected file system.

5.3 Windows File System

When the Windows Operating System is installed on the computer system the NTFS file system should be selected. This file system provides the highest level of file security.

If the Windows Operating System was previously installed with the standard FAT32 file system then it is possible to convert to the NTFS file system by using a Windows file conversion utility.

This procedure is described in the Windows Operating System manual.

5.4 Auxiliary Equipment

The POS Business Application has been verified to operate with the following auxiliary equipment:

1. Bar Code Scanner
2. Printers

5.4.1 Bar Code Scanner

The following Bar Code Scanners have been verified:

PSSR-1000-01
Handheld Bar Code Scanner
PSC Powerscan Keyboard Scanner + keyboard cable

PSC-8042403 8" + 3" KBW AT/PS2 CABLE
8-0424-03

PSC-PWRSCN10KBW   Powerscan, Standard Keyboard

Manufacturer: PSC Inc.   Tel: (541) 683-5700
                959 Terry Street   Fax: (541)345-7140
                Eugene   WWW: www.psc.com
                OR 97402-9150

Most keyboard scanners should operate correctly with this software. If any keyboard scanner operating errors occur please inform Quantum Blue Technology and we will attempt to resolve the problem.

5.4.2 Printers

The following printers have been verified:

HP LaserJet 4050
HP OfficeJet 7130
Dell 924
Star 300

Most printers should operate correctly with this software. If any printer operating errors occur please inform Quantum Blue Technology and we will attempt to resolve the problem.

5.5 Error Messages

This section identifies specific fault conditions and the manner in which they may be resolved.

5.5.1 Printer Not Available

If a new printer driver has been installed and the POS Business Application lists the printer as being available. When the printer is selected and an attempt is made to print to the new printer, an error message is displayed indicating that the printer is not available.

Solution

When a new printer driver is installed, the operating system does not fully recognize the printer until the computer system is restarted. Restart the computer system and the printer should now be available under all conditions and operate correctly.

5.5.2 Server Not Available

This operating system dependent situation can occur when the client computer is powered up prior to the server computer. Although the POS Business Application software attempts to map to the networked server directory, the operating system indicates that the client has incorrect authority to perform the mapping. This can occur even when using valid authority (network user name and password – if so required).

Solution

Restart the client computer system and the server directory should be correctly mapped and accessible

Point-Of-Sale Business Application

System Architecture

Project: Point-Of-Sale Business Application
Date: January 28th 2008
Revision: 1.0.1
Company: Quantum Blue Technology LLC.

Copyright Notice

Copyright ©2005, 2006, 2007, 2008 Quantum Blue Technology LLC. – All rights reserved worldwide. This document is proprietary to **Quantum Blue Technology LLC.** And may contain information that is to be maintained as Trade Secret. It is intended for use only by **Quantum Blue Technology LLC.** Employees and its' contractors, customer employees, and authorized personnel. It may not be copied, translated, or transcribed in whole or in part without the express permission of the copyright holder **Quantum Blue Technology LLC.**

Quantum Blue Technology LLC
1424 Welsh Way, Ramona
California 92065
U.S.A.

Phone: USA (858) 837-2160
Email: info@QuantumBlueTechnology.com
Web: www.QuantumBlueTechnology.com

Please Note:

Due to ongoing design and development, **Quantum Blue Technology LLC.** May, at any time, and without notification, amend and update either this document and/or the associated "POS Business Application" software package.

Change History

Date	Version	Author	Reason for Change
1/11/08	1.0.0	Steve McClure	Initial Draft.
1/28/08	1.0.1	Steve McClure	Added Process Description.

Table of Contents

1 **SCOPE** 1
   1.1 GENERAL 1
   1.2 ABBREVIATIONS 1

2 **SYSTEM DEVELOPMENT TOOLSETS** 2
   2.1 PROGRAM DEVELOPMENT ENVIRONMENT 2
      2.1.1 Hardware System 2
         2.1.1.1 Development Work Station 2
         2.1.1.2 Test Work Station 2
      2.1.2 Software System 3
         2.1.2.1 Compiler 3
         2.1.2.2 CodeWright Editor 3
         2.1.2.3 Qsetup Composer 3
   2.2 PROGRAM DEVELOPMENT PROCESS 4
   2.3 PROGRAM EXECUTION ENVIRONMENT 4
      2.3.1 Operating Systems 4
      2.3.2 Hardware Requirements 4

3 **SYSTEM ARCHITECTURE** 5
   3.1 LIMITATIONS WITH CURRENT POS PACKAGES 5
      3.1.1 Server / Network Hardware Failures 5
      3.1.2 Transaction Posting data can be lost 5
      3.1.3 Slow Report Generation and Database Size Limitations 6
      3.1.4 Database Backup and Restore Operations 6
      3.1.5 POS Systems are designed for accountants instead for business owners ... 6
   3.2 SERVER / CLIENT OPERATION 7
   3.3 DISTRIBUTED DATABASES 7
      3.3.1 System Database Header 7
      3.3.2 Server System Databases 8
      3.3.3 Client System Databases 8
      3.3.4 Quote Databases 8
         3.3.4.1 Client Quote Database 8
         3.3.4.2 Server Quote Database 8
   3.4 PROCESSES (TASKS) 9
      3.4.1 Timer Process 9
      3.4.2 Network Process 9
         3.4.2.1 Server Network Operations 10
            3.4.2.1.1 Auto Initiate specific database downloads 10
            3.4.2.1.2 Monitor Specific Database 10
            3.4.2.1.3 Build POS Quote Database Summary 10
         3.4.2.2 Client Network Operations 10
            3.4.2.2.1 Server Drive Remap Attempt 11
            3.4.2.2.2 Auto Initiate specific database downloads 11

	3.4.2.2.3	Monitor Specific Server Database 11
	3.4.2.2.4	Verify License Registration 11
	3.4.2.2.5	Obtain Updated POS Quote Database 11

3.5 DRIVERS 12
   3.5.1 Cash Register Till Printer Driver 12
   3.5.2 Cash Drawer Driver 12

POS Business Application — System Architecture

1 Scope

This document is the System Architecture Manual for the Point-Of-Sale Business Application. This manual describes the internal operation of the application.

1.1 General

The Point-Of-Sale (POS) Business Application is designed for the small business and provides networking capabilities not normally available to general Point-Of-Sale systems.

The principal features which set this POS Business Application Software apart from other POS accounting software systems are the following:

- Ease of Use
- Distributed Encrypted Databases
- Quicker Data Access via Calendar Indexed Databases
- Re-Posting of POS Sales transactions if database recovery is required
- Safe Non-Destructive Database Backup and Restore Operations

Please refer to the Overview document for a more detailed description of these features.

1.2 Abbreviations

CSV	Comma Separated Variable
IDE	Integrated Development Environment
PC	Personal Computer
POS	Point-Of-Sale
POSBA	Point-Of-Sale Business Application
UPS	Uninterruptible Power Supply

2 System Development Toolsets

2.1 Program Development Environment

This section describes the hardware and software which was utilized to develop the Point-Of-Sale Business Application software.

2.1.1 Hardware System

2.1.1.1 Development Work Station

The work station computer hardware used was an IBM compatible Personal Computer system utilizing the following configuration:

- Intel Motherboard
- 2.0 GHz Pentium 4 CPU
- 1 GByte RAM Memory
- 160 GByte Hard Drive
- 3 DVI Graphics Adapter cards
- Serial and Parallel Interfaces
- LAN Interface
- Keyboard and optical wireless mouse
- 3 Sony LCD Monitor Screens (19")

2.1.1.2 Test Work Station

A second computer system was used for testing Server/Client interaction and had the following configuration:

- Intel Motherboard
- 2.0 GHz Pentium 4 CPU
- 1 GByte RAM Memory
- 160 GByte Hard Drive
- 1 Graphics Adapter card
- Serial and Parallel Interfaces
- LAN Interface
- KVM to interface to development work station keyboard and mouse

2.1.2 Software System

2.1.2.1 Compiler

The POS Business Application (also called "POSBA") was designed using the Borland C++ Builder IDE development package. This package provides a source code editor and C++ compiler/linker as well as a built-in debugger for testing.

The IDE details are as follows:

    Borland C++ Builder Ver 6.0

2.1.2.2 CodeWright Editor

The CodeWright editor was also used to develop this package. When this editor is installed it attaches itself to the Borland C++ Builder IDE such that it is possible to swap between the editors with ease.

The editor details are as follows:

    CodeWright Editor Ver 7.5

2.1.2.3 Qsetup Composer

The Qsetup Composer package was used to build a single executable file which could be located on a web page (or a CD-ROM). When accessed on the web page, the executable file would be automatically downloaded and installed on the customer's computer system.

The Qsetup details are as follows:

    Qsetup Installation Suite Ver: 7.5.0.8
    Pantaray Research LTD.
    www.pantaray.com

POS Business Application   System Architecture

2.2 Program Development Process

Using a three monitor computer development workstation greatly aided the development process. The three LCD monitor screen were generally set up as follows:

- The CodeWright editor on the left screen
- Borland C++ IDE on the middle screen
- POSBA product display on the right screen / second computer system

The LCD monitors each contained three input channels – DVI plus two VGA interfaces. The right hand monitor could be switch between the main development computer and a second test computer when Server/Client testing was required.

2.3 Program Execution Environment

This section describes the hardware and associated software required to execute the Point-Of-Sale Business Application.

2.3.1 Operating Systems

The POS Business Application software is designed to execute on a standard IBM Personal Computer System (or compatible) which executes one of the following operating systems:

1. Windows Vista
2. Windows XP (Professional or Home Editions, or later versions)
3. Windows 2000 (or later versions)
4. Windows 2000 Server (or later versions)

Note: The POS Business Application may operate correctly on previous versions of Windows, however, at this time it has not been verified.

2.3.2 Hardware Requirements

The following minimum IBM PC compatible computer features are required:

- Pentium III 1GHz
- 512MB RAM
- LAN Network Interface
- Video Monitor (800 x 600 minimum)
- Mouse
- Keyboard

3 System Architecture

3.1 Limitations with current POS Packages

The POS Business Application was designed as an improvement to current POS systems by having features which are presently not available to small business operations.

When talking with small business owners it became apparent that most Point-Of-Sale systems suffered from problems in the following areas:

1. Server / Network Hardware Failures
2. Transaction Posting data can be lost
3. Slow Report Generation and Database Size Limitations
4. Database Backup and Restore Operations
5. POS Systems are designed for accountants instead for business owners

3.1.1 Server / Network Hardware Failures

The main restriction with many Point-Of-Sale accounting systems is their reliance on both the network and on the Server computer system. These accounting systems locate their central database on the server computer and the client computer systems must access this database via the network in order to perform any Point-Of-Sale operations.

A major cause for concern with users of such systems is with regard to what would happen if the network or the server were to fail. If either of these failures were to occur then the client computer systems would not be able to access the central database and would therefore not be able to perform Point-Of-Sale transactions. In this situation, the counter staff would then be required to make hand written sales receipts and refer to previously printed (and perhaps outdated) price lists. This method of operation is tedious, slow and can easily generate errors.

Later, when the Server and/or network are once more operational, the handwritten sale transactions have to be manually entered into the accounting system – another time consuming operation which is also fraught with possible errors.

3.1.2 Transaction Posting data can be lost

Most POS accounting systems use the Server to contain the central accounting databases. This database usually also includes the Point-Of-Sale transactions for each POS terminal. At the end of a business period, thee POS sales transactions are posted to the sales history database and certain inventory database parameters (eg. the "On Hand" quantity) are updated. Once this posting operation has completed, the original information is then deleted since it is no longer required.

POS Business Application — System Architecture

Normally this approach is successful, except under conditions when the database has had to be recovered due to system related problems (eg. disk drive failure).

If the database is to be recovered, the current day's posted (and un-posted) sales transactions for each POS Terminal may be deleted during the database backup restoration process. The sales data for the period between the backup date and the current date will then have to be manually re-entered in order to bring the database up to date. This is another time consuming operation which is also fraught with possible errors.

3.1.3 Slow Report Generation and Database Size Limitations

General POS accounting systems are very responsive when the system is first installed. However, as the days and months progress, more and more history data is created and the system can start to get sluggish. After several years of history data has been collected, the system can take a long time to scan an entire database in order to access and obtain specific information pertaining to a report.

In order to minimize this effect, some accounting systems impose database size limitations which restrict the amount of data history which may be retained.

3.1.4 Database Backup and Restore Operations

During Database Backup operations, some POS Accounting systems use the same backup storage file name and/or location, which may result in the previous backup file being overwritten.

During Database Restore operations the same POS Accounting system's active directory database is overwritten.

With this procedure a healthy database can easily be destroyed if an incorrect restore operation was performed.

3.1.5 POS Systems are designed for accountants instead for business owners

In many cases the Point-Of-Sale software is Accountant "friendly" but not small business person "friendly". Any associated documentation is written likewise such that POS operational instructions are quite vague and ambiguous to the general user.

POS Business Application — System Architecture

3.2 Server / Client Operation

The POS Business Application computer program was designed to be installed on either the Server computer hardware or the Client computer hardware. With this in mind, the software was designed to execute "Installation Screens" which would allow the installer to select the required Server/Client environment.

Many POS systems use TCP/IP as an interface with which to create a communications channel between the Server computer system and the various client computer systems. During Point-Of-Sale operations, the TCP/IP interface would carry product, transaction and report information between the computer systems.

Although TCP/IP is effective it is also highly confusing to the average home business user – setting up IP addresses. With this in mind it was determined to use a directory mapping procedure such that server computer system directories may be shared with the client computer systems – this also seemed applicable since entire databases were going to be transferred between the server and the client computer systems.

3.3 Distributed Databases

In order to allow a client computer system to function during server and / or network hardware failure conditions it would be necessary to provide the client computer system with a copy of the relevant server databases. These client databases would need to be updated whenever a changed was made to the primary server database.

3.3.1 System Database Header

The database header is used to indicate the lock status of the associated system database. When a system database is locked, the system user and the corresponding computer system's name is stored in the header. If another user attempts to edit the same system database, they are informed that it is locked and also provided with the user name and computer name of the person responsible for the lock. This feature was implemented to overcome the limitations of other POS applications which simply state that the database is locked and provide no indication of which user is responsible.

The database header also contains a lock timestamp which is used to automatically unlock a database if it has been locked for an excessive amount of time. If a system database is being modified then the lock timestamp will be automatically refreshed by the relevant computer system. However, if this client system was to become inactive, the locked database timestamp would no longer be refreshed and once the timestamp was several minutes old the database lock could be overridden and the file re-accessed. Other POS systems would require the Server to be reboot to overcome this problem..

POS Business Application — System Architecture

3.3.2 Server System Databases

The principal system databases are stored on the POS Business Application Server computer system. When any principal system database is edited, all modifications are performed only on the database which resides on the Server computer system.

3.3.3 Client System Databases

The POS Business Application program executing on a Client computer system constantly monitors the timestamps of all the system databases residing on the Server. This monitoring process is controlled by a background process which periodically checks every system database file on the Server computer system. If the timestamp of any specific Server database is changed, (ie. the database has been updated), the Client will automatically copy the database file and any associated database index files down from the Server on to the Client's local disk drive. The downloaded files are given a specific file extension to indicate that they are newly downloaded database files ready for installation.

If the Client determines that these specific database files are not currently being used in a POS transaction, it will proceed to install these files in the system. When the files are being installed, the active database files status are changed to "Backup" status and the new database files are marked as "Active". The newly installed database file lists are also loaded into all drop down and search lists.

This process occurs on each client computer system. It is the Client's responsibility to monitor the Server system files for any database updates. The Server does not play any role in ensuring that the Client system databases are up to date.

3.3.4 Quote Databases

Each Server and Client computer system controls its own respective Quote database.

3.3.4.1 Client Quote Database

When a new Quote has been created on the Client computer system, the quote is appended to the local Quote database. The Client periodically transfers the local Quote database up to the Server computer system for incorporation into the system wide Quote database. The Client periodically checks the Server's system wide Quote database to see if it has been updated and if so, downloads the database.

3.3.4.2 Server Quote Database

When the Server's Quote database has been updated, or the Server determines that it has received a Client's updated Quote database, it will proceed to collate its own and all other Client Quote databases into a combined single system wide Quote database. During this collating process, any duplicate and expired Quote entries will be discarded.

POS Business Application — System Architecture

3.4 Processes (Tasks)

When simultaneous operation of various events are required, these events are best placed in separate tasks – also called processes or threads.

The following proccesses are used:

1. Timer Process
2. Network Process

3.4.1 Timer Process

The Timer Process was created in order to keep accurate timing. If the timers were controlled in the main task by a Ttimer event, timer errors might creep in due to main task loading.

When the Timer Process is created it installs a 100ms event timer which generates 10 timer messages every second. The process thread's main loop waits for these messages and then adjusts all the system timers accordingly.

This implies that each system timer is accurate to 0.1 of a second.

The system timers ar 32 bit variables and therefore permit a timing range between 0.1 of a second and 429496729.5 seconds (4899.57 years).

3.4.2 Network Process

The Network Process was created in order to monitor the various server databases and to control the download process as required.

When the Network Process is created it installs a 1 second event timer which generates a single timer message every second. The process thread's mail loop waits for these messages.

If the POS Business Application is being shut down, the network control variable may be placed into a deactivating state. If this state is detected, the network control variable will be placed into the deactivated state and all future network operations blocked.

During normal network operations the network process thread's main loop will determine if the POS Business Application is operating as a Server or as a Client and perform the relevant operations.

3.4.2.1 Server Network Operations

When this function executes it performs the following operations:

1. Auto Initiate specific database downloads
2. Monitor specific database
3. Build POS Quote Database Summary

3.4.2.1.1 *Auto Initiate specific database downloads*

There is a function of this type for every inventory database which may undergo an auto initiate download. When a user on the POS Business Application Server wishes to auto-initiate the download of any specific database to the Clients, the relevant function is called to mark the database file ready for download.

3.4.2.1.2 *Monitor Specific Database*

There is a function of this type which monitors if a specific database has been modified. If the database has been modified a flag is set to force the reload of the list files associated with this specific database.

The main program monitors this flag and if in a safe state (eg. not processing a sale) controls the load operation to all revevant list boxes after which the flag is reset.

3.4.2.1.3 *Build POS Quote Database Summary*

This function first determines the name of all the POS Quote Register Files for the server and all the clients. It then builds a combined POS Quote Register File by combining all the entries in each of these files into a single file. Any duplicate quotes are deleted, as are voided and expired quotes. The final combined POS Quote Database Summary file is then made available to all systems for download. During the Quote database summary build process, stable sorts are used to ensure that the quote date entries are kept in order.

3.4.2.2 Client Network Operations

When this function executes it performs the following operations:

1. Server Drive Remap Attempt
2. Auto Initiate specific database downloads
3. Monitor Specific Server Database
4. Verify License Registration
5. Obtain updated POS Quote Database

POS Business Application System Architecture

3.4.2.2.1 *Server Drive Remap Attempt*

If the Server is inactive, an attempt will be made to try and access the Server and map onto the server drive.

3.4.2.2.2 *Auto Initiate specific database downloads*

There is a function of this type for every inventory database which may undergo an auto initiate download. When a user on the POS Business Application Client wishes to auto-initiate the download of any specific database from the Server, the relevant function is called to mark the database file ready for download.

3.4.2.2.3 *Monitor Specific Server Database*

There is a function of this type which monitors if a specific server database has been modified. If the database has been modified the revevant database files are downloaded to the client system and a flag is set to force the reload of the database and list files associated with this specific database.

The main program monitors this flag and if in a safe state (eg. not processing a sale) controls the installation of the updated database as well as updating all the associated list boxes after which the flag is reset.

3.4.2.2.4 *Verify License Registration*

This function ensures that any changes to the product license is implemented. For example, if a new product key is installed on the Server to permit additional accounting modules, this function then permits these same modules to be operational on the client system.

3.4.2.2.5 *Obtain Updated POS Quote Database*

This function determine if a new POS Quote Summary database has been created on the Server and, if so, downloads and installs this database on the client system.

3.5 Drivers

3.5.1 Cash Register Till Printer Driver

The Cash Register Till Printer Driver is used to communicate directly with the cash register printer. The driver interfaces with serial or parallel printers and also caters for ESC/POS printers utilizing standard ESC/POS commands.

3.5.2 Cash Drawer Driver

The Cash Drawer Driver is used to communicate directly with the cash register drawer. The driver interfaces with serial or parallel cash register drawers and, when required, transmits the character "A" in order to open the drawer.

Some cash register drawers are not controlled directly by the PC computer system and simply monitor the cash register printer communication channel. If communication is detected, (ie. a sale has been made), the drawer automatically opens.

This document is under construction…

Point-Of-Sale Business Application

System Build Procedure

Project: Point-Of-Sale Business Application
Date: January 29th 2008
Revision: 1.0.0
Company: Quantum Blue Technology LLC.

Copyright Notice

Copyright ©2005, 2006, 2007, 2008 Quantum Blue Technology LLC. – All rights reserved worldwide. This document is proprietary to **Quantum Blue Technology LLC.** And may contain information that is to be maintained as Trade Secret. It is intended for use only by **Quantum Blue Technology LLC.** Employees and its' contractors, customer employees, and authorized personnel. It may not be copied, translated, or transcribed in whole or in part without the express permission of the copyright holder **Quantum Blue Technology LLC.**

Quantum Blue Technology LLC
1424 Welsh Way, Ramona
California 92065
U.S.A.

Phone: USA (858) 837-2160
Email: info@QuantumBlueTechnology.com
Web: www.QuantumBlueTechnology.com

Please Note:

Due to ongoing design and development, **Quantum Blue Technology LLC.** May, at any time, and without notification, amend and update either this document and/or the associated "POS Business Application" software package.

Change History

Date	Version	Author	Reason for Change
1/29/08	1.0.0	Steve McClure	Initial Draft.

Table of Contents

1 **SCOPE** 1
   1.1 GENERAL 1
   1.2 ABBREVIATIONS 1

2 **SYSTEM BUILD PROCESS** 2
   2.1 BUILD ENVIRONMENT 2
      2.1.1 Work Station 2
      2.1.2 Operating Systems 2
      2.1.3 Compiler 2
      2.1.4 Qsetup Composer 3
   2.2 BUILD OPERATION 3

3 **APPENDIX – A** 6
   3.1 CD-ROM PROJECT FILES 6
   3.2 SOURCE CODE MODULES 7
      3.2.1 Header Files 7
         3.2.1.1 Definition Files 7
         3.2.1.2 Module Header Files 7
      3.2.2 Module Files 11
      3.2.3 Configuration File 15

POS Business Application   System Build Procedure

1 Scope

This document is the System Build Manual for the Point-Of-Sale Business Application and describes the manner in which the Application is built and placed on the Web Site.

1.1 General

The Point-Of-Sale (POS) Business Application is designed for the small business and provides networking capabilities not normally available to general Point-Of-Sale systems.

The principal features which set this POS Business Application Software apart from other POS accounting software systems are the following:

- Ease of Use
- Distributed Encrypted Databases
- Quicker Data Access via Calendar Indexed Databases
- Re-Posting of POS Sales transactions if database recovery is required
- Safe Non-Destructive Database Backup and Restore Operations

Please refer to the Overview document for a more detailed description of these features.

1.2 Abbreviations

IDE	Integrated Development Environment
PC	Personal Computer
POS	Point-Of-Sale
POSBA	Point-Of-Sale Business Application

# POS Business Application	System Build Procedure

2　System Build Process

2.1　Build Environment

2.1.1　Work Station

The POS Business Application software was developed on an IBM PC compatible computer system utilizing the configuration identified below.

- Intel Motherboard (or compatible)
- Pentium 4 CPU 2.0 GHz (or compatible)
- 1 GByte RAM Memory (RIMM)
- 160 GByte Hard Drive
- Graphics Adapter card
- LAN Interface
- Keyboard and mouse
- LCD Monitor Screen

2.1.2　Operating Systems

The POS Business Application software was developed on an IBM compatible computer system using the Windows XP Professional operating system.

Please Note: Service Pack 2 and all other operating system updates were also installed.

It should also be possible to build this product on other Windows Operating Systems.

2.1.3　Compiler

The POS Business Application was developed using the Borland C++ Builder IDE development package. This package provided an Integrated Development Environment (IDE) which included a source code editor, a C++ compiler/linker as well as a source code debugger for testing.

The IDE details are as follows:

> Borland C++ Builder Ver 6.0 Professional Package
>
> Available from: www.codegear.com/products/cppbuilder

POS Business Application   System Build Procedure

2.1.4 Qsetup Composer

The Qsetup Composer package was used to build a single executable file which could be located on a web page (or a CD-ROM). When accessed on the web page, the executable file would be automatically downloaded and installed on the customer's computer system.

The Qsetup details are as follows:

     Qsetup Installation Suite Ver: 7.5.0.8
     Pantaray Research LTD.
     www.pantaray.com

2.2 Build Operation

The POS Business Application is built as follows:

1. First open the POS Business Application project in Borland's C++ Builder.

   a) Start Borland C++ Builder.
   b) Select the "File / Open Project" menu option.
   c) The "Open Project" dialog box will be displayed.

   d) Select the POS Business Application source code directory .
   e) Select and open the "POS_Business_Application.bpr" project file.

2. Build the POS Business Application Project.

   a) Select the "Project / Build POS_Business_Application" menu option.

       The project build process will be started.
       Each program module will be compiled and then linked.
       After a few minutes the process should complete (± 3.5 million lines of code).
       There should be 0 Hints, 0 Warnings and 0 Errors.

       Press [OK] to complete the process.

   b) The Borland C++ Builder program may now be closed.

   c) The POS Business Application executable program "POS_Business_Application.exe" will reside in the same directory as the source code files.

       Copy the "POS_Business_Application.exe" file to the Qsetup "Installation Files" directory.

POS Business Application   System Build Procedure

3. The Qsetup Composer should contain the following sub-directories:

   a) The "Installation Files" Directory.

   This directory should contain the following files:

File	Description
Cash_Register.wav	Sound wave file
POS_Business_Application.exe	Application
POS_Configuration.ini	Application configuration
POS_License.lic	Application license
POS_Upgrade_Utility.exe	Application upgrade utility
The Computer Says No.wav	Sound wave file

   b) The "PDFs" Directory.

   This directory should contain the following files:

File	Description
Accounts_Receivable.pdf	PDF File
Brochure_Full_Overview.pdf	PDF File
Import_Database.pdf	PDF File
Installation.pdf	PDF File
Inventory.pdf	PDF File
Overview.pdf	PDF File
Point_Of_Sale.pdf	PDF File
System.pdf	PDF File

   Note: Any updates to the above documents should be converted into PDF format and placed in the "PDFs" directory. These files are incorporated into the POS Business Application Web installation file. The PDF files will be installed on the users computer when the POS Business Application is downloaded and installed via the web.

POS Business Application   System Build Procedure

4. Use the Qsetup Composer utility to build the Web installation file

    a) Start the Qsetup Composer utility.
    b) Select [Open Project} and select "POS Business Application Installation.qsp".
    c) Adjust any of the Qsetup features (not normally required).
    d) Select [Compile] to build the Web installation file.

    > **Note:** The POS Business Application Web Installation file will be created and placed in the Qsetup "Project" directory.

    > **Note:** The file is called "POSBAInstall_New.exe".

    e) Close the Qsetup Composer utility.

5. The Web Installation file may now be copied to the Web server directory.

POS Business Application   System Build Procedure

3 Appendix – A

3.1 CD-ROM Project Files

The following CD-ROM Project Directories are used:

File	Description
Data Exchange with CFG Definitions	Import configuration files
Eula	End Users License Agreement
QBT Web Pages	Quantum Blue Technology FrontPage Web
Qsetup	Qsetup project files
Upgrade Utility	Source code for building the POS upgrade utility used when installing POS Business Application software upgrades.
Version Stamp	Source code for building the Version Stamp utility used to attach a version stamp containing version and checksum information to the POS Business Application executable program.
Work	This directory contains all the POS Business Application source code files and document files.

POS Business Application   System Build Procedure

3.2 Source Code Modules

3.2.1 Header Files

The POS Business Application CD-ROM "Work \ Code" sub-directory contains the following header files:

3.2.1.1 Definition Files

Header File	Description
Definitions.h	Literal definitions
Externals.h	External variable definitions
Macros.h	Macro definitions
Publics.h	Public variable definitions
Typedefs.h	Typedef definitions

3.2.1.2 Module Header Files

Header File	Description
POS_Accounts_Payable.h	Class and/or Prototype definitions
POS_Accounts_Payable_Report_Parameters.h	Class and/or Prototype definitions
POS_Accounts_Receivable.h	Class and/or Prototype definitions
POS_Accounts_Receivable_Report_Parameters.h	Class and/or Prototype definitions
POS_AR_Refresh_Statistics.h	Class and/or Prototype definitions
POS_Backup_Databases.h	Class and/or Prototype definitions
POS_Bank_Reconciliation.h	Class and/or Prototype definitions
POS_Bar_Codes.h	Class and/or Prototype definitions
POS_Build_Client_Accounts_Payable_Lists.h	Class and/or Prototype definitions
POS_Build_Client_Accounts_Receivable_Lists.h	Class and/or Prototype definitions
POS_Build_Client_Inventory_Lists.h	Class and/or Prototype definitions
POS_Build_Server_Accounts_Payable_Lists.h	Class and/or Prototype definitions
POS_Build_Server_Accounts_Receivable_Lists.h	Class and/or Prototype definitions
POS_Build_Server_Inventory_Lists.h	Class and/or Prototype definitions
POS_Calendar.h	Class and/or Prototype definitions
POS_Cash_Register_Drawer_Interface.h	Class and/or Prototype definitions
POS_Client_Installation.h	Class and/or Prototype definitions
POS_Communications.h	Class and/or Prototype definitions
POS_Conversion.h	Class and/or Prototype definitions
POS_Credit_Card_Codes.h	Class and/or Prototype definitions
POS_CSV_Functions.h	Class and/or Prototype definitions

POS Business Application   System Build Procedure

Module Header Files (Cont'd)

Header File	Description
POS_Database_Edit.h	Class and/or Prototype definitions
POS_Database_Initial_Download_Message.h	Class and/or Prototype definitions
POS_Database_Parms.h	Class and/or Prototype definitions
POS_DB_Functions.h	Class and/or Prototype definitions
POS_Demo_Trial_Reminder.h	Class and/or Prototype definitions
POS_Display_License_Registrations.h	Class and/or Prototype definitions
POS_Eula.h	Class and/or Prototype definitions
POS_Export.h	Class and/or Prototype definitions
POS_Files.h	Class and/or Prototype definitions
POS_Find.h	Class and/or Prototype definitions
POS_General_Ledger.h	Class and/or Prototype definitions
POS_Help.h	Class and/or Prototype definitions
POS_Identify_Users.h	Class and/or Prototype definitions
POS_Import.h	Class and/or Prototype definitions
POS_Import_Correction.h	Class and/or Prototype definitions
POS_Import_Log.h	Class and/or Prototype definitions
POS_Import_Parameters.h	Class and/or Prototype definitions
POS_Information_Loading_Database.h	Class and/or Prototype definitions
POS_Installation_Welcome.h	Class and/or Prototype definitions
POS_Inventory.h	Class and/or Prototype definitions
POS_Inventory_File_Maintenance.h	Class and/or Prototype definitions
POS_Inventory_Report_Parameters.h	Class and/or Prototype definitions
POS_Invoice_Number.h	Class and/or Prototype definitions
POS_Invoice_Options.h	Class and/or Prototype definitions
POS_License_Configuration_Create.h	Class and/or Prototype definitions
POS_License_Configuration_View.h	Class and/or Prototype definitions
POS_License_Key_Create.h	Class and/or Prototype definitions
POS_License_Key_Enter.h	Class and/or Prototype definitions
POS_License_Registration.h	Class and/or Prototype definitions
POS_Log.h	Class and/or Prototype definitions
POS_Login.h	Class and/or Prototype definitions
POS_main.h	Class and/or Prototype definitions
POS_Multiple_Computer_Installation.h	Class and/or Prototype definitions
POS_Network.h	Class and/or Prototype definitions
POS_Network_Monitor_Client.h	Class and/or Prototype definitions
POS_Network_Monitor_Server.h	Class and/or Prototype definitions
POS_Network_Registration_Error.h	Class and/or Prototype definitions
POS_Options.h	Class and/or Prototype definitions
POS_Password.h	Class and/or Prototype definitions
POS_Payroll.h	Class and/or Prototype definitions
POS_Printer.h	Class and/or Prototype definitions

POS Business Application — System Build Procedure

Module Header Files (Cont'd)

Header File	Description
POS_Printer_Index.h	Class and/or Prototype definitions
POS_Printer_Selection.h	Class and/or Prototype definitions
POS_Project_Selection.h	Class and/or Prototype definitions
POS_Purchase_Order.h	Class and/or Prototype definitions
POS_Quote_Number.h	Class and/or Prototype definitions
POS_Quote_Options.h	Class and/or Prototype definitions
POS_Receipt_Number.h	Class and/or Prototype definitions
POS_Receipt_Options.h	Class and/or Prototype definitions
POS_Reentrancy_Test.h	Class and/or Prototype definitions
POS_Register.h	Class and/or Prototype definitions
POS_Register_Account_Payment_Receipt.h	Class and/or Prototype definitions
POS_Register_Balance.h	Class and/or Prototype definitions
POS_Register_Change.h	Class and/or Prototype definitions
POS_Register_Check_Info.h	Class and/or Prototype definitions
POS_Register_Credit_Exceeded.h	Class and/or Prototype definitions
POS_Register_Credit_Info.h	Class and/or Prototype definitions
POS_Register_Currency.h	Class and/or Prototype definitions
POS_Register_Customer_Info.h	Class and/or Prototype definitions
POS_Register_Files.h	Class and/or Prototype definitions
POS_Register_Item.h	Class and/or Prototype definitions
POS_Register_Item_Discount.h	Class and/or Prototype definitions
POS_Register_No_Account_Customers.h	Class and/or Prototype definitions
POS_Register_No_Inventory_Items.h	Class and/or Prototype definitions
POS_Register_Notes.h	Class and/or Prototype definitions
POS_Register_Number.h	Class and/or Prototype definitions
POS_Register_Paid_In.h	Class and/or Prototype definitions
POS_Register_Paid_Out.h	Class and/or Prototype definitions
POS_Register_Posting_Progress.h	Class and/or Prototype definitions
POS_Register_Quote_EndDate.h	Class and/or Prototype definitions
POS_Register_Recall_Quote.h	Class and/or Prototype definitions
POS_Register_Recall_Sale.h	Class and/or Prototype definitions
POS_Register_Recall_Sale_History.h	Class and/or Prototype definitions
POS_Register_Report_Parameters.h	Class and/or Prototype definitions
POS_Register_Reports.h	Class and/or Prototype definitions
POS_Register_Sale_Date.h	Class and/or Prototype definitions
POS_Register_Selection.h	Class and/or Prototype definitions
POS_Register_Start.h	Class and/or Prototype definitions
POS_Register_Total_Discount.h	Class and/or Prototype definitions
POS_Registry.h	Class and/or Prototype definitions
POS_Repost_Register_Transactions.h	Class and/or Prototype definitions
POS_Reset_Current_POS_Sale_Files.h	Class and/or Prototype definitions

POS Business Application   System Build Procedure

Module Header Files (Cont'd)

Header File	Description
POS_Restore_Database_From_Directory.h	Class and/or Prototype definitions
POS_Restore_Database_From_File.h	Class and/or Prototype definitions
POS_Sale_Types.h	Class and/or Prototype definitions
POS_Search_For_PDF_Reader.h	Class and/or Prototype definitions
POS_Server_Installation_Multiple.h	Class and/or Prototype definitions
POS_Server_Installation_Single.h	Class and/or Prototype definitions
POS_Single_Computer_Installation.h	Class and/or Prototype definitions
POS_Source_Document_Number.h	Class and/or Prototype definitions
POS_Source_Document_Options.h	Class and/or Prototype definitions
POS_System.h	Class and/or Prototype definitions
POS_System_Configuration_Editor.h	Class and/or Prototype definitions
POS_System_INI_Settings.h	Class and/or Prototype definitions
POS_System_Login.h	Class and/or Prototype definitions
POS_System_Override.h	Class and/or Prototype definitions
POS_System_Registry.h	Class and/or Prototype definitions
POS_System_Wide_Options.h	Class and/or Prototype definitions
POS_Tax_Codes.h	Class and/or Prototype definitions
POS_Term_Codes.h	Class and/or Prototype definitions
POS_Timers.h	Class and/or Prototype definitions
POS_Transaction_Codes.h	Class and/or Prototype definitions
POS_Transaction_Sources.h	Class and/or Prototype definitions
POS_Version_Stamp.h	Class and/or Prototype definitions
POS_Welcome_Demo.h	Class and/or Prototype definitions
POS_Welcome_Limited.h	Class and/or Prototype definitions
POS_Welcome_Server_Client_Overview.h	Class and/or Prototype definitions
POS_Welcome_Single_Multiple_Installation.h	Class and/or Prototype definitions
POS_Welcome_Unlimited.h	Class and/or Prototype definitions

3.2.2 Module Files

Module File	Description
POS_Accounts_Payable.cpp	Form Class Functions
POS_Accounts_Payable_Report_Parameters.cpp	Form Class Functions
POS_Accounts_Receivable.cpp	Form Class Functions
POS_Accounts_Receivable_Report_Parameters.cpp	Form Class Functions
POS_AR_Refresh_Statistics.cpp	Form Class Functions
POS_Backup_Databases.cpp	Form Class Functions
POS_Bank_Reconciliation.cpp	Form Class Functions
POS_Bar_Codes.cpp	Barcode Generation Functions
POS_Build_Client_Accounts_Payable_Lists.cpp	Form Class Functions
POS_Build_Client_Accounts_Receivable_Lists.cpp	Form Class Functions
POS_Build_Client_Inventory_Lists.cpp	Form Class Functions
POS_Build_Server_Accounts_Payable_Lists.cpp	Form Class Functions
POS_Build_Server_Accounts_Receivable_Lists.cpp	Form Class Functions
POS_Build_Server_Inventory_Lists.cpp	Form Class Functions
POS_Calendar.cpp	Form Class Functions
POS_Cash_Register_Drawer_Interface.cpp	Form Class Functions
POS_Client_Installation.cpp	Form Class Functions
POS_Communications.cpp	RS232 Communications Functions
POS_Conversion.cpp	Form Class Functions
POS_Credit_Card_Codes.cpp	Form Class Functions
POS_CSV_Functions.cpp	General CSV Functions
POS_Database_Edit.cpp	Form Class Functions
POS_Database_Initial_Download_Message.cpp	Form Class Functions
POS_Database_Parms.cpp	Form Class Functions
POS_DB_Functions.cpp	General Database Functions
POS_Demo_Trial_Reminder.cpp	Form Class Functions
POS_Display_License_Registrations.cpp	Form Class Functions
POS_Eula.cpp	Form Class Functions
POS_Export.cpp	Form Class Functions
POS_Files.cpp	Form Class Functions
POS_Find.cpp	Form Class Functions
POS_General_Ledger.cpp	Form Class Functions
POS_Help.cpp	Form Class Functions
POS_Identify_Users.cpp	Form Class Functions
POS_Import.cpp	Form Class Functions
POS_Import_Correction.cpp	Form Class Functions
POS_Import_Log.cpp	Form Class Functions
POS_Import_Parameters.cpp	Form Class Functions
POS_Information_Loading_Database.cpp	Form Class Functions

POS Business Application   System Build Procedure

Module Files (Cont'd)

Module File	Description
POS_Installation_Welcome.cpp	Form Class Functions
POS_Inventory.cpp	Form Class Functions
POS_Inventory_File_Maintenance.cpp	Form Class Functions
POS_Inventory_Report_Parameters.cpp	Form Class Functions
POS_Invoice_Number.cpp	Form Class Functions
POS_Invoice_Options.cpp	Invoice Options Functions
POS_License_Configuration_Create.cpp	Form Class Functions
POS_License_Configuration_View.cpp	Form Class Functions
POS_License_Key_Create.cpp	Form Class Functions
POS_License_Key_Enter.cpp	Form Class Functions
POS_License_Registration.cpp	License Registration Functions
POS_Log.cpp	Form Class Functions
POS_Login.cpp	Form Class Functions
POS_main.cpp	Form Class Functions
POS_Multiple_Computer_Installation.cpp	Form Class Functions
POS_Network.cpp	Network Process Functions
POS_Network_Monitor_Client.cpp	Form Class Functions
POS_Network_Monitor_Server.cpp	Form Class Functions
POS_Network_Registration_Error.cpp	Form Class Functions
POS_Options.cpp	General Options Functions
POS_Password.cpp	Form Class Functions
POS_Payroll.cpp	Form Class Functions
POS_Printer.cpp	General Print Functions
POS_Printer_Index.cpp	Printer Index Functions
POS_Printer_Selection.cpp	Form Class Functions
POS_Project_Selection.cpp	Form Class Functions
POS_Purchase_Order.cpp	Form Class Functions
POS_Quote_Number.cpp	Form Class Functions
POS_Quote_Options.cpp	Quote Options Functions
POS_Receipt_Number.cpp	Form Class Functions
POS_Receipt_Options.cpp	Receipt Options Functions
POS_Reentrancy_Test.cpp	Form Class Functions
POS_Register.cpp	Form Class Functions
POS_Register_Account_Payment_Receipt.cpp	Form Class Functions
POS_Register_Balance.cpp	Form Class Functions
POS_Register_Change.cpp	Form Class Functions
POS_Register_Check_Info.cpp	Form Class Functions
POS_Register_Credit_Exceeded.cpp	Form Class Functions
POS_Register_Credit_Info.cpp	Form Class Functions
POS_Register_Currency.cpp	Form Class Functions
POS_Register_Customer_Info.cpp	Form Class Functions

POS Business Application — System Build Procedure

Module Files (Cont'd)

Header File	Description
POS_Register_Files.cpp	Register File Functions
POS_Register_Item.cpp	Form Class Functions
POS_Register_Item_Discount.cpp	Form Class Functions
POS_Register_No_Account_Customers.cpp	Form Class Functions
POS_Register_No_Inventory_Items.cpp	Form Class Functions
POS_Register_Notes.cpp	Form Class Functions
POS_Register_Number.cpp	Form Class Functions
POS_Register_Paid_In.cpp	Form Class Functions
POS_Register_Paid_Out.cpp	Form Class Functions
POS_Register_Posting_Progress.cpp	Form Class Functions
POS_Register_Quote_EndDate.cpp	Form Class Functions
POS_Register_Recall_Quote.cpp	Form Class Functions
POS_Register_Recall_Sale.cpp	Form Class Functions
POS_Register_Recall_Sale_History.cpp	Form Class Functions
POS_Register_Report_Parameters.cpp	Form Class Functions
POS_Register_Reports.cpp	Form Class Functions
POS_Register_Sale_Date.cpp	Form Class Functions
POS_Register_Selection.cpp	Form Class Functions
POS_Register_Start.cpp	Form Class Functions
POS_Register_Total_Discount.cpp	Form Class Functions
POS_Registry.cpp	Registry Access Functions
POS_Repost_Register_Transactions.cpp	Form Class Functions
POS_Reset_Current_POS_Sale_Files.cpp	Form Class Functions
POS_Restore_Database_From_Directory.cpp	Form Class Functions
POS_Restore_Database_From_File.cpp	Form Class Functions
POS_Sale_Types.cpp	Form Class Functions
POS_Search_For_PDF_Reader.cpp	Form Class Functions
POS_Server_Installation_Multiple.cpp	Form Class Functions
POS_Server_Installation_Single.cpp	Form Class Functions
POS_Single_Computer_Installation.cpp	Form Class Functions
POS_Source_Document_Number.cpp	Form Class Functions
POS_Source_Document_Options.cpp	Source Document Functions
POS_System.cpp	General System Functions
POS_System_Configuration_Editor.cpp	Form Class Functions
POS_System_INI_Settings.cpp	Form Class Functions
POS_System_Login.cpp	Form Class Functions
POS_System_Override.cpp	Form Class Functions
POS_System_Registry.cpp	Form Class Functions
POS_System_Wide_Options.cpp	Form Class Functions
POS_Tax_Codes.cpp	Form Class Functions

Module Files (Cont'd)

Header File	Description
POS_Term_Codes.cpp	Form Class Functions
POS_Timers.cpp	Timer Process Functions
POS_Transaction_Codes.cpp	Form Class Functions
POS_Transaction_Sources.cpp	Form Class Functions
POS_Version_Stamp.cpp	Form Class Functions
POS_Welcome_Demo.cpp	Form Class Functions
POS_Welcome_Limited.cpp	Form Class Functions
POS_Welcome_Server_Client_Overview.cpp	Form Class Functions
POS_Welcome_Single_Multiple_Installation.cpp	Form Class Functions
POS_Welcome_Unlimited.cpp	Form Class Functions

3.2.3 Configuration File

Header File	Description
POS_Configuration.ini	Configuration Settings

Program Style
and
Methodology

Project: General Use
Date: February 5th 2008
Revision: 2.1.0
Company: Quantum Blue Technology LLC.

Copyright Notice

Copyright ©2005, 2006, 2007, 2008 Quantum Blue Technology LLC. – All rights reserved worldwide. This document is proprietary to **Quantum Blue Technology LLC.** And may contain information that is to be maintained as Trade Secret. It is intended for use only by **Quantum Blue Technology LLC.** Employees and its' contractors, customer employees, and authorized personnel. It may not be copied, translated, or transcribed in whole or in part without the express permission of the copyright holder **Quantum Blue Technology LLC.**

Quantum Blue Technology LLC
1424 Welsh Way, Ramona
California 92065
U.S.A.

Phone: USA (858) 837-2160
Email: info@QuantumBlueTechnology.com
Web: www.QuantumBlueTechnology.com

Please Note:

Due to ongoing design and development, **Quantum Blue Technology LLC.** May, at any time, and without notification, amend and update either this document.

Change History

Date	Version	Author	Reason for Change
1/5/06	1.0.0	Steve McClure	Initial Draft.
1/8/06	1.1.0	Steve McClure	Added more detail.
2/1/08	2.0.0	Steve McClure	First Release.
2/5/08	2.1.0	Steve McClure	Minor updates.

Table of Contents

1 **SUMMARY** 1
   1.1 SCOPE 1
   1.2 ABBREVIATIONS 1

2 **SOFTWARE DEVELOPMENT METHODOLOGY** 2
   2.1 *HEADER FILES* 2
      2.1.1 Module Title Block 3
      2.1.2 System Constants (Definitions) 3
         2.1.2.1 Integer Definitions 3
         2.1.2.2 Compiler Defaults 3
         2.1.2.3 Example 4
      2.1.3 System Types (Typedefs) 6
         2.1.3.1 Example 6
      2.1.4 System Global Variables (Publics) 8
         2.1.4.1 Example 8
      2.1.5 System Global Variables (Externals) 10
         2.1.5.1 Example 10
      2.1.6 Module Prototypes 12
         2.1.6.1 Example 12
   2.2 *SOURCE FILES* 13
      2.2.1 Module Title Block 13
      2.2.2 Function Title Block 13
      2.2.3 Function Parameters 14
         2.2.3.1 Passed Parameters 14
         2.2.3.2 Return Parameter 15
      2.2.4 Function Code Layout 15
         2.2.4.1 For Construct 15
         2.2.4.2 While Construct 16
         2.2.4.3 Do While Construct 16
         2.2.4.4 Switch Construct 16
         2.2.4.5 If Construct 17
      2.2.5 Error Detection 17
      2.2.6 Pseudocode 18
      2.2.7 Comments 18
      2.2.8 Example 19

3 **APPENDIX** 52
   3.1 CODE EDITOR 52
      3.1.1 Use of Tabs versus Spaces 52

Program Style and Methodology

1 Summary

This document describes the Quantum Blue Technology LLC. programming methodology used in developing company software.

1.1 Scope

This document identifies the layout of the program unit structure. This includes the module header, function headers, and general code constructs.

1.2 Abbreviations

IDE   Integrated Development Environment
PC   Pseudo Code (also known as Structured English)
PDL   Program Design Language.

Program Style and Methodology

2 Software Development Methodology

The purpose of programming is to develop a set of instructions, which make logical sense to both a computer system used to execute the instructions and to a human being who has to develop and maintain these instructions.

With this regard, the use of logical clear concise unambiguous names for modules, structures, variables and functions can not be overemphasized.

A program is built from the following types of files:

1. Header Files
2. Source Files

2.1 Header Files

In this methodology, the following types of header files are used:

1. The system constants header file
2. The system types header file
3. The system global variable header file
4. The module prototype header file

The advantage in this methodology is that it is a clean approach with specific definitions only existing in specific locations - a programmer immediately knows which file to edit for a given definition.

The disadvantage in this methodology is that a change to one of these files may result in the entire system having to be rebuilt. On current computer system this may result in having to wait an additional few seconds longer for the entire system build to complete - this additional time delay is hardly an issue in regard to the conceptual gain in code layout clarity.

Program Style and Methodology

2.1.1 Module Title Block

Each header file contains a descriptive title block, which identifies:

1. The module name
2. The customer's copyright information
3. The project name
4. The original author
5. The module creation date
6. A brief description of the module
7. The module version history information

2.1.2 System Constants (Definitions)

A project system constants header file is identified by the name "Definitions.h". This file is included in every source module.

2.1.2.1 Integer Definitions

A common programming problem exists with the manner in which a specific compiler defines the integer variable type. For instance, one compiler may identify an `int` as a 32-bit quantity whereas another compiler identifies it as a 16-bit quantity.

This confusion can easily develop into programming errors.

To bypass this problem the `uint` and `sint` literal definitions have been created as shown below:

```
/* Variable Integer definitions */
#define   uint8          unsigned char
#define   uint16         unsigned int
#define   uint32         unsigned long

#define   sint8          signed char
#define   sint16         signed int
#define   sint32         signed long
```

These literal definitions are located in the system definition header file.

2.1.2.2 Compiler Defaults

Compilers usually have specific default settings - for example, when defining a `char` variable, one compiler may default this to an `unsigned char`. However, another compiler may default to a `signed char`. It is also possible to further complicate the situation by overriding the compiler defaults at compile time.

To remove this confusion the integer definitions are used as discussed above.

Program Style and Methodology

2.1.2.3 Example

The following extract is an example of a system constants definition header file:

```
//----------------------------------------------------------------------------
// Project: POS Business Application
//  Module: Definitions.h
//  Author: Stephen W. McClure
//    Date: Oct 2005
//----------------------------------------------------------------------------
// Description:
//
// This header file contains the system definitions.
//----------------------------------------------------------------------------
// Version History:
//
// Version: 1.00        Date: 10/10/2005        Author: Steve McClure
//   Reason: Initial release.
//----------------------------------------------------------------------------
// Version: 1.01        Date: 02/12/2006        Author: Steve McClure
//   Reason: Added matrix changes.
//----------------------------------------------------------------------------
// This program is the exclusive property of Quantum Blue Technology LLC.
//   Copyright(c) 2005, 2006, 2007, 2008.
//
// Reproduction, disclosure, or use, in whole or in part, are not to be
// undertaken except with prior written authorization from the owner
// Quantum Blue Technology LLC.
//
// Contact Information:   Quantum Blue Technology LLC
//                        1424 Welsh Way
//                        Ramona
//                        CA 92065
//
//                        Phone: (858) 837-2160
//                        Email: info@quantumbluetechnology.com
//----------------------------------------------------------------------------

#ifndef SysdefsH
#define SysdefsH

/* Variable Integer definitions */
#define   uint8                     unsigned char
#define   uint16                    unsigned int
#define   uint32                    unsigned long

#define   sint8                     signed char
#define   sint16                    signed int
#define   sint32                    signed long


/* General Definitions */
#define   TRUE                      1
#define   FALSE                     0

#define   ON                        1
#define   OFF                       0

#define   SUCCESS                   1
#define   FAILURE                   0
```

Program Style and Methodology

```
/* DSP Register Addresses */
#define   TIMER_CTL0_REG_ADDRESS        0x01940000
#define   TIMER_PRD0_REG_ADDRESS        0x01940004
#define   TIMER_CNT0_REG_ADDRESS        0x01940008

/* Test LED State */
#define   LED_OFF                       0
#define   LED_HEARTBEAT_ON              1
#define   LED_ERROR_ON                  2
#define   LED_ERROR_OFF                 3

#endif
```

Discussion

1. The use of the definitions `#ifndef SysdefsH`, `#define SysdefsH` and at the end of the file `#endif` ensure that the include file will not generate a compiler error if it is included multiple times.

2. When defining various common device states, use the device as the first part of the state name - this keeps the various device states distinct from each other.

3. Column alignment aids in readability and reduces the likelihood of mistakes.

Program Style and Methodology

2.1.3 System Types (Typedefs)

A project system types header file is identified by the name "Typedefs.h". This file is included in every source module.

2.1.3.1 Example

The following extract is an example of a system types header file:

```
//-----------------------------------------------------------------------
// Project: POS Business Application
//  Module: Typedefs.h
//  Author: Stephen W. McClure
//    Date: Oct 2005
//-----------------------------------------------------------------------
// Description:
//
// This header file contains the various system typedef definitions.
//
// Note:   System Variable sizes are as follows:
//
//              char         1 byte
//
//              short int    2 bytes
//              int          4 bytes
//              long int     4 bytes
//
//              float        4 bytes
//
//              DWORD        4 bytes
//
//              double       8 bytes
//              long double  10 bytes
//
//-----------------------------------------------------------------------
// Version History:
//
// Version: 1.00       Date: 10/10/2005       Author: Steve McClure
//  Reason: Initial release.
//-----------------------------------------------------------------------
// Version: 1.01       Date: 02/12/2006       Author: Steve McClure
//  Reason: Added matrix changes.
//-----------------------------------------------------------------------
// This program is the exclusive property of Quantum Blue Technology LLC.
//   Copyright(c) 2005, 2006, 2007, 2008.
//
// Reproduction, disclosure, or use, in whole or in part, are not to be
// undertaken except with prior written authorization from the owner
// Quantum Blue Technology LLC.
//
// Contact Information:   Quantum Blue Technology LLC
//                        1424 Welsh Way
//                        Ramona
//                        CA 92065
//
//                        Phone: (858) 837-2160
//                        Email: info@quantumbluetechnology.com
//-----------------------------------------------------------------------
```

Program Style and Methodology

```
#ifndef SystypesH
#define SystypesH

/* SETUP Data Message */
typedef struct SETUP_DATA_
   {
   uint8          request_type;
   uint8          request;
   uint16         value;
   uint16         index;
   uint16         length;
   SETUP_DATA_  * next_record;

   }
   SETUP_DATA;

#endif
```

Please note the following:

1. The use of the definitions `#ifndef SystypesH`, `#define SystypesH` and at the end of the file `#endif` ensure that the include file will not generate a compiler error if it is included multiple times.

2. The `typedef` construct is used to permit a variable to be defined simply by using the typedef name, for example:

   ```
   SETUP_DATA    setup_data;
   ```

3. In order to help reduce the number of different variable names, the typedef is written using capital letters and the variable of that type uses the same name but in lowercase letters.

4. When the typedef is defined, the typedef name with an underscore, for example `SETUP_DATA_` follows the `struct` reserved word. This permits the compiler to recognize pointer variables, which point to the same structure as that is being defined.

5. Column alignment aids in readability and reduces the likelihood of mistakes.

Program Style and Methodology

2.1.4 System Global Variables (Publics)

A project system global variables public header file is identified by the name "Publics.h".

2.1.4.1 Example

The following extract is an example of a system global variables public header file:

```
//---------------------------------------------------------------------
// Project: POS Business Application
//  Module: Publics.h
//  Author: Stephen W. McClure
//    Date: Oct 2005
//---------------------------------------------------------------------
// Description:
//
// This header file contains the global public variable definitions.
//---------------------------------------------------------------------
// Version History:
//
// Version: 1.00      Date: 10/10/2005      Author: Steve McClure
//   Reason: Initial release.
//---------------------------------------------------------------------
// Version: 1.01      Date: 02/14/2006      Author: Steve McClure
//   Reason: Added matrix changes.
//---------------------------------------------------------------------
// This program is the exclusive property of Quantum Blue Technology LLC.
//    Copyright(c) 2005, 2006, 2007, 2008.
//
// Reproduction, disclosure, or use, in whole or in part, are not to be
// undertaken except with prior written authorization from the owner
// Quantum Blue Technology LLC.
//
// Contact Information:   Quantum Blue Technology LLC
//                        1424 Welsh Way
//                        Ramona
//                        CA 92065
//
//                        Phone: (858) 837-2160
//                        Email: info@quantumbluetechnology.com
//---------------------------------------------------------------------

#ifndef PublicsH
#define PublicsH

#include "Typedefs.h"

#include "POS_Inventory.h"
#include "POS_Timers.h"
#include "POS_Network.h"
#include "POS_Printer_Index.h"
#include "POS_Communications.h"

#include <dos.h>
#include <SyncObjs.hpp>


/* System Variables */
HANDLE  single_task_execution_mutex = NULL;
```

Program Style and Methodology

```
int   network_registration_error      = FALSE;
int   network_licenses_all_used_error = FALSE;

#endif
```

Discussion

1. The use of the definitions `#ifndef PublicsH`, `#define PublicsH` and at the end of the file `#endif` ensure that the include file will not generate a compiler error if it is included multiple times.

2. Note the use of descriptive typedef and variable names. Unambiguous names greatly add to the readability of program code and the myth of self-documented code could actually become a reality. The time saving in program maintenance is enormous.

3. Column alignment aids in readability and reduces the likelihood of mistakes.

Program Style and Methodology

2.1.5 System Global Variables (Externals)

A project system global variables external header file is identified by the name "Externals.h".

2.1.5.1 Example

The following extract is an example of a system global variables external header file:

```
//---------------------------------------------------------------------
// Project: POS Business Application
//  Module: Externals.h
//  Author: Stephen W. McClure
//    Date: Oct 2005
//---------------------------------------------------------------------
// Description:
//
// This header file contains external variable definitions.
//---------------------------------------------------------------------
// Version History:
//
// Version: 1.00      Date: 10/10/2005     Author: Steve McClure
//  Reason: Initial release.
//---------------------------------------------------------------------
// Version: 1.01      Date: 02/14/2006     Author: Steve McClure
//  Reason: Added matrix changes.
//---------------------------------------------------------------------
// This program is the exclusive property of Quantum Blue Technology LLC.
//   Copyright(c) 2005, 2006, 2007, 2008.
//
// Reproduction, disclosure, or use, in whole or in part, are not to be
// undertaken except with prior written authorization from the owner
// Quantum Blue Technology LLC.
//
// Contact Information:   Quantum Blue Technology LLC
//                        1424 Welsh Way
//                        Ramona
//                        CA 92065
//
//                        Phone: (858) 837-2160
//                        Email: info@quantumbluetechnology.com

//---------------------------------------------------------------------

#ifndef ExternalsH
#define ExternalsH

#include "POS_Timers.h"
#include "POS_Network.h"
#include "POS_Printer_Index.h"
#include "POS_Communications.h"

#include <dos.h>
#include <SyncObjs.hpp>

/* System Variables */
extern HANDLE  single_task_execution_mutex;
```

Program Style and Methodology

```
extern int    network_registration_error;
extern int    network_licenses_all_used_error;

#endif
```

Discussion

1. The use of the definitions `#ifndef ExternalsH`, `#define ExternalsH` and at the end of the file `#endif` ensure that the include file will not generate a compiler error if it is included multiple times.

2. Note the use of descriptive typedef and variable names. Unambiguous names greatly add to the readability of program code and the myth of self-documented code could actually become a reality. The time saving in program maintenance is enormous.

3. Column alignment aids in readability and reduces the likelihood of mistakes.

Program Style and Methodology

2.1.6 Module Prototypes

Each source code module (ie. ".c", or ".cpp" file) which contains function definitions will have an associated prototype header file. The name of the file will be identical to the source code module except it will utilize the ".h" suffix.

For example:

    digital.c - The digital source code functions definitions.
    digital.h - The digital source code function prototype definitions.

2.1.6.1 Example

The following extract is an example of a module prototype header file:

```
//---------------------------------------------------------------------------
// Project: POS Business Application
//  Module: POS_System.h
//  Author: Stephen W. McClure
//    Date: Oct 2005
//---------------------------------------------------------------------------
// Description:
//
// This header file contains the POS System function prototypes.
//---------------------------------------------------------------------------
// Version History:
//
// Version: 1.00      Date: 10/10/2005      Author: Steve McClure
//  Reason: Initial release.
//---------------------------------------------------------------------------
// Version: 1.01      Date: 02/14/2006      Author: Steve McClure
//  Reason: Added matrix changes.
//---------------------------------------------------------------------------
// This program is the exclusive property of Quantum Blue Technology LLC.
//   Copyright(c) 2005, 2006, 2007, 2008.
//
// Reproduction, disclosure, or use, in whole or in part, are not to be
// undertaken except with prior written authorization from the owner
// Quantum Blue Technology LLC.
//
// Contact Information:   Quantum Blue Technology LLC
//                        1424 Welsh Way
//                        Ramona
//                        CA 92065
//
//                        Phone: (858) 837-2160
//                        Email: info@quantumbluetechnology.com
//---------------------------------------------------------------------------

#ifndef POS_SystemH
#define POS_SystemH
```

Program Style and Methodology

```
int     POS_MessageBox (void      * Null_ptr,
                        const char * Text,
                        const char * Caption,
                        int         Flags);

int     Status_display_clear (void);
int     Status_display (char * status_string, int  timeout);
int     Status_display_beep (char * status_string, int  timeout);

#endif
```

Please note the following:

1. The use of the definitions `#ifndef POS_SystemH`, `#define POS_SystemH` and at the end of the file `#endif` ensure that the include file will not generate a compiler error if it is included multiple times.

2.2 Source Files

The source module is comprised of the following sections:

1. Module Title Block
2. Function Title Block
3. Function Parameters
4. Function Code Layout
5. Comments

2.2.1 Module Title Block

Each source module contains a descriptive title block, which identifies:

1. The module name
2. The customer's copyright information
3. The project name
4. The original author
5. The module creation date
6. A brief description of the module
7. The module version history information

2.2.2 Function Title Block

Each function is proceeded by a descriptive title block, which identifies:

1. The function name
2. A brief description
3. The passed parameters
4. The returned parameter

Program Style and Methodology

The following style should be used:

```
//------------------------------------------------------------------------
// Status Display Clear
//
// This function removes any displayed message from the status display.
//
// Returns: SUCCESS
//------------------------------------------------------------------------

int  Status_display_clear (void)
{

/* Erase the Status display message */
Status_display ("", INDEFINITELY);

/* Note that the display is inactive */
status_display = INACTIVE;

return (SUCCESS);
}
```

2.2.3 Function Parameters

Each function may utilize the following types of parameter:

1. Passed Parameters
2. Returned Parameters

2.2.3.1 Passed Parameters

The following style is used to define the function name and associated parameters:

```
int  status_display (char * status_string, int  timeout)

{
  uint8    key;
  uint8    digit;

  ...   code ...
  ...   code ...
}
```

Program Style and Methodology

If there are too many parameters to list on one line, the following style is used:

```
int   status_display (char * status_string,
                      char * error_message,
                      int    timeout)
{
  uint8   key;
  uint8   digit;

  ... code ...
  ... code ...
}
```

2.2.3.2 Return Parameter

The return parameter is to be used for returning the function status.

The function status is either:

1. SUCCESS
2. FAILURE

These literal constants are defined in the "systypes.h" file as follows:

```
#define   SUCCESS    1
#define   FAILURE    0
```

2.2.4 Function Code Layout

The function code layout style for the following constructs will now be discussed:

1. The For Construct
2. The While Construct
3. The Do… While Construct
4. The IF Construct
5. The Switch Construct

2.2.4.1 For Construct

The code layout style of the FOR construct is as follows:

```
for (index = 0; index < MAX_ITERATIONS; index++)
  {
    key = rs232_getch();
    ...
    ...
  }
```

Program Style and Methodology

2.2.4.2 While Construct

The code layout style of the WHILE construct is as follows:

```
index = 0;
while (index < MAX_ITERATIONS)
  {
    key = rs232_getch();
    ...
    ...
    index++;
  }
```

2.2.4.3 Do While Construct

The code layout style of the Do .. WHILE construct is as follows:

```
index = 0;
do
  {
    key = rs232_getch();
    ...
    ...
    index++;
  }
while (index < MAX_ITERATIONS);
```

Note: This construct is rarely used.

2.2.4.4 Switch Construct

The code layout style of the switch construct is as follows:

```
switch (digit)
  {
   case TEST_INVALID:
         return (FAILURE);
   case TEST_ONCE:
         perform_flash_memory_test_once();
         break;
   case TEST_REPEATEDLY:
         perform_flash_memory_test_repeatedly();
         break;
   default:
         return (FAILURE);
  }
```

Program Style and Methodology

2.2.4.5 If Construct

The code layout style of the various IF constructs are as follows:

```
if (index < MAX_ITERATIONS
   function_1();


if (index < MAX_ITERATIONS
   function_1();
else
   function_2();


if (index < MAX_ITERATIONS
   function_1();
else if (index = = MAX_ITERATIONS)
   function_2();
else
   function_3();



if (index < MAX_ITERATIONS
  {
   function_1a();
   function_1b();
  }
else if (index = = MAX_ITERATIONS)
  {
   if (test = = ACTIVE)
     {
      test_function_1();
      test_function_2();
     }
  }
else
   function_3();
```

2.2.5 Error Detection

There are many ways to handle error situations, which are detected within a function.

The manner, which will be utilized, is to exit from the function as soon as the error has been detected. This permits a clear concise logic flow exiting the function.

```
...
/* Test if error occurred */
if (error = = DETECTED)
   return (FAILURE);
...
```

The method whereby the error condition is delegated to the distant else part of an IF condition is discouraged since such code becomes difficult to read when the function is of a significant size.

Program Style and Methodology

2.2.6 Pseudocode

Pseudocode (also known as structured English) should be used to provide a description of the function of the subsequent lines of code, as shown below:

```
/* Do Forever */
while (1)
  {
  /* Wait for a key press */
  key = rs232_getch();

  /* If [ESC] key pressed - exit */
  if (key = = ESC_KEY)
     return (FAILURE);

  /* If [ENTER] key pressed - return number */
  if (key = = ENTER_KEY)
     {
     *number = result;
     return (SUCCESS);
     }
  }
```

2.2.7 Comments

Comments should only be used where it is necessary to explain in detail the actions of a code fragment. The comments should be well to the right of the code such that the code and the comments are clearly delineated. Both `/* comment */` and `// Comment` styles are permitted:

```
TCR.BIT.IEDG = SET;                /* Input Capture interrupts triggered on positive edge */

disable_fan_fault_interrupt();     // Only enabled when fan switched on, otherwise switch
                                   // generates interrupt in inactive state !!!
```

Quantum Blue Technology LLC.

Program Style and Methodology

2.2.8 Example

The following example illustrates the overall code layout style:

```cpp
//---------------------------------------------------------------------------
// Project: POS Business Application
//  Module: POS_System.cpp
//  Author: Stephen W. McClure
//    Date: Oct 2007
//---------------------------------------------------------------------------
// Description:
//
// This module contains the POS system functions.
//---------------------------------------------------------------------------
// This program is the exclusive property of Quantum Blue Technology LLC.
//   Copyright(c) 2005, 2006, 2007, 2008.
//
// Reproduction, disclosure, or use, in whole or in part, are not to be
// undertaken except with prior written authorization from the owner
// Quantum Blue Technology LLC.
//
// Contact Information:  Quantum Blue Technology LLC
//                       1424 Welsh Way
//                       Ramona
//                       CA 92065
//
//                       Phone: (858) 837-2160
//                       Email: info@quantumbluetechnology.com
//---------------------------------------------------------------------------

#include <windows.h>                // This is required
#undef GetEnvironmentVariable       // for proper operation of the GetEnvironmentVariable
#include <vcl.h>
#pragma hdrstop

#include "Definitions.h"
#include "Typedefs.h"
#include "Externals.h"

#include "POS_System.h"
#include "POS_Main.h"
#include "POS_Log.h"
#include "POS_Files.h"
#include "POS_Accounts_Payable.h"
#include "POS_Accounts_Receivable.h"
#include "POS_Bank_Reconciliation.h"
#include "POS_General_Ledger.h"
#include "POS_Inventory.h"
#include "POS_Payroll.h"
#include "POS_Purchase_Order.h"
#include "POS_Register.h"
#include "POS_Registry.h"
#include "POS_Import.h"
#include "POS_Invoice_Number.h"
#include "POS_Register_Reports.h"

#include <process.h>
#include <sysutils.hpp>
#include <dir.h>
#include <fcntl.h>
#include <io.h>
#include <sys\stat.h>
#include <stdio.h>
#include <mem.h>
#include <errno.h>
#include <math.hpp>
#include <Inifiles.hpp>
```

Program Style and Methodology

```
//---------------------------------------------------------------------------
// POS MessageBox
//
// This function displays an error message box.
//
// Returns: status of MessageBox key press.
//---------------------------------------------------------------------------
int   POS_MessageBox (void * Null_ptr, const char * Text, const char * Caption, int Flags)
{
int   status;


Application->NormalizeTopMosts();
status = MessageBox(Null_ptr, Text, Caption, Flags | MB_TASKMODAL);
Application->RestoreTopMosts();

return (status);
}




//---------------------------------------------------------------------------
// Status Display Clear
//
// This function removes any displayed message from the status display.
//
// Returns: SUCCESS
//---------------------------------------------------------------------------

int   Status_display_clear (void)
{

/* Erase the Status display message */
Status_display ("", INDEFINITELY);

/* Note that the display is inactive */
status_display = INACTIVE;

return (SUCCESS);

}




//---------------------------------------------------------------------------
// Status Display Beep
//
// This function beeps and places the passed data into the status bar for the
// specified timeout period.
//
// Returns: SUCCESS
//---------------------------------------------------------------------------

int   Status_display_beep (char * status_string, int  timeout)
{

/* The status display is now active */
status_display = ACTIVE;

/* Sound the warning */
MessageBeep(MB_ICONEXCLAMATION);

/* Display the status message */
Status_display (status_string, timeout);

/* SUCCESS */
return (SUCCESS);
}
```

Program Style and Methodology

```
//-------------------------------------------------------------------------
// Status Display Blank
//
// This function displays the new status message only if the currently
// displayed status message is blank.
//
// Returns: SUCCESS
//-------------------------------------------------------------------------

int  Status_display_blank (char * status_string, int  timeout)
{

/* Is the Status Message currently blank? */
if (status_display == INACTIVE)
   {
     /* Status display is now active */
     status_display = ACTIVE;

     /* Yes - Display the status message */
     Status_display (status_string, timeout);

     /* SUCCESS */
     return (SUCCESS);
  }

/* FAILURE */
return (FAILURE);
}




//-------------------------------------------------------------------------
// Status Display Beep Blank
//
// This function beeps and places the passed data into the status bar for the
// specified timeout period only if the currently displayed status message is
// blank.
//
// Returns: SUCCESS
//-------------------------------------------------------------------------

int  Status_display_beep_blank (char * status_string, int  timeout)
{

/* Is the Status Message currently blank? */
if (status_display == INACTIVE)
   {
     /* Status display is now active */
     status_display = ACTIVE;

     /* Yes - Display the status message */
     Status_display_beep (status_string, timeout);

     /* SUCCESS */
     return (SUCCESS);
  }

/* FAILURE */
return (FAILURE);
}
```

Program Style and Methodology

```
//---------------------------------------------------------------------------
// Clean Up String
//
// This function cleans up the parameter string by removing leading and
// trailing spaces, multiple embedded spaces are replaced by a single space,
// and all control characters are removed.
//
// Returns: SUCCESS or FAILURE
//---------------------------------------------------------------------------

int   clean_up_string (AnsiString *  parameter)
{
int     parameter_length;
char    buffer [MAX_STRING_SIZE];
char *  read_ptr;
char *  write_ptr;

AnsiString  local_parameter;
AnsiString  trimmed_parameter;


/* Set Text to Uppercase */
local_parameter = *parameter;

/* Remove leading and trailing spaces and any control characters */
trimmed_parameter = local_parameter.Trim();

/* Make a copy of the parameter string */
strcpy (buffer, trimmed_parameter.c_str());

/* Initialize pointers */
read_ptr  = buffer;
write_ptr = buffer;

/* Scan string and remove excess spaces */
while (*read_ptr != 0x00)
  {
    /* Copy non-blank characters */
    if (*read_ptr != ' ')
      *write_ptr++ = *read_ptr++;

    /* Copy single space character */
    if (*read_ptr == ' ')
      {
        /* Copy single space character */
        *write_ptr++ = *read_ptr++;

        /* Remove any excess spaces */
        while (*read_ptr == ' ')
          {
            /* Step to next character */
            read_ptr++;
          }
      }
  }

/* Null terminate the updated string */
*write_ptr = 0x00;

/* Return updates string */
*parameter = buffer;

/* All is well... */
return (SUCCESS);
}
```

Program Style and Methodology

```
//-------------------------------------------------------------------------
// Read System Registry File
//
// This function reads the system configuration registry for specific
// system variables.
//
// Note: The POS variable is set to UPPER CASE.
//
// Returns: SUCCESS or FAILURE
//-------------------------------------------------------------------------

int  read_system_registry_parameters (void)
{

/* Note: Only the Computer Name is currently obtained from the System Registry */
POS_computer_name = AnsiUpperCase(get_registry_string

("SYSTEM\\CurrentControlSet\\Control\\ComputerName\\ComputerName",
                       "ComputerName"));

/* Is the Computer Name defined? */
if (POS_computer_name == "")
  {
    /* No - Set the computer name to "Undefined" */
    POS_computer_name =  "UNDEFINED";
  }


/* Success */
return (SUCCESS);
}
```

Program Style and Methodology

```
//-----------------------------------------------------------------------
// Read Configuration
//
// This function reads the specified configuration parameter from the
// configuration file.  If the configuration parameter does not exist then
// the default is returned.
//
// Returns: Configuration Parameter
//-----------------------------------------------------------------------

AnsiString   Read_configuration (AnsiString   section_name,
                                 AnsiString   configuration_name,
                                 AnsiString   default_setting)
{
int   index;
int   start_of_section;
int   end_of_section;
int   number_of_configuration_lines;
AnsiString   full_section_name;
AnsiString   configuration_string;
AnsiString   first_token;
AnsiString   second_token;
AnsiString   third_token;


/* Load local configuration file into Memo Box */
POS_Main_Form->System_Configuration_Memo->Lines->Clear();
POS_Main_Form->System_Configuration_Memo->Lines
->LoadFromFile(system_configuration_file_name);

/* Initialization */
index = 0;
start_of_section = 0;
end_of_section = 0;
number_of_configuration_lines = POS_Main_Form->System_Configuration_Memo->Lines->Count;
full_section_name = "[" + section_name + "]";


/* Scan for section name */
while (index < number_of_configuration_lines)
   {
     /* Section Name found? */
     if (AnsiUpperCase(POS_Main_Form->System_Configuration_Memo->Lines->Strings[index]) ==
         AnsiUpperCase(full_section_name))
       {
         /* Start of section found */
         start_of_section = index + 1;
         break;
       }

     /* Step to next configuration entry */
     index++;
   }

/* Section name not found? */
if (index >= number_of_configuration_lines)
   {
     /* Return default value */
     return (AnsiUpperCase(default_setting));
   }

/* Step to next line */
index++;
```

Program Style and Methodology

```
/* Scan for subsequent section name or end of file */
while (index < number_of_configuration_lines)
  {
    /* Next section name detected? */
    if (POS_Main_Form->System_Configuration_Memo->Lines->Strings[index].c_str()[0] == '[')
      {
        /* End of section found */
        break;
      }

    /* Step to next configuration entry */
    index++;
  }

/* End of section found */
end_of_section = index;

/* Search through section for required configuration variable */
for (index = start_of_section; index < end_of_section; index++)
   {
     /* Get the next configuration string */
     configuration_string = POS_Main_Form->System_Configuration_Memo->Lines->Strings[index];
     configuration_string = configuration_string.Trim();

     /* Check that configuration string is not null and is not a comment */
     if ((configuration_string != "") &&
         (configuration_string.c_str()[0] != ';'))
       {
         /* Extract tokens from string */
         if (extract_token (configuration_string, &first_token,  0) == FAILURE)
           return (default_setting);
         if (extract_token (configuration_string, &second_token, 1) == FAILURE)
           return (default_setting);
         if (extract_token (configuration_string, &third_token,  2) == FAILURE)
           return (default_setting);

         /* Check for configuration variable name */
         if (AnsiUpperCase(first_token) == AnsiUpperCase(configuration_name))
           {
             /* Check that second token is the "=" sign */
             if (second_token == "=")
               {
                 /* Return configuration setting */
                 return (AnsiUpperCase(third_token));
               }

             /* Error detected */
             return (AnsiUpperCase(default_setting));
           }
       }
   }

/* Configuration variable name not found - return default value */
return (AnsiUpperCase(default_setting));
}
```

Program Style and Methodology

```c
//---------------------------------------------------------------------------
// Write Configuration
//
// This function writes the specified configuration parameter to the
// configuration file.  If the configuration parameter exists then its value
// is changed.  If the configuration parameter does not exist then a new
// parameter is written.
//
// Returns: SUCCESS or FAILURE
//---------------------------------------------------------------------------

int  Write_configuration (AnsiString   section_name,
                          AnsiString   configuration_name,
                          AnsiString   configuration_value)
{
int  index;
int  start_of_section;
int  end_of_section;
int  number_of_configuration_lines;
AnsiString   full_section_name;
AnsiString   configuration_string;
AnsiString   first_token;
AnsiString   new_configuration_section;
AnsiString   new_configuration_variable;


/* Initialization */
new_configuration_section  = "[" + section_name + "]";


/* Does the configuration value contain a space? */
if (StrPos (configuration_value.c_str(), " ") == NULL)
   {
     /* No - Just use the configuration value */
     new_configuration_variable  = configuration_name + " = " + configuration_value;
   }
else
   {
     /* Yes - Place the configuration value in double quotes */
     new_configuration_variable  = configuration_name + " = \"" + configuration_value + "\"";
   }



/******************************************************************/
/* First determine if the configuration name exists in the section */
/******************************************************************/

/* Load local configuration file into Memo Box */
POS_Main_Form->System_Configuration_Memo->Lines->Clear();
POS_Main_Form->System_Configuration_Memo->Lines->LoadFromFile(system_configuration_file_name);

/* Initialization */
index = 0;
start_of_section = 0;
end_of_section = 0;
number_of_configuration_lines = POS_Main_Form->System_Configuration_Memo->Lines->Count;
full_section_name = "[" + section_name + "]";
```

Program Style and Methodology

```
/* Scan for section name */
while (index < number_of_configuration_lines)
   {
     /* Section Name found? */
     if (AnsiUpperCase(POS_Main_Form->System_Configuration_Memo->Lines->Strings[index]) ==
        AnsiUpperCase(full_section_name))
       {
         /* Start of section found */
         start_of_section = index + 1;
         break;
       }

     /* Step to next configuration entry */
     index++;
   }

/* Section name not found? */
if (index >= number_of_configuration_lines)
   {
     /* Create New Section Name */
     POS_Main_Form->System_Configuration_Memo->Lines->Add(" ");
     POS_Main_Form->System_Configuration_Memo->Lines->Add(new_configuration_section);

     /* Write New Configuration Variable */
     POS_Main_Form->System_Configuration_Memo->Lines->Add(new_configuration_variable);

     /* Save Configuration File */
     POS_Main_Form->System_Configuration_Memo->Lines->SaveToFile
(system_configuration_file_name);

     /* Return */
     return (SUCCESS);
   }

/* Step to next line */
index++;

/* Scan for subsequent section name or end of file */
while (index < number_of_configuration_lines)
   {
     /* Next section name detected? */
     if (POS_Main_Form->System_Configuration_Memo->Lines->Strings[index].c_str()[0] == '[')
       {
         /* End of section found */
         break;
       }

     /* Step to next configuration entry */
     index++;
   }

/* End of section found */
end_of_section = index;


/* Search through section for required configuration variable */
for (index = start_of_section; index < end_of_section; index++)
   {
     /* Get the next configuration string */
     configuration_string = POS_Main_Form->System_Configuration_Memo->Lines-
>Strings[index];
     configuration_string = configuration_string.Trim();

     /* Check that configuration string is not null and is not a comment */
     if ((configuration_string != "") &&
        (configuration_string.c_str()[0] != ';'))
       {
         /* Extract tokens from string */
         if (extract_token (configuration_string, &first_token,  0) == FAILURE) return (FAILURE);
```

Program Style and Methodology

```
            /* Check for configuration variable name */
            if (AnsiUpperCase(first_token) == AnsiUpperCase(configuration_name))
              {
                /* Configuration variable found - Delete it */
                POS_Main_Form->System_Configuration_Memo->Lines->Delete(index);
                break;
              }
          }
      }

/* The configuration variable was deleted or did not exist.      */
/* Append a New configuration variable to the end of the section */
POS_Main_Form->System_Configuration_Memo->Lines->Insert(index,
new_configuration_variable);

/* Save Configuration File */
POS_Main_Form->System_Configuration_Memo->Lines->SaveToFile
(system_configuration_file_name);

/* Success */
return (SUCCESS);
}
```

Program Style and Methodology

```c
//---------------------------------------------------------------------------
// Read System Configuration File
//
// This function reads the system configuration file and sets all the system
// variables.
//
// Note: The POS variable is set to UPPER CASE.
//
// Returns: SUCCESS or FAILURE
//---------------------------------------------------------------------------

int   read_system_configuration_file (void)
{
/* Access [System] Section Variables */
// Note: Computer name is found from the Registry.

POS_application       = Read_configuration ("System", "Application",      "Client");
POS_daylight_savings  = Read_configuration ("System", "Daylight_Savings", "On");
POS_sound             = Read_configuration ("System", "Sound",            "OFF");

/* Access [Drives] Section Variables */
POS_server_drive            = Read_configuration ("Drives", "Server",                  "C:");
POS_server_name             = Read_configuration ("Drives", "Server_Name",             "");
POS_server_shared_directory = Read_configuration ("Drives", "Server_Shared_Directory", "");

POS_local_drive_low_limit   = Read_configuration ("Drives", "local_drive_low_limit",   "2.0");
POS_server_drive_low_limit  = Read_configuration ("Drives", "server_drive_low_limit",  "2.0");

/* Access [Directory] Section Variables */
POS_project_directory_name          = Read_configuration ("Directories", "Project", "PROJ");

/* Fixed directory names */
POS_system_directory_name              = "System";
POS_log_directory_name                 = "Log";
POS_license_directory_name             = "License";
POS_inventory_directory_name           = "Inventory";
POS_accounts_payable_directory_name    = "Accounts_Payable";
POS_accounts_receivable_directory_name = "Accounts_Receivable";
POS_point_of_sale_directory_name       = "POS";
POS_general_ledger_directory_name      = "General_Ledger";
POS_bank_reconciliation_directory_name = "Bank_Reconciliation";
POS_purchase_order_directory_name      = "Purchase_Order";

POS_pdf_directory_name = "PDF";

/* Access [Options] Section Variables */
POS_register              = Read_configuration ("Options",  "Register", "0");

/* Access [General] Section Variables */
POS_currency_symbol       = Read_configuration ("General",  "Currency_Symbol", "$");

POS_minimize_screens      = Read_configuration ("General",  "Minimize_Screens",        "OFF");
POS_fixed_forms           = Read_configuration ("General",  "Fixed_Forms",             "Fixed");
POS_display_network_messages = Read_configuration ("General", "Display_Network_Messages", "OFF");

POS_auto_pos              = Read_configuration ("General",  "Auto_POS",                "OFF");
POS_auto_shutdown         = Read_configuration ("General",  "Auto_Shutdown",           "OFF");
POS_exit_block            = Read_configuration ("General",  "Exit_Block",              "OFF");


/* Access [Programs] Section Variables */
POS_PDF_Reader            = Read_configuration ("Programs", "PDF_Reader",    AcroRd32.exe");

/* Success */
return (SUCCESS);
}
```

Program Style and Methodology

```
//---------------------------------------------------------------------------
// Log
//
// This function appends the log_entry to the end of the current system log.
//
// Returns: SUCCESS or FAILURE
//---------------------------------------------------------------------------

int  Log (char * log_entry)

{
int    file_handle;
int    bytes_written;
char   buffer[MAX_STRING_SIZE + 100];


/* Test if log file operational */
if (log_file_status == INACTIVE)
   {
     /* Log file is not available */
     return (FAILURE);
   }

/* Does the Log file exist? */
if (file_exists (system_log_file_name) == FAILURE)
   {
     /* No - Do nothing otherwise infinite loop can occur!!! */
     return (FAILURE);
   }

else
   {
     /* Attempt to open the existing training log file */
     if (file_open (system_log_file_name, &file_handle, OPEN_READ_WRITE_EXCLUSIVE) == FAILURE)
        {
          /* Display error message */
          sprintf (buffer, "Could not open Log File '%s'!!! [errno = %d, %s]",
                   system_log_file_name,
                   errno,
                   _sys_errlist[errno]);

          POS_MessageBox (NULL, buffer, "System Log File Error", MB_OK|MB_ICONEXCLAMATION);
          return (FAILURE);
        }
   }

/* Prepend the data and time stamp to the log entry */
TimeSeparator    = ':';
LongTimeFormat   = "hh:mm:ssam/pm";
ShortTimeFormat  = "hh:mm:ssam/pm";

DateSeparator    = '/';
LongDateFormat   = "mm/dd/yyyy";
ShortDateFormat  = "mm/dd/yyyy";


/* Create the log file entry */
sprintf (buffer, "%s  %s", DateTimeToStr(Now()).c_str(), log_entry);

/* Restore time format to normal setting */
LongTimeFormat   = "hh:mm:ss am/pm";
ShortTimeFormat  = "hh:mm:ss am/pm";

/* Place file pointer at end of file */
if (file_seek_end (file_handle) == FAILURE)
   {
     sprintf (buffer, "Could not seek to end of Log File '%s'.", system_log_file_name);
     POS_MessageBox (NULL, buffer, "System Log File Error", MB_OK|MB_ICONEXCLAMATION);
     return (FAILURE);
   }
```

Program Style and Methodology

```
/* File opened successfully - Append log entry */
if (file_write (file_handle, buffer, strlen(buffer)) == FAILURE)
   {
     /* Display error message */
     sprintf (buffer, "Log: Error detected when writing log entry to file '%s'!!! [errno = %d, %s]",
              system_log_file_name,
              errno,
              _sys_errlist[errno]);

     POS_MessageBox (NULL, buffer, "System Log File Error", MB_OK|MB_ICONEXCLAMATION);
     file_close (file_handle);
     return (FAILURE);
   }

/* System log entry appended - now append a <CR> */
if (file_write (file_handle, "\n", 1) == FAILURE)
   {
     /* No - Display error message */
     sprintf (buffer, "Log: Error detected when writing <CR> to file '%s'!!! [errno = %d, %s]",
              system_log_file_name,
              errno,
              _sys_errlist[errno]);

     POS_MessageBox (NULL, buffer, "System Log File Error", MB_OK|MB_ICONEXCLAMATION);
     file_close (file_handle);
     return (FAILURE);
   }

/* All is well, close the file */
file_close (file_handle);

return (SUCCESS);
}
```

Program Style and Methodology

```
//-------------------------------------------------------------------------
// Start Calculator
//
// This function spawns the calculator.
//
// Returns: SUCCESS or FAILURE
//-------------------------------------------------------------------------
void   start_calculator (void)
{
int    result;
char   buffer [MAX_STRING_SIZE];
char   executable [MAX_STRING_SIZE];

AnsiString   system_root;


/* Get System Root environment variable */
system_root = GetEnvironmentVariable("SystemRoot");

/* Build executable file name */
strcpy (executable, system_root.c_str());
strcat (executable, "\\System32\\calc.exe");

/* Start the Calculator */
result = spawnlp (P_NOWAIT, executable, executable, NULL);

/* Success? */
if (result == INVALID)
   {
     /* No - Tell User to start Windows Calculator manually */
     POS_MessageBox (NULL,
                "Windows Calculator not found...  Please start manually.",
                "Calculator",
                 MB_OK|MB_ICONEXCLAMATION);

     /* Could not start Windows Calculator */
     sprintf (buffer,
            "Could not start 'calc.exe' process  [errno = %d, %s].",
             errno,
             _sys_errlist[errno]);

     Log_error (1, buffer);
   }

}
```

Program Style and Methodology

```
//--------------------------------------------------------------------------
// Start Windows Explorer
//
// This function spawns the Microsoft Windows Explorer.
//
// Returns: SUCCESS or FAILURE
//--------------------------------------------------------------------------

void   start_windows_explorer (void)
{
int    result;
char   buffer [MAX_STRING_SIZE];
char   executable [MAX_STRING_SIZE];

AnsiString system_root;


/* Get System Root environment variable */
system_root = GetEnvironmentVariable("SystemRoot");

/* Build executable file name */
strcpy (executable, system_root.c_str());
strcat (executable, "\\explorer.exe");

/* Start Windows Explorer */
result = spawnlp (P_NOWAIT, executable, executable, NULL);

/* Success? */
if (result == INVALID)
  {
    /* No - Tell User to start Windows Explorer manually */
    POS_MessageBox (NULL,
                   "Windows Explorer not found...  Please start manually.",
                   "Windows Explorer",
                    MB_OK|MB_ICONEXCLAMATION);

    /* Could not start Windows Explorer */
    sprintf (buffer,
            "Could not start 'explorer.exe' process  [errno = %d, %s].",
             errno,
             _sys_errlist[errno]);

    Log_error (1, buffer);
  }

}
```

Program Style and Methodology

```
//-------------------------------------------------------------------------
// Start Auto Shutdown
//
// This function starts the auto shutdown process.
//
// Returns: SUCCESS or FAILURE
//-------------------------------------------------------------------------

void   start_auto_shutdown (void)
{
int    result;
char   buffer [MAX_STRING_SIZE];


// !!! Only an Administrator or a user who is part of the Administrators Group can use tsshutdn !!!


/* Start the shutdown process */
result = spawnlp (P_NOWAIT, "tsshutdn.exe", "20", "/powerdown", NULL);

/* Was an error detected? */
if (result == INVALID)
   {
     /* Yes - Log error */
     sprintf (buffer,
              "Could not start the Auto Shutdown process  [errno = %d, %s].",
               errno,
              _sys_errlist[errno]);

     Log_error (1, buffer);
     return;
   }

/* Log Auto Shutdown process started */
Log_info ("Auto Shutdown process started...");
}




//-------------------------------------------------------------------------
// Play Cash Register Sound
//
// This function plays the cash register sound clip.
//-------------------------------------------------------------------------

void   play_cash_register_sound (void)
{
char   sound_file_name [MAX_STRING_SIZE];


/* Build path using system startup drive and directory */
fnmerge (sound_file_name,
         system_startup_drive.c_str(),
         system_startup_directory.c_str(),
        "Cash_Register",
        ".wav");

try {
     POS_Register_Form->MediaPlayer1->FileName = sound_file_name;
     POS_Register_Form->MediaPlayer1->Open();
     POS_Register_Form->MediaPlayer1->Play();
    }

catch (...)
    {
      Status_display ("Sound not found...", TIMEOUT_5_SECONDS);
    }
}
```

Program Style and Methodology

Quantum Blue Technology LLC.   Page 34

Program Style and Methodology

```
//-------------------------------------------------------------------------
// Play Computer Says No Sound
//
// This function plays "The Computer Says No" sound clip.
//-------------------------------------------------------------------------

void  play_computer_says_no_sound (void)
{
char  sound_file_name [MAX_STRING_SIZE];


/* Are we signed on as a SUPERVISOR? */
if (SUPERVISOR_override)
   {
     /* Yes - Build path using system startup drive and directory */
     fnmerge (sound_file_name,
              system_startup_drive.c_str(),
              system_startup_directory.c_str(),
              "The Computer Says No",
              ".wav");

     try {
            POS_Register_Form->MediaPlayer1->FileName = sound_file_name;
            POS_Register_Form->MediaPlayer1->Open();
            POS_Register_Form->MediaPlayer1->Play();
         }

     catch (...)
         {
            Status_display ("Sound not found...", TIMEOUT_5_SECONDS);
         }
   }
}




//-------------------------------------------------------------------------
// Limit String Size
//
// This function shortens the string to the specified limit value.  This is
// used when printing long strings in short fields.  If the string is too
// long it is truncated with the last two string characters being displayed
// as "..".
//
// Returns:  SUCCESS or FAILURE
//-------------------------------------------------------------------------

int  limit_string_size (char * text, int  limit)
{
int  text_length;


/* Get string length */
text_length = strlen (text);

/* Determine if text exceeds limit */
if (text_length > limit)
  {
    /* Abbreviate text string */
    text[limit - 2] = '.';
    text[limit - 1] = '.';
    text[limit] = 0x00;
  }


/* Success */
return (SUCCESS);
}
```

Program Style and Methodology

```
//--------------------------------------------------------------------------
// Limit String Size No Dots
//
// This function shortens the string to the specified limit value.  This is
// used when printing long strings in short fields.  If the string is too
// long it is simply truncated.
//
// Returns:  SUCCESS or FAILURE
//--------------------------------------------------------------------------

int   limit_string_size_no_dots (char * text, int   limit)
{
int   text_length;


/* Get string length */
text_length = strlen (text);

/* Determine if text exceeds limit */
if (text_length > limit)
   {
     /* Abbreviate text string */
     text[limit] = 0x00;
   }


/* Success */
return (SUCCESS);
}




//--------------------------------------------------------------------------
// Move Cursor to Home Position
//
// This function moves the cursor to the top of the MemoBox.
//
// Returns:  SUCCESS or FAILURE
//--------------------------------------------------------------------------

int   move_cursor_to_home_position (TMemo   * MemoBox)
{
AnsiString   AnsiBuffer;


/* Abort if memobox does not exist */
if (MemoBox == NULL)
  return (FAILURE);

/* Display top of report */
MemoBox->SelStart = 0;

/* Success */
return (SUCCESS);
}
```

Program Style and Methodology

```
//--------------------------------------------------------------------------
// Set Timer
//
// This function sets the timer to the specified timeout value.  Since the
// timers are decremented by a separate thread, a locking mechanism is used
// to ensure correct operation.
//
// Returns:  SUCCESS or FAILURE
//--------------------------------------------------------------------------

void  set_timer (UINT32 *  timer, UINT32  timeout)
{
/* Obtain sole access to the timers */
timer_access->Acquire();

/* Initialize the timer */
*timer = timeout;

/* Release sole access to the timers */
timer_access->Release();
}




//--------------------------------------------------------------------------
// Get Timer
//
// This function gets the timeout count left in the specified timer.
// Since the timers are decremented by a separate thread, a locking mechanism
// is used to ensure correct operation.
//
// Returns:  SUCCESS or FAILURE
//--------------------------------------------------------------------------

UINT32  get_timer (UINT32 *  timer)
{
UINT32  timer_value;


/* Obtain sole access to the timers */
timer_access->Acquire();

/* Get the current timer value */
timer_value = *timer;

/* Release sole access to the timers */
timer_access->Release();

/* Return the timer value */
return (timer_value);
}
```

Program Style and Methodology

```
//----------------------------------------------------------------------
// Insert Money Symbol
//
// This function takes the specified string and inserts a money symbol at the
// beginning of the number (if space permits).
//
// Returns:  SUCCESS or FAILURE
//----------------------------------------------------------------------

int   insert_money_symbol (char *  buffer)
{
char    money_symbol;
char *  pointer;


pointer = buffer;

while (*pointer != 0x00)
   {
    /* Test for the first numeric digit */
    if (*pointer != ASCII_SPACE)
      {
        /* Step to the previous character */
        pointer--;

        /* Are we still within the buffer? */
        if (pointer >= buffer)
           {
             /* Yes - Replace character with a money symbol */
             money_symbol = POS_currency_symbol.c_str()[0];
             *pointer = money_symbol;
             return (SUCCESS);
           }

        /* No - Buffer string not large enough for money symbol */
        return (FAILURE);
      }

    /* Step to next character */
    pointer++;
  }

/* No non-space characters in buffer */
return (FAILURE);
}
```

Program Style and Methodology

```
//-------------------------------------------------------------------------
// Remove Money Symbol
//
// This function takes the specified string and removes the money symbol
// (if it exists).
//
// Returns:  SUCCESS or FAILURE
//-------------------------------------------------------------------------

AnsiString   remove_money_symbol (AnsiString   money_string)
{
char    input_buffer  [MAX_STRING_SIZE];
char    output_buffer [MAX_STRING_SIZE];
char    money_symbol;

AnsiString   result_string;


/* Get the money symbol */
money_symbol = POS_currency_symbol.c_str()[0];

/* Get the money string without additional spaces */
strcpy (input_buffer, money_string.Trim().c_str());

/* Is a money symbol used? */
if (input_buffer[0] == money_symbol)
   {
    /* Yes - Set the output buffer to the money string without the money symbol */
    strcpy (output_buffer, &money_string.c_str()[1]);
   }
else
   {
    /* No - Set the output buffer to the full money string */
    strcpy (output_buffer, &money_string.c_str()[0]);
   }

/* Convert money string back to an AnsiString */
result_string = output_buffer;

/* No non-space characters in buffer */
return (result_string);
}
```

Program Style and Methodology

```
//------------------------------------------------------------------------
// Random Initialize
//
// This function random initializes the specified data structure.
//
// Returns:  SUCCESS or FAILURE
//------------------------------------------------------------------------

int  random_initialize (void *  data_structure, long size)
{
char *  random_structure;
long    index;
time_t  random_seed;


/* Re-Seed the random number generator */
srand((unsigned) time(&random_seed));

/* Initialization */
random_structure = (char *) data_structure;

/* Randomize the entire data structure */
for (index = 0; index < size; index++)
   {
      /* Randomize each string in the structure */
      *random_structure++ = (char) RandomRange (0x00, 0xFF);
   }

/* Success */
return (SUCCESS);
}
```

Program Style and Methodology

```c
//---------------------------------------------------------------------------
// Determine Days In Month
//
// This function determines the number of days in a given month [1..12].
//
// Returns:  Number of days in the specified month.
//           FAILURE - Date is not valid.
//---------------------------------------------------------------------------

int   determine_days_in_month (int   month, int   year)
{
int   days_in_month;
int   days_in_february;


/*****************************////
/* Determine days in february */
/*****************************////

/* Is this a leap year? */
if ((year % 4) == 0)
   {
     /* Yes - Is this a new century? */
     if ((year % 100) == 0)
        {
          /* Yes - Is this century divisible by 400? */
          if ((year % 400) == 0)
             {
               /* Yes - It is a true leap year */
               days_in_february = 29;
             }
          else
             {
               /* No - It is not a true leap year */
               days_in_february = 28;
             }
        }
     else
        {
          /* Not a new century but still a true leap year */
          days_in_february = 29;
        }
   }
else
   {
     /* Not a leap year */
     days_in_february = 28;
   }


/* Determine days in month */
switch (month)
   {
     case  1: days_in_month = 31;  break;            // Jan
     case  2: days_in_month = days_in_february;  break;   // Feb
     case  3: days_in_month = 31;  break;            // Mar
     case  4: days_in_month = 30;  break;            // Apr
     case  5: days_in_month = 31;  break;            // May
     case  6: days_in_month = 30;  break;            // Jun
     case  7: days_in_month = 31;  break;            // Jul
     case  8: days_in_month = 31;  break;            // Aug
     case  9: days_in_month = 30;  break;            // Sep
     case 10: days_in_month = 31;  break;            // Oct
     case 11: days_in_month = 30;  break;            // Nov
     case 12: days_in_month = 31;  break;            // Dec
     default: days_in_month = 0;
   }

/* Return number of days in the month */
return (days_in_month);
}
```

Quantum Blue Technology LLC.

Program Style and Methodology

```
//-----------------------------------------------------------------------
// Convert To Double
//
// This function converts the text in an EditBox into a double number.  If
// no text is present then the number is set to the default value.
//
// Returns:  SUCCESS or FAILURE
//-----------------------------------------------------------------------

int  Convert_To_Double (TEdit * EditBox, double *  number, double  default_value)
{
char    buffer [MAX_STRING_SIZE];
double  result;

AnsiString   text_number;


/* Convert the EditBox text to a double number */
try {
      /* Remove leading and trailing spaces */
      text_number = EditBox->Text.Trim();

      /* Is this a null string? */
      if (EditBox->Text.Length() == 0)
        {
          /* Yes - No text entered - set to default */
          *number = default_value;
          return (SUCCESS);
        }

      /* Is the first text character a currency symbol? */
      if (text_number.c_str()[0] == POS_currency_symbol.c_str()[0])
        {
          /* Yes - Remove any leading currency symbol */
          strcpy (buffer, &text_number.c_str()[1]);
          text_number = buffer;
        }

      /* Try to convert text into a number */
      result = text_number.ToDouble();
      *number = result;
      return (SUCCESS);
   }

catch (...)
    {
      /* Invalid number - Inform the user */
      return (FAILURE);
    }
}
```

Program Style and Methodology

```
//-------------------------------------------------------------------------
// Convert To Int
//
// This function converts the text in an EditBox into a integer number.  If
// no text is present then the number is set to the default value.
//
// Returns:  SUCCESS or FAILURE
//-------------------------------------------------------------------------

int  Convert_To_Int (TEdit * EditBox, double *  number, int  default_value)
{
char   buffer [MAX_STRING_SIZE];
int    result;

AnsiString   text_number;


/* Convert the EditBox text to an integer number */
try {
      /* Remove leading and trailing spaces */
      text_number = EditBox->Text.Trim();

      /* Is this a null string? */
      if (EditBox->Text.Length() == 0)
        {
          /* Yes - No text entered - set to default */
          *number = default_value;
          return (SUCCESS);
        }

      /* Is the first text character a currency symbol? */
      if (text_number.c_str()[0] == POS_currency_symbol.c_str()[0])
        {
          /* Yes - Remove any leading currency symbol */
          strcpy (buffer, &text_number.c_str()[1]);
          text_number = buffer;
        }

      /* Try to convert text into a number */
      result = text_number.ToInt();
      *number = result;
      return (SUCCESS);
    }

catch (...)
    {
      /* Invalid number - Inform the user */
      return (FAILURE);
    }
}
```

Program Style and Methodology

```
//---------------------------------------------------------------------------
// Get Version Numbers
//
// This function reads the version information table.
//
// Returns:  SUCCESS or FAILURE
//---------------------------------------------------------------------------
int  get_version_numbers (char *  file_name,
                          char *  version_numbers)
{
char       * version_table;
char       * version_number_string;
DWORD        version_table_size;
unsigned int parameter_length;
AnsiString   version_search_string;
AnsiString   file_version;



/* Initialization */
strcpy (version_numbers, "0.0.0.0");

/* Get the version table size */
version_table_size = GetFileVersionInfoSize(file_name, &version_table_size);

/* Does the version table exist? */
if (version_table_size == 0)
  {
    /* No - Exit */
    return (FAILURE);
  }

/* Allocate dynamic memory for the version table */
version_table = (char *) malloc(version_table_size);

/* Was the version table memory allocated okay? */
if (version_table == NULL)
  {
    /* No - Exit */
    return (FAILURE);
  }

/* Build version table search string */
version_search_string  = "StringFileInfo\\040904E4\\";
version_search_string += "FileVersion";

/*Read the Version Table */
if (GetFileVersionInfo(file_name, 0, version_table_size, version_table) == 0)
  {
    /* Failed - Exit */
    free (version_table);
    return (FAILURE);
  }

/* Obtain the version numbers */
if (VerQueryValue (version_table,
                   version_search_string.c_str(),
         (void **)&version_number_string,
                   &parameter_length))
  {
    /* Get the version number string */
    strcpy (version_numbers, version_number_string);
  }

/* Release version table memory */
free (version_table);

/* Success */
return (SUCCESS);
}
```

Quantum Blue Technology LLC.

Program Style and Methodology

```
//-------------------------------------------------------------------------
// Extract Quad Numbers
//
// This function extracts four integer numbers from a quad string such as
// "1234.2.34341.2".
//
// Returns:  SUCCESS or FAILURE
//-------------------------------------------------------------------------

int   extract_quad_numbers (char *  quad_number_string,
                            int  *  number1,
                            int  *  number2,
                            int  *  number3,
                            int  *  number4)
{
char *  string_ptr;
char *  decimal_point_ptr;


/*****************/
/* First Number */
/*****************/

/* Initialize */
string_ptr = quad_number_string;

/* Find first decimal point */
decimal_point_ptr = StrPos (string_ptr, ".");

if (decimal_point_ptr == NULL)
  return (FAILURE);

/* Set decimal point to string terminator */
*decimal_point_ptr = 0x00;

/* Extract first number */
*number1 = atoi (string_ptr);


/*****************/
/* Second Number */
/*****************/

/* Set string ptr to start of second number */
string_ptr = ++decimal_point_ptr;

/* Find next decimal point */
decimal_point_ptr = StrPos (string_ptr, ".");

if (decimal_point_ptr == NULL)
  return (FAILURE);

/* Set decimal point to string terminator */
*decimal_point_ptr = 0x00;

/* Extract second number */
*number2 = atoi (string_ptr);
```

Program Style and Methodology

```
/*****************/
/* Third Number */
/*****************/

/* Set string ptr to start of third number */
string_ptr = ++decimal_point_ptr;

/* Find next decimal point */
decimal_point_ptr = StrPos (string_ptr, ".");

if (decimal_point_ptr == NULL)
  return (FAILURE);

/* Set decimal point to string terminator */
*decimal_point_ptr = 0x00;

/* Extract third number */
*number3 = atoi (string_ptr);


/*****************/
/* Fourth Number */
/*****************/

/* Set string ptr to start of fourth number */
string_ptr = ++decimal_point_ptr;

/* Extract fourth number */
*number4 = atoi (string_ptr);

/* Success */
return (SUCCESS);
}
```

Program Style and Methodology

```
//---------------------------------------------------------------------------
// Get Major Version Number
//
// This function reads the version information table and extracts the major
// version number.
//
// Returns:  SUCCESS or FAILURE
//---------------------------------------------------------------------------

int   get_major_version_number (char *  file_name,
                                int  *  major_version_number)
{
int    number1;
int    number2;
int    number3;
int    number4;
char   version_numbers [MAX_STRING_SIZE];


/* Initialization */
*major_version_number = 0;

/* Obtain version numbers */
if (get_version_numbers (file_name, version_numbers) == FAILURE)
  return (FAILURE);

/* Extract the four independent version numbers */
if (extract_quad_numbers (version_numbers, &number1, &number2, &number3, &number4) == FAILURE)
  return (FAILURE);

/* Extract major version number */
*major_version_number = number1;

/* Success */
return (SUCCESS);
}
```

Program Style and Methodology

```
//----------------------------------------------------------------------
// Get Minor Version Number
//
// This function reads the version information table and extracts the minor
// version number.
//
// Returns:  SUCCESS or FAILURE
//----------------------------------------------------------------------

int   get_minor_version_number (char *  file_name,
                                int  *  minor_version_number)
{
int    number1;
int    number2;
int    number3;
int    number4;
char   version_numbers [MAX_STRING_SIZE];


/* Initialization */
*minor_version_number = 0;

/* Obtain version numbers */
if (get_version_numbers (file_name, version_numbers) == FAILURE)
  return (FAILURE);

/* Extract the four independent version numbers */
if (extract_quad_numbers (version_numbers, &number1, &number2, &number3, &number4) == FAILURE)
  return (FAILURE);

/* Extract minor version number */
*minor_version_number = number2;

/* Success */
return (SUCCESS);
}
```

Program Style and Methodology

```c
//-----------------------------------------------------------------------
// Print MemoBox
//
// This function prints the specified MemoBox on to the printer.
//
// Returns: SUCCESS or FAILURE
//-----------------------------------------------------------------------

int  print_memobox (TPrinter *  OUT_Printer, int  orientation, TStrings * Document, char
*  Title)
{
int    index;
int    line_count;
int    max_pages;
int    page_count;
int    page_width;
int    page_height;
int    text_height;
int    max_document_lines;
int    max_document_pages;
int    max_printed_lines_per_page;
int    max_document_lines_per_page;
int    number_of_document_lines;
int    number_of_document_pages;
char   buffer [MAX_STRING_SIZE];
struct date d;
struct time t;


/* Get number of lines in document */
number_of_document_lines = Document->Count;

/* Is the document empty? */
if (number_of_document_lines == 0)
  return (FAILURE);

/* Get current Date and Time Information */
getdate(&d);
gettime(&t);

/* Determine maximum number of lines to the page */
page_width  = OUT_Printer->PageWidth  - PRINTER_LEFT_MARGIN; // - PRINTER_RIGHT_MARGIN;
page_height = OUT_Printer->PageHeight - PRINTER_TOP_MARGIN;  // - PRINTER_BOTTOM_MARGIN;


OUT_Printer->Canvas->Font->Name = "Courier";
OUT_Printer->Canvas->Font->Pitch = fpFixed;
OUT_Printer->Canvas->Font->Size  = 10;

text_height = OUT_Printer->Canvas->TextHeight(Document->Strings[0]);

if (text_height == 0)
  {
    for (index = 0; index < number_of_document_lines; index++)
        {
          /* Get the text height of another line */
          text_height = OUT_Printer->Canvas->TextHeight(Document->Strings[index]);

          /* Is the text height > 0 ? */
          if (text_height > 0)
            break;
        }
  }

/* Did we obtain a valid text height? */
if (text_height == 0)
  {
    /* No - Cancel print */
    return (FAILURE);
  }
```

Program Style and Methodology

```c
/* Is Portrait orientation required? */
if (orientation == PORTRAIT)
  {
    /* Yes - Print page in Portrait Format */
    OUT_Printer->Orientation = poPortrait;

    /* Determine printing parameters */
    max_printed_lines_per_page = page_height / text_height;
    max_document_lines_per_page = max_printed_lines_per_page - 4;    //2 lines for header and
                                                                    //2 lines for footer

    number_of_document_pages = (number_of_document_lines / max_document_lines_per_page) + 1;
  }
else
  {
    /* No - Print page in Landscape Format */
    OUT_Printer->Orientation = poLandscape;

    /* Determine printing parameters */
    max_printed_lines_per_page = page_width / text_height;
    max_document_lines_per_page = max_printed_lines_per_page - 4;    //2 lines for header and
                                                                    //2 lines for footer

    number_of_document_pages = (number_of_document_lines / max_document_lines_per_page) + 1;
  }


/* Initialization */
line_count = 0;
page_count = 1;

/* Start Printing */
OUT_Printer->Title = Title;
OUT_Printer->BeginDoc();

/* Output each line */
for (index = 0; index < number_of_document_lines; index++)
  {
    /* Print next line of document */
    OUT_Printer->Canvas->TextOut (PRINTER_LEFT_MARGIN,
                                  PRINTER_TOP_MARGIN + (line_count++ * text_height),
                                  Document->Strings[index]);

    /* Print document and footer */
    if (line_count >= max_document_lines_per_page)
      {
        /* Print Blank Line */
        OUT_Printer->Canvas->TextOut (PRINTER_LEFT_MARGIN,
                                      PRINTER_TOP_MARGIN + (line_count++ * text_height),
                                      "");

        /* Print Footer */
        sprintf (buffer, "Date: %4d-%02d-%02d   Time: %02d-%02d-%02d   Page: %d / %d",
                 d.da_year, d.da_mon, d.da_day, t.ti_hour, t.ti_min, t.ti_sec, page_count,
                 number_of_document_pages);

        OUT_Printer->Canvas->TextOut (PRINTER_LEFT_MARGIN,
                                      PRINTER_TOP_MARGIN + (line_count * text_height),
                                      buffer);

        /* Reset line counter */
        line_count = 0;

        /* Increment page counter */
        page_count++;
```

Program Style and Methodology

```
    /* Still more to print? */
           if (index + 1 < number_of_document_lines)
              {
                /* Yes - Start a new page */
                OUT_Printer->NewPage();
              }
        }
    }

/* Write blank lines until end of page */
for (index = line_count; index <= max_document_lines_per_page; index++)
    {
      /* Print Blank Line */
      OUT_Printer->Canvas->TextOut (PRINTER_LEFT_MARGIN,
                                    PRINTER_TOP_MARGIN + (line_count++ * text_height),
                                    "");
    }

/* Print Footer */
sprintf (buffer,
        "Date: %4d-%02d-%02d    Time: %02d-%02d-%02d    Page: %d / %d",
         d.da_year,
         d.da_mon,
         d.da_day,
         t.ti_hour,
         t.ti_min,
         t.ti_sec,
         page_count,
         number_of_document_pages);

OUT_Printer->Canvas->TextOut (PRINTER_LEFT_MARGIN,
                              PRINTER_TOP_MARGIN + (line_count * text_height),
                              buffer);

/* Stop Printing */
OUT_Printer->EndDoc();

/* Success */
return (SUCCESS);
}
```

Program Style and Methodology

3 Appendix

3.1 Code Editor

3.1.1 Use of Tabs versus Spaces

The code editor each programmer uses must be configured such that it replaces the TAB character with the equivalent number of space characters. This will permit a file, which has been modified by different programmers/editors to be displayed and/or printed with the correct indentation.